Praise for *Your Soul's Compass*

"An elegant, simple, and practical guide to get in touch with your higher self and experience the field of infinite possibilities."

— **Deepak Chopra,** the author of *Buddha: A Story of Enlightenment*

"Your Soul's Compass by Joan Borysenko and Gordon Dveirin refreshingly challenges the 'light unto ourselves' sensibilities of much of the modern spiritual marketplace. It points us all to the simple truth that direction from an intelligence greater than our own ego is critical for authentic spiritual evolution. The book's greatest message is that not only do we have to open ourselves to the experience of direct revelation, but even more important, if we want our world in crisis to change, we must have the courage to act on what is revealed to us."

— **Andrew Cohen,** the founder of EnlightenNext and *What Is Enlightenment?* magazine

"Your Soul's Compass is a treasure—a book that will change the way you move through your life. Beautiful and provocative, it explores in completely original ways the most important questions: How do you lead a life that's guided by love? How can you distinguish between authentic guidance and the desires of the ego? How can leaders as radically opposed as Hitler and Gandhi both feel they're being divinely inspired? Simple yet profound, pragmatic and transforming, this is a book you'll want to reread and keep close at hand."

— **Sara Davidson,** the author of *Leap!* and *Loose Change*

"Surely no journey is more promising, yet more problematic, than the journey into our own hearts. In this marvelous and insightful book, Joan and Gordon have done us the immense service of distilling the guidance of 27 sages from a wide array of spiritual lineages. A delicious feast awaits the reader—a true pleasure to partake!"

— **William Ury**, the author of *The Power of a Positive No*

"As a Christian, my beliefs in God and the consciousness that we're all spiritual beings yearning for a deeper connection to our Source draws me into this mind-expanding book. The convictions of 27 sages sharing their insights on the spiritual journey and our soul's maturation gives us clarifying revelations into our understanding and imagination of how you and I can draw closer to God."

— entertainer **Naomi Judd**

"This book is such a gift to the world! It makes a significant contribution by launching the first real interfaith dialogue on identifying what spiritual guidance is and perceiving the potential it has in helping the world in its evolution toward greater compassion."

— **Reverend Dr. Ruth Ragovin**

Also by Joan Borysenko, Ph.D.

Books
Minding the Body, Mending the Mind
Guilt Is the Teacher, Love Is the Lesson
Fire in the Soul
Pocketful of Miracles
The Power of the Mind to Heal (with Miroslav Borysenko, Ph.D.)*
On Wings of Light (with Joan Drescher)
7 Paths to God*
A Woman's Book of Life
A Woman's Journey to God
Inner Peace for Busy People*
Inner Peace for Busy Women*
Saying Yes to Change: Essential Wisdom for Your Journey
(with Gordon Dveirin, Ed.D.)*

Audio Programs
Seventy Times Seven: On the Spiritual Art of Forgiveness
A Woman's Spiritual Retreat
Menopause: Initiation into Power
The Power of the Mind to Heal
Your Spiritual Quest

(And please see the Hay House catalog for
over a dozen guided-meditation CDs, unabridged
books on CD, and inspirational lectures.)

Video Programs
Inner Peace for Busy People*
The Power of the Mind to Heal*

*Available from Hay House

Your Soul's Compass

What Is Spiritual Guidance?

Joan Borysenko, Ph.D.

and

Gordon Dveirin, Ed.D.

HAY HOUSE, INC.

Carlsbad, California • New York City
London • Sydney • Johannesburg
Vancouver • Hong Kong • New Delhi

Published and distributed in the United States by: Hay House, Inc.: www.hayhouse.
com • *Published and distributed in Australia by:* Hay House Australia Pty. Ltd.:
www.hayhouse.com.au • *Published and distributed in the United Kingdom by:* Hay
House UK, Ltd.: www.hayhouse.co.uk • *Published and distributed in the Republic
of South Africa by:* Hay House SA (Pty), Ltd. • www.hayhouse.co.za • *Distributed
in Canada by:* Raincoast: www.raincoast.com • *Published in India by:* Hay House
Publishers India: www.hayhouse.co.in

Editorial supervision: Jill Kramer • *Design:* Tricia Breidenthal

Library of Congress Cataloging-in-Publication Data

Borysenko, Joan.
  Your soul's compass : what is spiritual guidance? / Joan Borysenko and Gordon
Franklin Dveirin. -- 1st ed.
      p. cm.
  Includes bibliographical references.
  ISBN-13: 978-1-4019-0776-1 (hardcover)
  ISBN-13: 978-1-4019-0777-8 (tradepaper) 1. Spiritual direction. 2. Spirituality.
I. Dveirin, Gordon F. II. Title.
  BL624.B6197 2007
  204--dc22   2007017648

Hardcover ISBN: 978-1-4019-0776-1
Tradepaper ISBN: 978-1-4019-0777-8

10 09 08 07   4 3 2 1
1st edition, October 2007

Printed in the United States of America

In memory of
Brother Wayne Teasdale
and his vision:

Creating a Civilization with a Heart

Contents

PART II: INTRODUCING THE SAGES

The Sages:

Preface

When in Doubt, Ask the Nearest Sage

As the year 2005 came to an end—a "dark" period marked by hurricanes, earthquakes, tsunamis, war, terrorism, and genocide—*Time* magazine ran an inspiring article on local heroes who'd made a difference in places such as New Orleans and Biloxi, and across the world in faraway Pakistan and Indonesia. One of these heroes, a Pakistani man named Ihsanullah Khan, rescued thousands of people who were injured by an earthquake that registered 7.6 on the Richter scale and killed more than 73,000 people in Pakistan in October 2005.

Fifteen years before, Khan, then a Washington, D.C., cab driver, had a dream in which winning (he thought) lottery numbers were revealed to him. He played them religiously every week, until he finally won a jackpot worth $55.2 million in 2001. Recalling the dying words of his mother, who told him that one day he was going to be somebody important, he decided to take his winnings and return home to the Himalayan town of Batagram. There he could do good for the local people, which was the most important thing he could think of.

He ran for mayor and won . . . and three days later the earthquake struck. The local hospital was destroyed, and injured people wandered around dazed, looking for help that wasn't there. Using his lottery cash, Khan immediately bought all the medicines and supplies he could find, rounded up health-care personnel, and established a field hospital. Using still more of his winnings, he set up tents for displaced families and is currently helping villagers rebuild their homes, fulfilling what he sincerely believes to be his divine destiny.

Throughout history, many influential people have believed that they were divinely guided—for better or worse. Hitler was convinced that he had a special mission and was guided and protected by divine Providence. His certainty had a hypnotic effect on the German people, much like the pronouncements of some modern religious figures that generate fear, hatred, and mass murder. The original founders of the United States, on the other hand, were guided by a vision that, while rooted in faith, transcended religiosity and invited equality and opportunity for all. Around the world, leaders are faced with the necessity—and the privilege—of aligning global and domestic policies with the very best in human nature. This is a task that requires a wisdom transcending the dichotomy between faith and reason, encompassing the best of both.

If there is such a thing as spiritual guidance that directs us to our best self individually and collectively, following it involves some serious questions:

- How do we tell the difference between spiritual guidance and the ego's need for control, certainty, and power—or from instinctive drives and social conditioning?

- Is there a divine attraction—a kind of grace—that pulls us forward on the journey of becoming an awake, compassionate, and purposeful human being . . . or are we the sole instigators of that quest?

- And, perhaps most important, is there a compass of love and wisdom within the soul that keeps us on track—and if so, how does it function?

In these dark times of global uncertainty and dogmatic religious fundamentalism, such perennial questions seem particularly compelling, since they're likely to be important determinants of our planet's future.

In order to get input on these questions, we set out initially to assemble a virtual Noah's ark of spiritual luminaries from a variety of religious backgrounds: a male and female rabbi; a male and female from the Sufi tradition (originally Islamic mysticism, but more broadly a religion of the heart); a pair of Hindus; a duo of Buddhists. . . . And although recruiting a Catholic priest of both genders was out of the question, we hoped that a female Episcopal priest would fill the bill. One of the greatest delights was learning more about the Society of Friends from four unprogrammed Quakers, who have no clergy at all. But somewhere along the way we abandoned our neat categorization and expanded the group to include a few other people who, we believed, were intimately involved with living spiritually guided lives themselves and, in most cases, with helping guide others in that quest.

While most of the people we interviewed are well-known lineage holders from established religious traditions, others range from shamans to poets. They also include a psychologist who studies past-life regression, a metaphysician, and two founding members of the Center for Purposeful Living, whose spiritual path is the service of others. (That group was named a Presidential Point of Light and is an example of spirituality as compassionate social action.) In Part II of this book, "Introducing the Sages," you'll read more about who these spiritual luminaries are and the perspectives they share. Each one is also listed in the Contents to make it easier for you if you choose to look them up along the way as you encounter them in the text.

When it came time to decide what to call them, we reasoned that some might be uncomfortable with being referred to as spiritual teachers or leaders. Over time, because of our profound respect for their wisdom, we started to call them the Sages—the wise ones. We sincerely hope that they won't mind. The first person we interviewed, Hindu Swami Adiswarananda—head of the Ramakrishna-Vivekananda Center of New York and a wonderfully clear teacher of Vedanta (an ancient Indian philosophy of self-knowledge)—told us that when people are in doubt about their dharma or purpose, they should ask the nearest sage. We loved that advice, and it kept us interviewing much longer than we'd originally planned to.

The conversations we had with the Sages were based on a dozen questions (they're listed at the end of the book) that we hoped would help us—and you—understand what spiritual guidance is, what forms it may take, how we can distinguish authentic guidance from less reliable impulses, what cultivates the ability to listen for and recognize guidance, what blocks it, and how it relates to our evolution as human beings and as a species. These conversations gave us hope that Homo sapiens is evolving into a nobler species: *Homo sapiens caritas*—Man (and Woman) of wisdom and compassion. We were especially interested in the benefits that this guidance might bring to the world in these troubled times of spiritual indirection and religious intolerance, and what it has to say in response to fundamentalist-inspired violence.

The conversations—which were lively and engaging—are a bit like a wheel. We were privileged to be at the hub, the only ones who had the opportunity to speak with all the others. As you read along, you'll notice that the majority of the book is written from the perspective of both of us (Joan and Gordon). However, some sections are written in our individual voices, which will be prefaced by **Joan:** or **Gordon:**. When the content goes back to being from both of our perspectives, this transition will be indicated by the designation **Joan and Gordon:**.

It's our hope that we've been true to what the Sages shared with us. They trusted us to render their words faithfully and to place them in the proper context. We've done our best to honor that trust. Nonetheless, we want to acknowledge two things:

1.   First, mistakes and/or misunderstandings may have crept into this book in spite of our best efforts. We take responsibility for that and offer our most heartfelt apologies for any errors in content, in interpretation, or of omission, which are bound to have occurred.

2. Second, the treasure we've been given is vast and would take the rest of our lifetimes to catalog and absorb—a task that we're eager to continue.

Our "Noah's ark" is far from complete. While we've interviewed two Sufis whose paths intersect with the inner mysticism of Islam, we haven't yet interviewed mainstream Sunni or Shiite Muslims. The same is true for many other religious and indigenous traditions. The book that you hold in your hands is far from the last word on what it means to live a spiritually guided life—rather, it's a very humble beginning. We have no doubt that this is precisely the kind of dialogue the world needs if we're to move from the destructive clash of worldviews so prevalent today toward a globally enlightened wisdom civilization. To change the world conversation is to change the world.

When time and resources permit, we'd love this conversation to become more inclusive, involving people across the spectrum of currently warring belief systems. It has pained us to see—on the large screen of current events—forest fires of fear and hatred, of passionate intensity, raging out of control in the minds of true believers toward anyone they see as "other." The world is divided, and *we* are divided within ourselves. Only truth can reconcile us—the truth of our shared humanity beneath the superficial differences that separate us, the truth of our sublime human potential. But how do we find it? That is what *Your Soul's Compass* is about.

As a married couple, we held the personal hope that in writing this book we'd be able to move from a more intellectual understanding of spiritual guidance to actually realizing the love and freedom to which it points. For us, this work was more than a self-directed continuing-education course and an opportunity to synthesize our different spheres of knowledge . . . it was a personal prayer for guidance. The writing has seemed purposeful—destined—what in our own Jewish tradition of origin is called *beshert. Your Soul's Compass* has been, and continues to be, an integral part of our own evolution as human beings, as a couple, and as professionals whose day jobs are in the health-care and corporate sectors, as well as in the growing domain of *interspirituality*—the common ground where all wisdom traditions meet.

The spiritual principles that emerged in our research and interviews are universal, revealing what our friend the late Catholic monk and Hindu sannyasin (renunciate) Brother Wayne Teasdale called the Mystic Heart. That heart emerges when we enter into the *now*—free of agenda and open to life as it is unfolding. The deepest essence of who we are then emerges like a sun that's been hidden behind clouds, connecting with a higher intelligence—whether you call it wisdom, God, or Ultimate Reality. Regardless of their traditions of origin, all the Sages described this same core spiritual experience: the Mystic Heart.[1]

The descriptions were, of course, flavored by the particular religious tradition that each Sage was rooted in. Father Thomas Keating, for instance, spoke about the teachings of Jesus and St. Paul, although his spirituality is so expansive and inclusive that at times he might even be mistaken for a Buddhist monk or a rabbi. Cecilia Montero, a Peruvian shaman with Incan ancestry, spoke of guidance as a force available to all people, called *Sami*. She teaches that when we're in a peaceful, harmonious state, rather than stressed and fragmented, we can connect to that sublime, pure, infinite form of energy that's the very force of guidance itself. The three rabbis, on the other hand, brought guidance to life using Hasidic stories, Torah teachings, and wisdom that spanned the gamut from evolutionary biology to Jungian psychology.

Inspired by the emerging field of intersprituality, we founded the Claritas Institute for Interspiritual Inquiry in the summer of 2004. By the summer of 2005, in collaboration with our colleague and friend Janet Quinn, R.N., Ph.D., we'd launched its first program—the Claritas Interspiritual Mentor Training Program. Almost every religion has a tradition of spiritual guidance in which people familiar with the journey and the art of deep, reflective listening and inquiry act as mentors or companions for others. Our intention was to train mentors who were deeply grounded in the common Mystic Heart and were interested in an authentic exploration of the perennial questions of who we are and what our souls' purpose is.

Physicist and spiritual teacher Peter Russell is reputed to have had a recording on his answering machine at one point that said something to the effect of: "This is not an answering machine. It's a questioning machine. Who are you, and what do you want?" After a brief pause, it continued: "In case you think these are trivial questions, most people come to Earth and leave it again without answering either one."

In reading this book and hearing our own reflections and those of the Sages, we hope that you'll be inspired to take a fresh look at these questions for yourself. We invite you to deeply ponder what living a spiritually guided life would look like for you—and therefore, for our fragile world—in this time when it's up to us whether we will evolve in humanity or die by our own hands.

❊　❊　❊

Introduction

Inner Light or True Nature

This is a book about connecting with the Inner Light that's the birthright of every human being. There are times when we've all been in touch with it: the exquisite sense of being in love—when you're "home" in your partner's arms, perfectly content and fully present; the ecstatic moment when you feel as if you're in the right place at the right time, living your purpose in a graceful way; the mystery of moonlight illuminating the landscape when you sense the living soul of the natural world.

These experiences of being at home in yourself, centered in some essential kernel of what it is to be human, are profoundly natural. They're both "inner" and "other," in the sense that when you're in that center of goodness within you, you also feel connected to a greater wholeness—a higher intelligence—that's hard to express in words but has been called many things, including wisdom, God, the Source of Being, or Ultimate Reality.

Sages from all of the world's wisdom traditions tell us that such experiences of "true nature" are expressions of our essential inborn humanity—like the nectar that's the subtlest and most exquisite essence of a flower. True nature lacks the self-consciousness, fear, and compulsive need to make things happen in *our* own way, which creates so much suffering and unhappiness. Aligning with true nature allows freedom to move into alignment with larger currents of wisdom and bring new ideas to fruition.

Think about Gandhi, Thomas Jefferson, or Martin Luther King, Jr.—their personal alignment with a larger Source was not only a matter of singular importance to them; it was the center out of which their lives, and their service to others, flowed. When there's alignment between personal essence and a greater intelligence, happiness and purposeful action well up like sweet water from an underground source.

Whether you realize it consciously or not, the experiences of daily life are a form of feedback about whether you're getting closer to that state or farther away from it. Are you all stressed out, with a mind that won't stop running in circles, or can you rest in the contentment of your own true nature and wait for wisdom to arise of its own accord? In one of the most ubiquitous spiritual metaphors, are you asleep, locked into your own fearful fantasies . . . or are you awake, present to conscious choice and the infinite possibilities that each moment contains?

Waking Up: The Hymn of the Pearl

The parable you're about to read will make the ancient spiritual concepts of being asleep and waking up—and of following guidance that's freely given by a loving Source—more transparent. Then we'll explain what your Soul's Compass is and how you can use it to guide you on the journey of becoming a *Homo sapiens caritas*: the kind of wise and loving being whom we believe is the ultimate perfection of human life.

Written in the 2nd century c.e., the Hymn of the Pearl—also known as the Hymn of the Soul—is a Gnostic poem that's a parable of the soul's journey and the essential questions *Who am I?* and *Why am I here?* Gnosticism was a 1st- and 2nd-century spiritual movement oriented to direct knowledge of the sacred, which the Greeks called *gnosis*. This tradition most likely predated Christianity but was also thought to reflect the experience of Jesus, although eventually it was considered a heresy. Nonetheless, the Hymn of the Pearl made its way into the apocryphal Christian gospel the Acts of Judas Thomas the Apostle. It's a map of the soul's journey home—the human migration out of a separate sense of self ruled by fear and the need to control (sometimes called the false or egoic self)—to true nature or the Inner Light, whose expression is love, clarity, and co-creation with wisdom itself.

The hero of the tale is a young prince who's the absolute delight of his parents, the King of the East and the Queen of the Dawn. The prince is lovingly outfitted with provisions and sent on a voyage to Egypt. His task—a classic ordeal of the sort typical of the archetypal "hero's journey"—is to find the one Pearl that lies in the sea, next to a "loud-breathing Serpent."[1] Upon his return with the hard-won prize, he'll become heir to his parents' kingdom.

The young prince makes the arduous journey to Egypt and settles down near the Serpent's lair, hoping to snatch the Pearl while the awful beast lies sleeping. In the meantime he puts on Egyptian clothes so as not to look suspicious, and the locals give him food. As soon as he eats it, he forgets that he's the King's son, loses all memory of the Pearl, and sinks into a deep sleep.

Meanwhile, his parents anxiously perceive what's happening from afar and are beside themselves with worry. They write a magical letter to arouse the prince from his sleep and to remind him of who he is and of the purpose of his journey—which is to get the Pearl, return home, and take his place in the Kingdom as a noble who can rule with wisdom and compassion. The letter takes the form of an eagle, which flies to their son and speaks the message of truth.

At the sound of its wings thrumming and its beautiful voice, the young prince awakens and remembers who he really is. He realizes that *the words of the letter are already written in his heart* (within him as true nature), and he heeds their guidance. At once he charms the Serpent, snatches up the Pearl, strips off his Egyptian clothing, and turns toward home. The magic letter guides him with its love, and at the journey's end the prince has matured. He has found the Pearl beyond price—his own divine nature—and the childish aspects of false identity are gone. Now he's ready to be a wise leader.

The Hymn of the Pearl suggests that we aren't wandering alone, strangers lost in a strange land. Some Higher Power or Greater Reality is looking after us, sending the guidance we need to awaken from our sleep and come home to ourselves and to our place in the family of all that lives. Even when we fall into materialism or despair, that loving Power is still there, emitting a mysterious force of attraction that we can learn to recognize, and respond to, as spiritual guidance. When we act on that guidance and move toward our center, it feels like the sweetest relief, akin to manna that falls from heaven and nourishes the hungry soul.

Sleep is represented allegorically in the Old Testament as enslavement in Egypt. The Hebrew word for Egypt is *Mitzrayim,* which means "the narrow place." It refers not to a country, but to the areas in ourselves that hold us back and keep us imprisoned. Those narrow places of habit—of the many false identities that we assume and the destructive emotions that take us over as a result—are ingrained. But we're not without resources. We're being watched out for—or drawn toward wholeness—and sent guidance in "magic letters" such as dreams, synchronicities, illnesses, and insights . . . the message of which is already engraved in our hearts.

Variants of the Hymn of the Pearl show up in a range of wisdom traditions. The Sufis tell a similar tale about a prince who ends up wandering in the Land of Lies, forgetting his true identity. In the Jewish tradition, there's the story of Zusya, who's a very pious man but has gotten stuck in his false self. His rabbi tells him, "When you die, God isn't going to ask you whether you were as brave as David or as wise as Solomon. He's only going to ask why you weren't Zusya."

A Christian counterpart to the Hymn of the Pearl is the understanding that it's the Father's pleasure to give us the Kingdom. The Holy Spirit, like the magic letter, functions as a guide to wake us up and reveal the way back home. Nonetheless, the journey is difficult because it's unknown. Sometimes we don't even know where we are, much less where we're going, and perhaps we fall into despair or confusion. But even so, when we're willing to look for wisdom or God, we finally discover that it was looking for *us* all along. It pulls us toward it as inexorably as iron filings are drawn to a magnet. That's how the Soul's Compass works.

Your Soul's Compass

A compass is an instrument that orients to magnetic north so that we can tell which way we're going. Migratory birds know how to find their way over thousands of miles of unknown territory because of small particles of magnetite (akin to tiny micromagnets) embedded in their brains. A hummingbird headed from Colorado for a winter sojourn in Mexico doesn't usually wind up in Chicago by mistake. Its guidance system is hardwired for precision. Many mystics believe that human beings have just such a built-in guidance system that takes us home to the Source of Being. We're hardwired for God. But rather than being embedded in our brain, the magnet for our spiritual journey is located in the heart.

There's a certain *felt sense* of being centered in the heart. *Felt sense* has been defined simply as "a bodily sensation that is meaningful."[2] When we're centered in true nature and our minds are as steadfastly present to the moment as a mountain is to changing weather, there's a feeling of peace and fullness in our being. When we say that our heart is full or that a person is "heartful," it's to this meaningful bodily sensation that we're referring. We know somehow that we're at home in the universe . . . that all is well. And as you'll read in later chapters, this felt sense is a source of wisdom beyond words.

When we're in the essential core (what some traditions refer to as the Self with a capital *S*), we organically align to True North—wisdom, God, or Ultimate Reality. It's as if our heart is at the center of the compass. When the needle is free to be in present time, rather than fearing the future or regretting the past, it moves effortlessly to True North. In that state of alignment with Source, we know—in a way that may be more intuitive than cognitive—what any situation requires. We're confident, competent citizens of the world; and whether we're sitting on a park bench gazing at the first cherry blossoms of spring, changing a baby's diaper, or passing a bill in Congress, there's an unmistakable felt sense of something larger moving through us.

Aligning true nature with Source is easy conceptually but difficult in practice—until a certain point. Think of a seesaw: You don't have to move it 100 percent in order for it to tip to the other side.

Because it rests on a fulcrum, when even a fraction more than 50 percent of the weight shifts, the seesaw instantly tilts in that direction. The 49.99999999 percent of the effort that you don't have to supply to taste Self-realization is grace. But until you get to the tipping point, skillful effort is required.

This book is about both grace and effort. Scientists tell us that a compass can be fooled by what they call *magnetic deviance*. If there are large lodes of iron ore in the ground, for example, and a migratory bird flies over it, it can attract the magnets in the bird's brain and lead it astray. The same is true for the magnet of true nature that resides in our hearts.

The biggest source of magnetic deviance is fear. When we tell ourselves frightening stories, it's hard to find the peaceful felt sense in the heart or to engage other forms of guidance, such as the sense of unease that may be signaling that we're going the wrong way. Other sources of misdirection, as you'll read about in the chapter on blocks to guidance, include habits of mind—for example, judgment, pride, willfulness, sloth, and desire.

The Secret of Life

When you clear away sources of magnetic deviance—obstructions to the Inner Light—then purposeful action and deep contentment arise as surely and naturally as day follows night. Contentment doesn't originate from outside, from being loved by others or from the solace of material items (as long as you have enough to meet survival needs); it comes only from within. That's the secret of life that mystics of every tradition know.

There's a difference we sometimes fail to notice between willing the good and willing the goods. The most common misconception about the secret of life is this: When you set your intention and decide what *you* want, you can control the universe—or at least your little corner of it—and find happiness. But rich people are often miserable, and powerful individuals may be seriously misguided. Our Buddhist Sages assured us that happiness and skillful action emerge from orienting to the Buddha Nature (the essential core) of love and wisdom within. Jesus expressed a similar idea when he suggested that if we put the Kingdom of Heaven first—if we orient to True North—then the rest of life's good things will follow.

Dr. Francis Collins, the physician and scientist who's the long-time director of the Human Genome Project—which has mapped the entire human genetic code within our DNA—tells a powerful story about orienting to True North in his book *The Language of God*. In the summer of 1989, he volunteered at a small hospital in Eku, Nigeria, hoping to make a positive difference by contributing his medical skills to this impoverished and underdeveloped area of the world. The conditions there were almost unimaginably primitive—diseases such as malaria and tuberculosis, as well as parasitic infestations, produced terrible suffering.

One day a seriously ill young farmer was brought to the hospital by his family. Even without modern diagnostic equipment, Dr. Collins was able to recognize that the man was suffering from a life-threatening accumulation of fluid in the pericardium—the sac that surrounds the heart. Left untreated, it would soon squeeze the life out of the young farmer. In a modern hospital, the fluid could be drained in relative safety by a skilled cardiologist guided by an ultrasound machine. But on the dirt floor of the Nigerian hospital, without access to medical equipment, the farmer's only hope was that Dr. Collins could manage to insert a large bore needle into his chest and draw off the fluid without puncturing his heart.

The procedure, risky though it was, saved the day. But even so, the long-term prognosis for the young man was poor. The fluid that had threatened to stop his heart was caused by tuberculosis. In spite of the fact that he was started on antitubercular drugs, there was a good chance that he'd be unable to pay for the two-year supply necessary to cure him—or that he'd die from some other cause related to the poverty, dirty water, and poor nutrition endemic to the area. Dr. Collins felt a sense of gloom. What use were his meager efforts to relieve suffering in the face of such dire conditions?

The next morning he found the young man sitting up in bed, reading the Bible. Somehow aware that Dr. Collins was new at the hospital, and remarkably tuned in to what the doctor was feeling, the young man looked at him and said, "I get the sense you are wondering why you came here. . . . I have an answer for you. You came here for one reason. You came here for me."[3]

The young man's words went directly to Dr. Collins's own heart, cutting through both his sense of futility and his "grandiose dreams of being the great white doctor, healing the African millions."[4] While each of us is called to reach out to others, Dr. Collins realized, it's in the small acts of kindness, rather than the rare deeds that occur on a grand scale, that we most commonly touch one another. He summed up his epiphany:

> The tears of relief that blurred my vision as I digested his words stemmed from indescribable reassurance—reassurance that there in that strange place for just that one moment, I was in harmony with God's will, bonded together with this young man in a most unlikely but marvelous way. Nothing I had from science could explain that experience. Nothing about the evolutionary explanations for human behavior could account for why it seemed so right for this privileged white man to be standing at the bedside of this young African farmer, each of them receiving something exceptional.[5]

The sense of *agape*—pure unselfish love seeking nothing in return—that Collins experienced was like a compass for his soul. It was a type of inner knowing, wisdom beyond words and concepts, that let him know he was on the right track in his life . . . in Christian terminology, in harmony with God's will. He realized that less noble motivations such as the admiration of his colleagues at home or of the Eku villagers had previously gotten in the way of the supremely meaningful experience of pure love and purpose that he found so transformational. He explained:

> A burden lifted. This was true north. And the compass pointed not at self-glorification, or at materialism, or even at medical science—instead it pointed at the goodness that we all hope desperately to find within ourselves and others.[6]

Realizing and experiencing that goodness is the secret of life. The revelation that Dr. Collins had was one of almost indescribable joy and homecoming. The false or conditioned self that drives the relentless search for affirmation, goods, and certainty stepped aside and something much more real and luminous shone forth. That experience is the common ground that mystics from all spiritual traditions describe.

Mysticism means the direct communion with the sacred, beyond any kind of dogma or doctrine. Regardless of whether a person believes in God, as Collins does; in a source of wisdom, as our Buddhist friends do; or simply in the possibility of wholeness, the experience of universal love and compassion is the same. It's life's most evident delight, and the true hope of our species. It's what we all discover, regardless of creed, when we touch the Mystic Heart and follow its guidance. When we encounter the goodness within our own hearts, we recognize our true identity as a unique and meaningful part of life's heart.

Seeking spiritual guidance is often misunderstood as consulting a cosmic Dear Abby or a universal Google for advice on relationships, health and illness, pathways to financial freedom, or even great car deals. While there's guidance out there about everything in life, the kind that we're most concerned with here sheds light on the spiritual journey itself. Are we going in a direction that helps us become less selfish, more compassionate, and peaceful? Or have we gone off on a tangent that keeps us tethered to old habits and perceptions, which perpetuate fear, greed, and ignorance?

We'll open our conversation with the Sages now and turn both our minds and our hearts to the nature of spiritual guidance . . . what Sage Rabbi Rami Shapiro defined as "discovering or experiencing the grain of the moment—like the grain of wood—what the forces are that are operative in this moment so that I can engage them directly and cleanly without having to go across the grain."

PART I

Orienting to True North

"Deeper and more fundamental than sexuality,
deeper than the craving for social power,
deeper even than the desire for possessions,
there is a more generalized and more universal craving
in the human make-up.
It is the craving for right direction—for orientation."

— William Sheldon, American psychologist

Chapter One

OPENING THE CONVERSATION

It was the summer of 2004, on a surpassingly beautiful day in Barcelona, Spain. We were privileged to be attending the Parliament of the World's Religions, where I (Joan)—as a scientist interested in consciousness studies—had been invited to participate on a panel about prayer. Perhaps the most fascinating session we attended at the Parliament was a conversation about fundamentalism. The participants were Rabbi Michael Lerner, a political activist and the editor of *Tikkun* magazine (*tikkun* is a Hebrew word meaning "to heal and repair the world"); former nun and respected writer on world religions Karen Armstrong; and female Islamic scholar Kamah Kamaruzzaman.

Drawing on her seminal book *The Battle for God*, Armstrong discussed the recent rise of virulent forms of fundamentalism in virtually all world religions, characterizing it as a reaction to a soulless and technologically driven Western worldview. Lerner described modernity itself as a form of secular fundamentalism. The Islamic scholar Kamaruzzaman, who was the last to speak, passionately affirmed that the way to transcend these two competing yet interrelated fundamentalisms was for us to discover the common ground of our shared humanity.

An awareness of that common ground can emerge from a special kind of spiritual conversation that goes beyond external differences in belief. One of the Sages whom you're about to meet in these pages, Father Thomas Keating, convened an annual conference at St. Benedict's Monastery in Snowmass, Colorado, in 1984, inviting participants from a variety of religious traditions to converse in just such a special way. One of the basic tenets of the Snowmass Conference is that participants speak *from* their tradition—sharing their experiences of God or Ultimate Reality—but not *for* their tradition in terms of dogma. This kind of dialogue is called *interspiritual,* and it's a profound form of interfaith understanding and communication.

Interfaith conversations occur at two levels:

1. Externally, they focus metaphorically on the varieties of flowers in the garden of faith and cultivating an appreciation for—or at least a tolerance of—the differences among them.

2. Internally, they focus on a shared spirituality that transcends differences in belief. These internal, interspiritual conversations reveal the common ground out of which the diverse flowers grow and the sunlight, wind, and water that nourishes them all.

In his beautiful book *The Mystic Heart,* Brother Wayne Teasdale writes:

> The real religion of humankind can be said to be spirituality itself, because mystical spirituality is the origin of all the world religions. If this is so, and I believe it is, we might also say that *interspirituality*—the sharing of ultimate experiences across traditions—is the religion of the third millennium. Interspirituality is the foundation that can prepare the way for a planet-wide enlightened culture, and a continuing community among the religions that is substantial, vital, and creative.[1]

The 15 spiritual leaders from the Snowmass Conference arrived at a consensus on the principles of authentic interreligious conversation—principles that you'll come to recognize as being interspiritual as you eavesdrop on some of the highlights of the discussions we had with the Sages in the pages that follow.

Father Thomas Keating outlined these guidelines in the book *Speaking of Silence*:

1) The world religions bear witness to the experience of the Ultimate Reality to which they give various names: Brahman, the Absolute, God, Allah, [the] Great Spirit, the Transcendent.

2) The Ultimate Reality surpasses any name or concept that can be given to It.

3) The Ultimate Reality is the source (ground of being) of all existence.

4) Faith is opening, surrendering, and responding to the Ultimate Reality. This relationship precedes every belief system.

5) The potential for human wholeness—or in other frames of reference, liberation, self-transcendence, enlightenment, salvation, transforming union, moksha, nirvana, fana—is present in every human person.

6) The Ultimate Reality may be experienced not only through religious practices but also through nature, art, human relationships, and service to others.

7) The differences among belief systems should be presented as facts that distinguish them, not as points of superiority.

8) In the light of the globalization of life and culture now in process, the personal and social ethical principles proposed by the world religions in the past need to be re-thought and re-expressed.[2]

The fourth basic principle—that "faith is opening, surrendering, and responding to the Ultimate Reality" and the recognition that this essential "relationship precedes every belief system"—is a way of saying that guidance is available to all human beings.

A dinner conversation that we had with our friends Sara and Rachael spoke to this guiding function of Ultimate Reality in a very down-to-earth way. Recounting some of the startling synchronicities that had occurred during the past year that had deepened her spiritual journey, Rachael—who's petite, vivacious, and seriously smart—laughed and told us, "God leaves bread crumbs to show us the way back home." In other words, we can count on a beneficent force—like the prince's parents in the Hymn of the Pearl from the Introduction—to help us find our way to becoming more skillful, loving human beings.

But if we can rely on spiritual guidance to lead us to a realization of our true identity, then how come the journey seems so difficult and the road so long and so often disheartening? As Dr. Ed Bastian, another one of our Sages, remarked with a laugh, "If we're the Buddha, then how come we don't know it?"

Perhaps the reason for our ignorance is that there's a second variable in the equation of spiritual growth (as the fourth principle of the Snowmass Conference states): surrender to, and cooperation with, the force of guidance. Surrender and cooperation aren't always easy. They entail letting go of our own agenda and waiting patiently for the path to open step-by-step.

Releasing ourselves into the unknown can be scary. Most of us would rather chart our own course if for no other reason than that it helps manage fear. But letting go of the steering wheel and trusting in a greater compassionate intelligence not only has the potential to be anxiety producing; it's also paradoxical.

On the one hand, surrendering to guidance involves the bone-deep realization that we're helpless—no matter how hard we try to control things, we're ultimately *not* the sole author of our experience. On the other hand, in some mysterious way entirely beyond the capacity of words or rational thought to convey, we're *one* with the author of all experience. The realization of that oneness is at the heart of the spiritual journey and our ability to trust that a wisdom greater than our own is helping us evolve.

The journey home to our true nature and to God-realization—which are one and the same thing—has three parts according to Father Thomas Keating:

1. First, as the journey begins, there's a compelling experience of a Mysterious Other.

2. Second, as we progress along the way, there's an effort to come into union with that Mysterious Other.

3. Third, at the point of realization, we understand that there never was an Other.[3]

Our own true Self—the answer to the question *Who am I?*—is the individualized expression of Ultimate Reality. If this sounds abstract, confusing, or heretical to you, you're in good company. From the beginning of time, people have struggled to find words for what can't be said but may only be realized in the laboratory of the heart. Our hope is to make this all as transparent and clear as we can, giving you the means for discerning your part in the ongoing symphony of life.

Both of us, your humble authors, as longtime students of the world's great wisdom traditions, are somewhat familiar with various theories and stages of the spiritual journey. But there's an enormous chasm between head knowledge—the rational concepts we have about things—and direct, embodied experience. The former is like a menu that describes what we *could* experience; the latter is the actual meal, which can only be appreciated when tasted. When rational thought gives way to direct experience, the events of daily life become a revelation and a mystical, mythical journey—whether (as you'll read about in the next chapter) spiritual guidance comes dressed in a robe of glory or in the rags of stress and disappointment.

Chapter Two

Magic Letters . . . the Anatomy of Revelation

In the Hymn of the Pearl (which is recounted in the Introduction), the parents of the forgetful prince send him a letter that takes the form of an eagle. It awakens their son and shows him the way home. The world's wisdom traditions are replete with different guises that such a letter of awakening and guidance might assume: dreams, signs, synchronicities, revelations, stress, illness, untoward events, and bodily sensations, to name just a few. Understanding a little bit about these and how to decipher their messages can help prevent simplistic misinterpretations, on the one hand, and missed opportunities—unread letters—on the other.

Shaman/poet Oriah Mountain Dreamer told us a story about something that happened when she was a young woman. An acquaintance was trying to decide whether or not to go to Mexico with a man she'd recently met. A truck passed by with the word *Mexico* written on the side, and the woman took it as a sign that she should make the trip. Off she went, only to get beaten up by her companion, who proved to be untrustworthy.

Oriah's advice about signs is to use them as questions to sit with in contemplation, rather than accepting them as pat answers. Spiritual guidance rarely comes as a given, we've learned, but more often as an invitation to feel for the movement of Spirit.

What greater wisdom does a particular life event suggest, and how can we best integrate its teaching into our lives? Some of the most common ways that the Sages discussed feeling for the movement of Spirit were by attending to felt sense (meaningful bodily sensations such as goose bumps, for instance, or feelings of peace, excitement, aliveness, or anxiety), intuition, dreams, signs, and synchronicities.

Everything Provides Guidance

While the Old Testament God appears to Moses as a burning bush, spiritual guidance is usually a lot more subtle. The counterpart to God the Father is God the Mother. In Judaic mysticism she's known as Shechinah . . . wisdom itself. And rather than being *up there,* she's *in here.* In you. In me. In the earth, the sky, the water, and the wind. She is in joy and in sorrow, in success and failure. Shechinah is the life force itself and can offer her wisdom in an infinite number of changing forms. Former Jesuit priest Wilkie Au commented:

> The whole material creation is the language of God. The spiritual life is coextensive with all of human life, so we have to look [for guidance] in a lot more places. It forces us to push our categories wide open. God can communicate with us in any way we come to know anything—through sexual energy, bodily sensations, and so forth. That's why I rely on [educational psychologist] Howard Gardner and his account of multiple intelligences.

Quaker educator Patricia Loring finds such a variety in guidance that it's impossible to name all the ways it can emerge. Often they can be named only in retrospect. She explains:

> At times I've felt an urging to do something very small, which develops ramifications that become more focused and clear over time. At other times people have named something they sense emerging in me or my life that I haven't particularly felt led to do,

spiritual guidance itself [referring here to being a spiritual guide or director for other people] being a case in point.

The first time someone came to me for spiritual guidance, I was shocked and sent them immediately to my own director [guide]. The third time I did that, my director said, "All right, maybe the first time was poor judgment on the part of the person who approached you, and the second time was a fluke; but somewhere along the line, you have to ask yourself whether they're naming something real."

And that was the beginning of a more focused process of discernment for her. "Then there are times when I've been guided by an accumulation of circumstances," she continued. "It was like being rounded up or corralled—guided in the sense of being directed or taught by a sequence of events. . . . Bad health has been an unanswerable guide—there's nothing that reveals as clearly and inescapably that I'm not in control of the universe or even a tiny corner of it."

Like many Friends (what Quakers call one another), she stresses that whatever guise the guidance may take, it's the quality of our attention and our willingness to listen with an open mind and heart that creates the conditions for recognizing and following it: "Spiritual guidance . . . involves an ever-increasing level of openness and awareness. Over a lifetime, we are led to open in the direction of absolutely everyone and everything around us as a potential messenger of God—a goal toward which we reach all our lives without expecting to reach it."

Opening to everyone and everything around us requires feline sensitivity. A cat's whiskers continually taste the air; ears orient to the subtlest sound. Muscles expand and contract in poetic harmony with the changing environment . . . not as it was a moment ago, but as it is now, and now, and now again. The tapetum (reflective layer) of the eyes creates visual acuity matched only by a cat's uncanny inner acuity. Even think about getting out the cat carrier for a trip to the vet and your precious pet stages a disappearing act worthy of Houdini. How does it know?

We asked our Sages a similar question: How do you know? What is your personal experience of guidance? Unlike cats, who tune in to multiple channels of knowing, most of us humans have a much more limited bandwidth. No two Sages answered the same way. Nonetheless, some had preferred methods for listening deeply to their lives to discern the wisest direction. Others spoke about using multiple channels to receive guidance. *You* may have your own methods, or perhaps reading about the experiences we've chosen to highlight here will help you recognize more about your own process of making choices and living with purpose and direction.

The Felt Sense

Sometimes you're so much in your head that you don't notice what's going on in your body—a subtle range of inner sensation called the *felt sense* that can give you an intuitive read of a situation. When you're thinking about whether or not to accept a job, how do you decide? One way is to list the pros and cons and consider the opportunities for advancement, the pay, the benefits, and so forth.

But rational thought alone often won't tell you the whole story. There's a more wide-ranging system at your disposal that includes tuning in to bodily sensations. Philosopher and psychotherapist Dr. Eugene Gendlin discovered that the difference between people who did well in psychotherapy and those who didn't was the ability of the former to pay attention to this interior information, which he called the *felt sense*.

Here are a few examples. . . .

Joan: A young woman goes on a blind date with a man who comes highly recommended by her own mother. Even though he's unfailingly polite and kind, she feels slightly restless and tense all evening—queasy even. Something just feels "off" inside. She ignores these feelings, since he's intelligent and good-looking, has a great pedigree, makes plenty of money, and seems to like her. On their second date, he takes her to his apartment and tries to rape her. She barely escapes. A form of wisdom different from rational thought was sending danger signals through the felt sense, but she chose to ignore it—at her peril, as it turned out. And, guess what . . . that young woman was me.

Several years later, when I was a young scientist doing cancer research at the Tufts University School of Medicine, I paid attention to felt sense. I was a competent medical researcher with an enviable track record, and in academia this meant that my experiments yielded interesting results published in fine scientific journals and that my grants got funded. When I wasn't in the lab, I taught histology—the microscopic anatomy of cells, tissues, and organs—to medical and dental students. Teaching and doing research was rewarding, but a vague sense of unease started to grow.

One day a phone call came from the National Cancer Institute to let me know that not only had my latest grant proposal been funded, but it had such a high-priority score that they were wondering whether I'd like more money for new equipment. When I burst into tears, the funding agent was touched. She thought that I was thrilled to get the good news, but the reality was that the grant suddenly felt like a three-year prison sentence. The felt sense of misery and disappointment in the face of seemingly great news was an invitation to sit with the question of what I *did* want to do with my career, since what I *didn't* want was suddenly clear.

Felt sense came into the picture again when I made the highly rational decision to attend Tufts University School of Dental Medicine when my grant research was complete. Why dental school, you ask? The reasons were eminently practical. My husband at that time, Miroslav Borysenko, also taught at the medical and dental schools, and as a faculty spouse, I would get my tuition waived. The university also offered to let me keep teaching histology and to pay me well. Our two boys were still young, and I reasoned that practicing dentistry part-time would make me more available to them while still generating a good income.

All systems seemed to be go, and there was an easy flow. The only problem was that I started waking up at night with butterflies in my stomach. The felt sense of anxiety and "wrongness" grew. After sitting with it for a month, I reluctantly concluded that dentistry wasn't my *dharma* (the path in life that leads both to spiritual growth and purposeful living) . . . or you might be sitting in my chair right now.

Quaker Deanne Butterfield, with her bright smile and gentle manner, described how she used attention to felt sense, what she calls the "emotional truth of the moment," in a job search:

> There are numerous times when I need guidance—maybe I have a decision to make and I'm thinking, *C'mon, God, give me a lightning bolt.* And because I'm a human being as well as a spiritual being, it doesn't just come.
>
> What we [Quakers] have in common is that we've experienced that there is a Source of Guidance. How we conceptualize it differs, and we each have to find the experience in our own way. I'm cerebral, so I have to have some concept of the steps. What works for me is to ground myself in the question *What's the truth of this situation?* This means that I need to stop worrying about the solution and focus on the emotional truth instead.
>
> Maybe I'm afraid or feeling vulnerable. If I can stay with that and just feel it without judging it or pushing it away, then I can move to a larger truth. As I'm able to sit with each level of the truth in a really vulnerable way, everything opens up. First truth, I'm scared. Then I can sit with the truth about the talents and gifts I was born with. As I expand the concentric circles, I feel like I'm closer to the larger truth.
>
> I use the word *truth* in connection with spiritual guidance. It's not the right word, but it's the closest I can get. If I can have the patience and faith to really move through these levels, guidance isn't a lightning bolt and seldom comes with an answer like *This is the job you need.* It's a bigger Truth that opens the way.
>
> There's not divine guidance about what job I should take. The guidance comes as I move out in the circle from what I know 200 percent to what I don't know 100 percent [in other words, she goes beyond a rational sense of absolute certainty to a position of openness]. I feel lighter, I have confidence, and the way opens. The phone rings and someone tells me about a job that's available.

The way opened in just such a synchronistic way for me when I decided not to go to dental school. I'd given up trying to figure out what to do with my life and was receptive to whatever might emerge. One day the phone rang . . . but *I* was the one who made the call.

I'd picked up a medical journal, and there was an article written by my former mentor Herbert Benson, M.D., with whom I'd done research in graduate school. The article was about the physiological benefits of meditation—what he and his colleague Keith Wallace, Ph.D., dubbed the *relaxation response.*

I'd been meditating for years and gave Dr. Benson a call to catch up on what he was doing. As fortune—or guidance—would have it, he'd written a grant proposal to retrain physicians and medical researchers in the newly emerging field of behavioral medicine. It had been funded that very morning. He offered me one of the two available fellowships, and as the Quakers would say, "the way opened." I took the position, went back to Harvard, and was able to use my research background to help people with cancer and other illnesses by cofounding a mind/body clinic with Dr. Benson and other colleagues.

It's important to recognize that the opportunity for such meaningful work didn't appear out of thin air. It was the result of a clear intention to follow guidance, a willingness to wait until the way revealed itself, and a strong desire to match my work in the world with my inner journey to God.

Signs and Synchronicities

Thomas Edison believed that chance favors the prepared mind. But is synchronicity chance or something more? Was it an accident that I called Dr. Benson on the very day that his grant was funded? The felt sense I had of that phone conversation was "rightness." There was peace, excitement, and gratitude—that delightful sense of life unfolding and evolving that Sage Hameed Ali might call "dynamism." I knew that I was on the right track.

Joan and Gordon: Carl Jung wrote about synchronicity more specifically as an out-picturing of something in the mind. For example, you're thinking about a friend whom you haven't seen for years and he or she calls you at that very moment. Or perhaps your dead mother dearly loved hummingbirds, and on the anniversary of her death, several appear and hover in your garden, even though they're rare where you live. Some such occurrences are bound to be simple chance, but others may be more meaningful. The important thing is to be patient before you decide that an instance of synchronicity is a sign that you're guided to do something—or not—since otherwise it's easy to jump to conclusions.

A friend of ours sent out wedding invitations, and they were inexplicably lost in the mail. Then the flowers that had been ordered for the ceremony didn't arrive. The minister ran into problems and barely made it to the church, and our friend's father-in-law to-be—who was supposed to give the bride away—arrived at the ceremony late and drunk. But the groom pushed forward anyway—even though he had serious concerns—and the marriage turned out to be a disaster.

"If I'm confronted with a pattern," shaman/poet Oriah Mountain Dreamer explained, "and something's off—if the path is blocked over and over, and there's no alignment and flow—I take it as a cue to stop pushing and take time to sit and discern."

Joan: Difficulties *per se* aren't always a sign that you're moving in the wrong direction. As Oriah says, they're an invitation for deep listening for the movement of Spirit, which sometimes moves *through* the difficulties. I was visiting Cortes Island in British Columbia one summer, where there's a reserve for the Klahoose band of Coastal Salish First Nation people. They'd received a grant to celebrate and nourish their culture by building a large, ocean-going canoe.

A skilled artisan was sent from Vancouver to oversee the project, and before he arrived, a huge cedar tree several feet in diameter had been felled for the purpose. Unfortunately, the people who cut it down were novices and hadn't cleared a bed for the behemoth to land on. When it fell crosswise over a log resting on the forest floor, the ancient tree cracked. Furthermore, it was badly rotted inside and little more than a shell. But since the band had a permit to take only one tree from the old-growth forest, the artisan had to make do with what he'd been given. As a result, the canoe would have to be very narrow—made from one of the intact walls of the tree—and pegged together where it was cracked.

The work was going very slowly, since most of the men who'd volunteered to help the artisan had become frustrated and given up. Nevertheless, he persisted patiently in the task. On the third or fourth day of my visit, once he and I had struck up an acquaintance, I sat down on a tree stump and observed, "If I had as much trouble as you're having and everything was going wrong, I'd be tempted to think that there wasn't any energy in the project. Maybe I'd just give up."

The young native artisan turned to me and wiped the sheen of sweat from his face with a bandana. He nodded solemnly. "It's not like that in my culture," he replied. "Sometimes the harder it is to accomplish something, the bigger the Spirit that's trying to be born. The Spirit of our people is being born again here." With that, he began again to patiently—and with single-minded concentration—chip away at the enormous tree with his hammer and chisel.

Perhaps the canoe wouldn't be as beautiful as it might have been were the tree intact, but it carried an energy absolutely fitting for the occasion—nobility, steadfastness, and patient acceptance. The Klahoose, like almost all First Nations people, had been through years of devastating cultural disruption. It might take years for cultural rebirth. And that was all in the flow of guidance for the artisan. Evaluating life according to external success is a particularly Western, materialist preoccupation. Understanding the inner story, as the artisan did, and flowing gracefully with Spirit as it's moving in your situation is *life* artistry.

The Intention to Listen for Guidance

Joan and Gordon: As we advance on the spiritual path and follow the guidance we're given, then according to Sufi Sheikh Kabir Helminski, more guidance shows up:

> To the degree to which we're conscious, coherent, and live with pure intention—this is very important—the more we have intention and devotion, that's the extent to which our life will take on greater and greater aspects of synchronicity. Life itself becomes meaningful. To the extent that we're willing and conscious students, the Educator of the Universe can give us deeper and richer instructions and teachings.

It all depends on our state. If a human being can be in that state of remembrance, referring back to the master truth of existence—that we live in a spiritual reality—the bottom line is that the inventory of spiritual qualities adds up to great mercy and generosity.

Or as Father Thomas Keating put it: "When people think of being guided . . . this seems to grow first out of the sincerity of one's practice and the depth of one's opening to a relationship with God."

A very rich part of the interviews with the Sages were the conversations that we—the interviewers—had together afterward. After speaking to Sheikh Kabir, we wondered, *What's it like to encounter the Ultimate Mystery in a way that invites it to reveal more and more of itself and of you, the questioner, at the same time? What kind of an amazing relationship—what kind of knowing—is that?*

Intuition: The Teaching That Happens on the Inside

We talked about that particular kind of knowing with Rabbi Zalman Schachter-Shalomi in the basement lair of his home, where he has a room for *davening,* or prayer, a room to entertain discussions with people like us, an office filled with workers busily transcribing his archive of teachings, a library, and a room overflowing with computers. He explained, "We have good *reason* words, but we have hardly any *intuition* words. And if somebody says, 'How do you know?' and it's an intuitive thing, I can't say how."

"Did G-d speak in a baritone?" Reb Zalman (*Reb* is an honorific term for "rabbi" or "teacher") continued, shrugging his shoulders. "No," he answered himself. "It's not necessary for G-d to move air against my eardrums. . . . Intuition is the teaching that you get on the inside. Most of us don't have good vocabularies, so we borrow. How do we know it? I know it like I know myself. How can you talk about this conceptually?"

Spiritual teacher and originator of the Diamond Approach to Self-Realization Hameed Ali tried valiantly to find words to describe his own subtle but clearly identifiable experience of guidance. In the Ridhwan School that he founded, he teaches about what he calls the *Diamond Guidance* in great depth. It's a penetrating process of revelation that cuts through surface appearances and human distortions as cleanly as a diamond. The guidance has a distinct quality that's clearly recognizable but is impossible to convey in general terms.

Here's what Hameed told us about this mode of knowing:

> It's a particular form in which the spiritual nature, whose function is revelation and guidance, manifests itself. Because it has a particular form, a particular feel to it, a particular kind of presence, it's recognizable for what it is. There's no subject/object in the experience of it. The presence is aware of itself, *knowing itself by being itself.* That's general about spiritual presence—the guidance is a particular way of having that *immediacy* and has its own flavor.

This direct experience that he calls Diamond Guidance isn't a noun. It's a verb, a happening, a flash that illuminates one's consciousness—like light and lightning, which are indistinguishable from each other. Furthermore, it seems to be different from what most of us experience as intuition. It seems more akin to an experience of *nondual awareness,* in which we're one with Source, rather than getting messages from a more distant perspective.

Nonduality is an example of a state that can be experienced but is impossible to put into words. We seem to be two: you and me, them and us, plants and people—and so forth. But at a certain level of perception, we're not two but one. As soon as we stop identifying with our emotions, thoughts, and desires, we drop beneath the superficial sense of separateness. Like a chain of islands that appear distinct above the surface of the sea, deeper down they're connected—part of the underlying earth—yet they maintain their individuality when seen from above. In such a way, all phenomena are part of a single Ground of Being that's more subtle than the physical reality of rock, but just as real.

Nina Zimbelman, whom we interviewed in part because of her exceptional intuitive capacity, made a clear distinction between spiritual guidance and intuition:

When I use my intuition, I go to a place of wisdom and use this ability, but when I experience guidance, true wisdom comes to me. I don't go looking. It accesses me like a bolt of lightning. *I* have to access intuition. There's a difference in the feeling, the experience. I use my intuition like others use their thought patterns and brains. Often I work as a medical intuitive and I go to this place in me that's wise, and from there I can experience more than the usual information.

Guidance accesses me—it's a different feeling. I don't initiate it. It's initiated by some embodiment of wisdom that says, *Pay attention!* Intuition is just an ability I have. I use it. Guidance uses *me.* Obviously the greater wisdom that is my guidance is the greater part of me that is steering my smaller self into directions it may not want to go—I have to speak in these dualistic terms, but there's only One.

In an attempt to delve deeper into the realm of direct knowing, we asked our Quaker Sages about what they call leadings. A leading focuses attention on a new possibility that, in some circumstances, can be life changing—Boulder Quaker Meeting member Mary Hey's transformation from being a lawyer to a full-time artist, for example. Leadings can be much less consequential, of course, such as being led to speak aloud in a meeting for worship. The key point we were able to glean about them is that they have "a sense of coming from somewhere else."

Deanne Butterfield described a leading as "both inner and other"—originating from both the Inner Light and from the larger ground of the Divine to which we're connected. Leadings can result in the "way opening," which can be like following a string of synchronicities. Sometimes we're faced with what seems to be an impenetrable wall, and then we discover doors.

We've all had moments of inner knowing, both the type of intuition that words can express and the ineffable kind that's described as *nonduality*—divine union or Diamond Guidance beyond articulation. Both modes of knowing also happen in the dream state where the conscious and unconscious mind meet in the realm of archetypes and symbols.

Dreams

Sufi guide Taj Inayat had a great deal to say about dreams and guidance. She's an accomplished teacher in her own right and is also the mother of the current Pir or spiritual head of the Sufi Order International. She told us that shortly after she was initiated into Sufism, she had a dream that paralleled a famous Sufi teaching story that she wasn't familiar with. "I didn't yet know the famous story of *The Congress of the Birds* [also called *The Conference of the Birds*]," she told us.

This 12th-century teaching story—a poem like the Hymn of the Pearl—tells an archetypal tale of the spiritual journey. The birds of the world are told by a guide that they have a great king, the *Simorgh,* who lives in a palace far, far away. Some birds decide not to attempt the journey. The finch is too cowardly, while the hawk remains entranced with the company of earthly kings. The rest band together and fly over seven mountains and seven valleys. Along the way they begin to discuss how, although all different, they're still birds and must have a common origin.

The journey is long and arduous, and of the innumerable birds that start out, only 30 finally arrive. When they get to the palace, the throne is empty, and they come to the realization that they themselves are the Simorgh. The very word *Simorgh* is a pun that reveals the hidden truth: *Si* means "thirty" and *morgh* translates as "birds."

As Sheikh Kabir Helminski told us, when we're in a state of strong spiritual intention—as Taj was when she had this dream—the Educator of the Universe gives us very rich teachings, and the fabric of a meaningful spiritual reality is revealed. At a later point in her journey, Taj Inayat asked, "What does my soul need to do in this life to complete itself?" She had another powerful dream in which she was going up in an elevator in a seven-story building. She got off at each floor and did what she had to do there. When she reached the seventh, she exited and two men stationed on either side of the door, their arms folded like bodyguards, denied her entry. They said that she'd failed, and Taj then realized that the only way to gain entrance to that floor was to know—to *really* know—that you belong there.

"You have to own your own being," she told us, "but not in a grandiose way." This owning your own being speaks to having the humility of inner authority, being able to sit on the throne of the Simorgh and know that the Divine is one with your own true Self.

Reb Tirzah Firestone is a Jungian and has been working with dreams for more than three decades. "Dreams are a G-d voice," she told us. (In the Jewish tradition, the word *God* is written "G-d" to avoid making an idol of the Divine Mystery and desecrating it when destroying the paper on which it's written.) The symbols and characters that show up in them are a powerful door to Spirit for Reb Tirzah. She told us about a huge lion that appeared in one dream. She didn't analyze it, a typical way to approach dreams, but instead engaged it as a Sacred Other—which yielded powerful insight and guidance. When we engage a symbol as a Sacred Other—talking to it and asking questions—we enter into an adventure with it. That intimate encounter can bring us to the edge of the known . . . to the rich mystery of the unknown.

"That edge is often paradoxical," Reb Tirzah told us. She explained that the unconscious mind is always looking for the tension of opposites, because we grow in the act of reconciling them. So, if we're committed to growth, the unconscious will set up a tension if we're getting too comfortable. If we can see it as a goad, an urging toward wholeness, then working with it becomes exciting rather than disconcerting or frightening.

Sally Kempton, who teaches an ancient Hindu philosophy asserting that the atman (the true Self) is one with Brahman (God or Ultimate Reality), also experiences dreams as a source of guidance. She agrees with Taj Inayat and Reb Tirzah that asking for insight or guidance before going to sleep and then seeing what comes up in dreaming is almost infallible.

In the Siddha Yoga tradition in which she spent many years as Swami Durgananda, as well as in Sufi and Tibetan Buddhist traditions, Sally explained, there's a lot of emphasis on divine dreams in which one's teacher appears. Having spent many years with a guide who operates on the subtle and dream planes, she told us that messages come through those planes when the teacher

22

is present in the dream state. At other times he or she appears symbolically—a Jungian symbol of the Self or atman—rather than through any conscious intention. Sally explained, "There's a lot of talk in the Indian traditions about divine dreams, the kind of dream where a guiding being appears and says something mysterious or koan-like, or shows you an image, or takes you on a journey—and about how you discern whether the dream message is a true one." Sally continued:

> Even when you have a close relationship with a teacher, there is wisdom that can be given in the dream state that can't be given face-to-face, because, in a sense, you have to get it yourself, from inside. That's just the reality of how human beings grow towards God. There are recognitions you have to come to yourself, just as there is a point when you realize that the true teacher is not a separate person, but a face that you put on your own inner Self. Whenever people are in a collective relationship with a divine personage like Christ, or with a guru as in some of the Eastern traditions, there's a tendency to project the Divine onto the teacher, to put grace outside of yourself. The dreaming process is one of the roads we take to realizing that the Divine is within us.

Each form of guidance that we've discussed—paying attention to felt sense, signs and synchronicities, intuition, and dreams—reveals deeper answers to the questions *Who am I?* and *Why am I here?* When the forgetful prince in the Hymn of the Pearl receives the magic letter from his parents, reminding him of who he is and providing guidance for the trip home, it takes the form of an eagle. The eagle speaks to him through many channels: a voice, the thrumming of its wings, and a certain kind of inner knowing. All these forms of guidance, and more, are given to us.

To the prince's amazement, the words in the magic letter are already inscribed in his heart. It is both "inner and other." The revelatory message of that paradox is that the Source of Guidance is both inside you as your true Self and outside you as All-That-Is. And the two are one.

This is wisdom that can't come through the mind—only the eyes of the heart can comprehend it. But if you sincerely want to know who you are and what your purpose in this world is, then there's one thing you can count on for sure: The quality of your longing to know will bring more guidance. Seek and you shall find. Knock and the door *will* be opened.

❋ ❋ ❋

Chapter Three

In "God" We Trust?

Spiritual guidance, as we understand it from our conversations with the Sages, is always available. But if you subscribe to the adage "Knock and it shall be opened," it's reasonable to ask who or what is opening the door. For some readers, a personal God Who loves you—and to Whom you can pray—is the energy behind the door. For others, the doorway opens to an intelligence or wisdom that's impersonal yet operates according to natural laws of cause and effect that human beings can gain insight into and learn to cooperate with in a way that diminishes suffering and increases compassion.

Perhaps you—like many people—periodically reevaluate your spiritual beliefs in the light of your lived experience. This curiosity about the nature of reality, and our relationship to it, is at the heart of living a spiritually guided life.

Joan: Several years ago I was hanging between the horns of an apparent dilemma. While I could appreciate the wisdom of Buddhism and its nontheistic approach to human development and spiritual awakening, I'd had many personal experiences of a loving energy, which—for want of a better term—I called God. In an attempt to come to peace with the fact that I couldn't easily articulate my experience—or reconcile its personal and nonpersonal aspects—for months I compulsively asked every friend or acquaintance I could corner, "What *is* God?"

The Gallup poll won't be hiring me as a researcher, since my sample was obviously skewed—made up of people who were genuine spiritual seekers. Most of my friends began their answer with something like this: "If you're talking about an old-fashioned, fire-and-brimstone God Who rewards, punishes, roots for particular football teams, and Whose ego is even bigger than mine, then no—I don't believe in the kind of God Who's made in our own image."

After that common disclaimer, their answers were divergent. Some invoked a conscious intelligence, others a Divine Beloved, still others a wisdom that operates according to natural laws. *But the bottom line—the take-away lesson from this "research"—was a sense that they could cultivate a meaningful relationship to the higher intelligence of their understanding and become freer and happier as a result.*

Joan and Gordon: Whether you view God or consciousness as personal or impersonal—and our Sages, like these friends, were divergent on this point—spiritual guidance itself (the relationship you have to that consciousness) is *intensely personal*. There's nothing abstract or general about it. There's an immediacy, a directness, a *felt sense* of contact in this level of communication that leaves little doubt that *you* are the intended receiver and that something important, fresh, and new is being revealed. Whether information comes through a dream, a synchronicity, a series of leadings, the process of inquiry, meditation, prayer, or as feedback from observing the results of your behavior, the guidance helps orient you to greater degrees of awareness, compassion, and skillful action.

In God We Trust?

Every religion has moral guidelines—a kind of one-size-fits-all prescription for living a good life. Those precepts are helpful as far as they go, but spiritual guidance provides a more personal level of direction that speaks to exactly where we are and what we need. This isn't the first time in history when, both as a society and as individuals, we've needed to look beyond political, religious, and social structures for specific guidance. The Protestant Reformation, for example, set the stage for the emergence of modern democracy by transferring power from corrupt external authorities to the individual conscience. In response to the same abuses of power, St. Ignatius of Loyola, while remaining in the Catholic fold, offered his spiritual exercises (which we'll consider when we discuss discernment) as a way to personally attune the individual soul—the seat of our inner authority—to universal or divine will.

Our current era is again one in which the external authority placed in business, government, and religion stands in many cases discredited, leaving us hungry for a source of wisdom and direction that we can trust. The decision to use the *Soul's Compass,* and to form a personal relationship to the Source of Guidance—however we conceptualize that—has always been a route to wisdom and a significant step toward spiritual maturation. And in these chaotic times, the understanding that spiritual guidance is always available, no matter how loud and insistent the voices of external authority may be, is crucial to finding our way.

In the hope of learning more about how the still, small voice of our own inner authority—our connection to a greater intelligence—functions, we asked our Sages if they'd be willing to share some of their personal experiences of spiritual guidance with us. As you read in the last chapter and will discover more about here, those experiences were quite varied and ranged from subtle leadings to untoward events; from divine union to Dark Nights of the Soul. But what the experiences had in common was that they were *up close and personal.* The guidance that our Sages received wasn't revelation meant for the masses, but for them personally. It was precise and, in some cases, totally transformative because it changed the person's basic view of reality.

The three major themes that came through most clearly were:

1. Trust in spiritual guidance is the foundation for following it. If you don't believe in some form of higher intelligence, whether it's personally aware of you or not, you won't be interested in being guided.

2. Guidance is a deeply personal relationship with the God (or wisdom principles) of your own understanding. It functions for people of any and all belief systems, as long as they maintain an open, curious attitude toward whatever may be revealed.

3. Guidance invites you to look beyond the surface of your immediate circumstances, and your attachment to a particular outcome, to see how wisdom—or Spirit—is moving in your life right now to help you develop greater insight, compassion, and effectiveness in the world.

Experiences of Trust in a Personal God

Episcopal priest Suzanne Fageol told us about a magnificent experience she had at the age of three. Because of her youth, she had few words to describe it and no real context to place it in. It was something that fell outside the boundaries of the known, yet it created a firm foundation—or ground on which she could stand and listen for guidance—for the rest of her life:

> I'd been napping in my grandmother's house, and it was thundering. I had my head under the pillow because I was afraid. When the storm was over, I pulled the pillow off my eyes and my immediate view was of a beautiful huge old oak tree outside. As I looked at the tree, the sun hit every drop of water and turned it into a crystal tree with rainbows shining out of each drop. The next thing, I was no longer me; I no longer had a body. I felt myself merged and enfolded in this incredible peak experience of love. From that I was shown my path of service—not as something

specific like "You'll be an Episcopal priest," but as a path of serving this love, this Mystery. That was my first intimation of coming back into a sense of separation from that union.

At first I was just in the union, and then I saw the calling—and then the next thing I knew, I was being slammed back into my body and I was on the bed. I was sobbing from a place of deep love. It was a sense of longing for the [Divine] Beloved. . . .

When I'm specifically asking to receive spiritual guidance, it's to that deepest state of partnership with the Beloved that I go as my grounding point, and from there I sit and open to receive. It's a very grounded experience as well as being transcendent—it's important to me that both are present. If one or the other is lacking, it's false guidance.

The presence of God that Reverend Suzanne described is a grace that has served her well through the years. It gave her a direct experience of a loving Presence that she could trust and relax into, letting go of her own agenda as she opened up to receive guidance from a larger source of intelligence.

Shaman/poet Oriah Mountain Dreamer also spoke of God as a steadfast companion on her journey: "From the time I was a young child, my earliest memories were of a Presence that was with me. There was a certain quality to it that was always the same—this kind of holding, loving, all-abiding, and all-inclusive quality."

Rabbi Rami Shapiro described an experience of Divine Presence that came to him as an adult, the result of his longing for the Divine Beloved. He told us that he'd repeated the Hebrew words *ahava rabah* (infinite love) daily for years to remind him that G-d's love is infinite.

Rabbi Rami—the type of man who works hard, does good, and is always pressing himself to do more and be better—laughed as he explained, "I'm used to earning, working on merit."

Joan: I nodded in recognition, since he's a mirror for my own overachieving patterns. From the place of deficiency where whatever you do doesn't ever seem to be enough, the idea that God's love is infinite—as well as personal and unconditional—is an abstraction. But a moment of grace gifted Rabbi Rami with a direct experience of that love . . . a living revelation.

"You can't earn G-d's love," he continued his story with conviction. "You can only accept it or reject it. I learned this through guidance, through getting the intense feeling of being loved just as I am. This experience was totally transformative, and it took away the last of [my] thinking that I needed a system to get enlightened. The word *kabbalah* means to receive—not just the tradition, but the actual act of receiving the unending, infinite love of G-d. It's about opening hand and heart to the love of G-d and becoming part of the divine flow. The feeling of being loved unconditionally by G-d is one of the most, or perhaps *the* most, transformative experiences I've ever had."

To Sufi guide Taj Inayat, the experience of divine union is so intensely personal and private that she could only point to it obliquely: "The very depth of my spiritual life is a deep, deep intimacy with God as my beloved. I've not found a way to teach about that without losing the essential truth of it. In Sufism there are dimensions of the heart. These dimensions within the heart, at the center there's a temple—a perfumed sanctuary where the mystical marriage happens poetically. This place is reserved for only the Soul and God—the bridal chamber. So there's no way to speak of these without," she hesitated uncomfortably while searching for the right word, ". . . soiling them."

Avoiding Spiritual Materialism

One way to "soil" experiences of Divine Presence is to treat them as goals to be achieved—merit badges that confer some kind of distinction upon the spiritual seeker. I had an experience that is a case in point. For a span of several years in my 40s, I had powerful visions of divine light, insightful lucid dreams (*lucidity* means that you awaken in the dream, know that you're dreaming, and have some control over what happens), and the breakthrough of psychic abilities called *siddhis*.

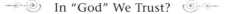

One night when I became lucid in a dream and decided to float upward into union with divine light, my head became lodged in a cloud. Since normal awareness is maintained in such a dream, I started to laugh at the obvious message: My head was, in reality, stuck in the clouds. I needed to come back down to Earth and work on some of the ways that the most limited aspect of identity—the ego—blocked me from being present to the intelligent dynamism that moves through every moment.

Joan and Gordon: Wanting to see mystical figures during meditation, developing psychic powers, and the like have long been viewed as red herrings on the path—or what we're calling *magnetic deviance.* They stroke the ego and make you feel special, rather than encouraging ego to step aside so that true nature can emerge in the ordinariness of daily life. As the old adage says, "If you meet the Buddha on the road, kill him."

A much more authentic criterion of spiritual growth is *interior freedom*—the willingness to stay present to what's happening in the moment instead of allowing yourself to get hooked by judgment, desire, fear, residue from the past, or thoughts about what you'd rather be experiencing. Reverend Cynthia Bourgeault explained the attitude of interior freedom quite simply: "The deep willingness to sit in this moment and find the complete fullness of it and realize that whatever is in your path is okay lets you surrender to the moment and allow guidance to emerge."

You may not know where the guidance is leading you, but when you become more aware of what it is, there's a growing inner confidence that certain steps feel right. As Reverend Cynthia describes it, you may be taking a leap of faith, but you know that you're not jumping into an empty swimming pool. If you're receptive to noticing the subtle messages—or *leadings*—that speak of a spiritual reality just beneath surface appearances, then the signals that guide you back to your true nature become progressively easier to spot, at least in retrospect. Trust in guidance deepens organically as the results of following it become more and more apparent.

Trusting Leadings

Sister Rose Mary Dougherty replied to our question about the personal experience of guidance by describing how she's often led from one step to the next when she's willing to pay attention and listen:

> I would say that most times in my life it's been more a retrospective look that has allowed me to recognize that, indeed, there was a leading. It was a moving, as it were, from Light to Light. The best I could say was, "I don't have a clue about what this really is about," but this step seemed right. And there was a deep inner confidence with that. When I looked back at the choices that I'd made out of that sense that didn't have their bases in a rational figuring-out sort of thing, I'm absolutely stunned sometimes at where that has gone.
>
> There are times I've been freer to hear that guidance or to be in touch with it. Sometimes I really have to pray for a sense of freedom or have to acknowledge to myself my own un-freedom. I have to let go of busyness and learn to listen more deeply—but it's been there when I'm in that listening place.
>
> I think the guidance is always available to us. It's always just there, but my I [ego] gets so far separated from my [true or higher] Self that I'm not in touch with it . . . so often I get caught in my own little, narrow constructs that I just don't see beyond them. Not only do I get caught in them, I get really pushy with my own agenda around them. But there's something [about guidance] . . . it's like the lotus opening to the Light, where I can see beyond this narrowness. That's when the interconnectedness is most real for me. It's always there—I only need to open to it.

"Opening in general is not about doing," Quaker Mary Hey explained. "It's about seeing what comes from sitting in silence. The only thing in the way of seeing leadings clearly is *me*. The Holy Spirit does intervene in some way and actually point in a direction."

To hear that direction, Mary continued, "we have to stop at both major and minor places. We learn when to pause, connect, and question, even in small ways."

Continual openness to what's new and fresh in each moment is anchored in the pure-process language that defines the Quaker attitude or stance toward the flow of spiritual guidance: seeking, listening, waiting, opening, discerning, witnessing, reviewing—all of which require a silencing of the noisy ego, with all its special interests and desires. That quelling of ego goes hand in hand with an almost radical trust in a larger intelligence—the Holy Spirit or Spirit of Guidance—that's trying valiantly to get a word in edgewise.

Quaker educator Patricia Loring told us two delightful stories about that radical trust. She described the first as a bit of Quaker folklore: "Folklore such as this is of doubtful provenance, but we're fond of retelling and rehearing many such stories. It's in the stories that ways of being with God that we cherish are preserved. . . .

> Back in colonial America, sometime in the 1700s or there-abouts, a Quaker man is traveling through the wilderness of the East Coast on foot, and he stumbles upon an old foundation from a ruined house deep within the forest. He curls up in its lee for a nap and wakes with the sense that he's supposed to speak out loud—kind of like a Friends' vocal ministry when there's a strong leading during a meeting to say what comes to mind.
>
> This seems totally ridiculous, since he's alone in the middle of nowhere—there's nothing there but him and the forest. But after some hesitation, he finally stands up and delivers the message anyway. Feeling relieved, he picks up his pack and goes on his way. The following day, having arrived at a settlement, he hears a story about a man who—just the day before—was sitting alone in the forest near the foundation of a tumbled-down house when he heard a voice telling him just what he needed to do to change the course of his life.

That story may be apocryphal, but Patricia told us that there are many recorded historical instances of Friends' willingness to trust unexpected leadings that arise during time spent in silent prayer, meditation, or worship.

One such story concerned getting relief to refugees in the Gaza Strip in 1948. The American Friends Service Committee went over all the requirements, took stock of their resources and manpower, and concluded that there was simply no possible way to carry it out. Saddened by this realization, they decided to sit in silent prayer together. When they reemerged, there was total unanimity that they'd go ahead with the project, even though they all concurred that it seemed impossible.

"So you pass beyond reason and utilitarianism," Patricia told us, "and you're trusting in something else, which is contrary to the prevailing 'wisdom' in our culture." It's hard to think or act outside the box—to be open to following a leading even though it seems nonsensical—unless you have firm spiritual ground to stand on. Faith in guidance comes down to recognizing that there's a pattern of growth and evolution that we can discern and cooperate with.

Trusting in the unknown—in something beyond what you can see, hear, and reason your way through—makes it possible to follow the subtle leadings that appear. In some cases, though, uncertainty and stress seem to block the way. But when seen rightly, even these uncomfortable states are allies on the journey, since the tension that they produce can crack open the ego and begin to let in the light of a new understanding.

Trusting Uncertainty and Stress

When we asked former Jesuit priest Dr. Wilkie Au whether he'd be willing to share a personal instance of spiritual guidance, he chose one where uncertainty became his guide:

> One of my most dramatic experiences came after a year in the seminary. I had this sudden impulse to leave, and I was quite shaken by that. I was underage when I entered, and my father had opposed it. One afternoon I wanted to get out, and I brought it up with my [spiritual] director. I was about to turn 21 and legally could stay, so this was the final opportunity to leave without taking vows. He suggested that I take vows of devotion—private vows.
>
> I did, and all my remorse and resistance ceased. Everything came back to peace. My unrest and disturbance disappeared. He

was able to see something in my experience, and I feel like it was a gift from God. This was one of the first times he [the spiritual director] was this directive. It was his intuition about what might have been going on in me. That's why I think it was divinely inspired—it seemed a little out of character, out of the way he usually functioned in terms of that kind of depth. It was so right on. After that, I was peaceful about being a Jesuit for a large number of years. That was one of the biggest bumps in the road.

"So your response was immediate and experiential: a sense of peace?" we reflected back.

"Yes," Dr. Au continued. "In fact, peace for Christians is a hallmark of the Spirit's presence—verifying the rightness of a decision. It has to be confirmed by peace; and if there's a radical unrest, we have to go back to the drawing board to see what's going on."

Dr. Au was fortunate in having a spiritual director—a soul friend skilled in deep listening—to help him use stress as a clarifier for where Spirit was moving in his life. For him, as well as for many of the other Sages, disquiet is considered an integral part of our built-in guidance system.

"If you feel lost, you are. If you have to ask if you're in harmony, you're not. You don't feel well. There's a feedback loop there," Buddhist monk Ajahn Sona explained.

If you're anxious, you can either continue to do more of what got you there, or begin to listen to the stress. It will tell you where the disharmony is, and then you can make healthier choices. Ajahn Sona quotes the Buddha in saying that *dhamma* (he uses the Pali word, rather than the more familiar Sanskrit *dharma*) is beautiful in the beginning, beautiful in the middle, and beautiful in the end. So if life isn't beautiful now, right where you are, that's a signal that you're not following the dhamma, or path of harmony. And like an alcoholic who hits bottom and then joins a 12-step program, the disharmony can be a wake-up call that launches you on a spiritual trajectory that you might otherwise never have discovered.

Stress, disharmony, and depression are all states in which divine love seems absent. But that very eclipse of the Light is a well-known part of the spiritual journey and has been called the Dark Night of the Soul. The 15th-century Christian mystic St. John of the Cross and his spiritual director St. Teresa of Avila spoke of these times as *la noche oscura*—the dark night—when we can't see the movement of Spirit and the reassuring connection to God seems to dry up. Rabbi Tirzah Firestone talked about these dry times using the Hebrew term *hester panim,* meaning "the eclipse or hiding of the face."

"There can be prolonged seasons of *hester panim,*" Reb Tirzah explained, "when we can't feel, discern, hear, or see the face of God, the One That we yearn for. There's something that's occluding that connection, and these are very trying times."

She worries a bit about people who always seem to be in the light without ever questioning their faith or entering those periods of darkness when the bright face of the moon yields to the shadow of the earth. It's the times of darkness, Reb Tirzah has observed, that make us deep and profound, that cultivate the compassion to relate to human doubts and wounds in a more thoughtful and authentic way.

"What can we make of hurricanes, tsunamis, and earthquakes that create such terrible suffering?" she mused.

What can we make of the cancer that threatens our life or that of our loved one? What can we make of war and genocide? Reb Tirzah compared the face of a tsunami to that of the fierce Hindu goddess Kali, who gives birth to the world and then eats her own children. Now *there's* an image that could undermine trust, unless you're willing to engage it directly and unflinchingly—something for which Reb Tirzah has a fascinating method. She'll occasionally invite people who are railing against the dark face of God to come into a sacred space and relate directly to their Creator . . . not to talk about what happened, but to converse intimately with the Source of life itself. That's *chutzpah*—the nerve to beard the lion in its own den.

To some people for whom she's the spiritual mentor or guide, Reb Tirzah suggests that they address God directly with the Hebrew word *Atah,* which means "You." Call out, *"Atah! Atah! Atah! You! You! You!"* and let loose with all your scathing recriminations. The image that comes to mind is of a wounded, confused, and furious Job shaking his fists at God. *You! You! You! What is this terrible suffering all about? Is there anyone there? Who am I talking to?* (By the way, we don't suggest trying this at home without an experienced spiritual mentor to guide you.)

This practice, Reb Tirzah finds, can open a floodgate to the Sacred Other. It brings to mind Jacob's wrestling with an angel of God on the banks of the Jabbok River. At the time, Jacob is a young family man, shaped by the bitter and altogether human experience of having been both the betrayer and the betrayed. He stole his brother Esau's birthright and then had to hide out in exile. His father-in-law to-be then robbed him of his bride, hiding his ugly daughter Leah beneath the wedding veil when it was the beautiful Rachel whom Jacob believed was his intended. Eventually, having worked himself to the bone for his father-in-law, Jacob earns the right to wed Rachel as well.

After years in exile, he's finally on his way home with his wives, his concubine, a gaggle of children, and a herd of livestock. But Jacob's problems aren't over yet. His brother Esau, the one who was cheated of his birthright, has heard that he's coming home and is out looking for him with his retinue. Night falls, and Jacob goes to the banks of the river to think. An angel appears to him, and they wrestle ferociously until dawn. The angel won't let go of Jacob, and Jacob won't let go of the angel until he's made sense of his predicament and understands his life. Finally satisfied, they disengage as the light dawns.

But Jacob is no longer his old self. He's crippled where the angel has held on to his thigh and, as Rabbi Rami Shapiro explained, now has to walk at the pace of the wounded, the lame, and the nursing mother. He's wiser, more compassionate, and ready both to forgive and to be forgiven. God gives him the new name *Israel,* which means "God wrestler." And sometimes that's what guidance feels like: a wrestling match with God.

Chronos and Kairos: A Deeper Level of Listening to Life

There are two ways of listening to stories such as Jacob's. The first is the linear, logical way—taking what's said at face value. We call this the *chronos* level, from the Greek word for "clock time." But there's a second level to the story, and that's the inner spiritual meaning. The Greek word for that dimension of experience is *kairos,* or eternal time. The kairos level of Jacob's story concerns his renaming. There's been a fundamental shift in identity during his struggle with the angel. He has left his limited false self behind and stepped into a larger version of who he is—his true nature.

While it might be tempting to think that inner growth is usually a movement from Light to Light that guarantees success, this is rarely the whole story. The shell of the ego usually has to be cracked open before the seed of Spirit can sprout. For example, rushed people who always feel a sense of urgency—compelled to get more and more done in less and less time—will eventually crash. Sooner or later, burned-out and overwhelmed, they'll hit bottom and experience the sacrament of helplessness. Only then is the situation ripe for authentic investigation of the possibility that there's an underlying, trustworthy movement of Spirit, with which they're in partnership.

The insight that they aren't the separate "doer" who gets things done through absolute control and heroic effort can finally arise. They're exhausted by the doing, and ready to let go because there simply isn't any more strength left to hang on; thus, the stage is set for perceiving the invisible wind beneath their wings. Then it's a matter of leaning into it and letting themselves be carried. By "letting go and letting God"—a condition that could only have been embodied through surrender—a divine co-creative partnership can emerge.

The hope in a spiritual-mentoring situation is that the mentor (who might prefer to call him- or herself an *anam cara,* soul friend, companion, guide, or spiritual director) can listen to a chronos, or ego story, and reflect back the underlying kairos, or soul story.

When we asked Professor Wilkie Au how such direction was helpful to him, he said, "When I felt that they heard my story and could offer a spiritual explanation of what might have been going on in my soul in a way that resonated with me."

"So it wasn't just a mirroring back of what was going on," we responded, "but it added a spiritual dimension to the interpretation of the events in your life. It lit up the inner meaning."

Listening to the stories of guidance that the Sages told, we heard an underlying soul theme, an inner meaning. Simply put, it's that God (wisdom or Ultimate Reality) is extending a hand to us and sending us directions for the journey home. As in the Hymn of the Pearl, the directions are already inscribed in our heart as our true Self, but God reaches out to us—the beloveds—and reminds us of what's already written in our spiritual DNA. Whether that outreach takes the form of divine union, subtle leadings, or overt stress, it's nonetheless a magic letter that comes to us personally from the Creator, the loving Spirit of Guidance.

Father Thomas Keating told us how the stories of the interfaith participants in his annual Snowmass Conference confirm the sense that the Divine Beloved is reaching out to us across time and space: "The experience of the Snowmass Conference, for over 20 years, has shown that deep dialogue among people who are advanced in their respective traditions reveals a common heart that is communicating or transmitting itself to everyone who is moving into that level of listening and relating and becoming intimate with that which is closer to us than we are to ourselves—the Divine Presence within us, around us, and everywhere else."

Our awakened human heart is the receiver that picks up the signal of the Divine Heart. We, in turn, transmit that love. The more love we generate—in the form of intimacy with life, gratitude, and compassionate action—the more open our hearts become, and the more direction we receive. Synchronicities appear as we come into coherence with a larger field, and guidance opens the way before us: The scientist receives inspiration for her experiment. The father sees a notice on the bulletin board of the health-food store about a new school that's just right for his child. The author has a conversation with a stranger that sparks an idea about the plot for a novel. Following the thread of love—excitement, passion, gratitude, a desire to know more about life—we find the treasure.

Listening for the Vector of Love

Rabbi Rami talked about *kabbalah* as "receiving"—the literal translation of the word. He called it the opening of hand and heart to God and becoming part of the divine flow. Tuning in to that divine flow—the kairos part of any story—might also be described as aligning with the vector of love.

The *vector of love* is a term that Sister Rose Mary Dougherty uses for how we can "listen one another" into a state of transparency to guidance. (The phrase *listen one another* is used frequently in spiritual mentoring—it refers to how listening for the movement of Spirit and then mirroring it back to others can help them understand how Spirit is guiding them.) She describes the vector of love as the prayer of God for us, unfolding within our hearts as guidance. Being fired from a job, for example, might open up a discussion of where a person's true gifts and talents reside. An addiction could be love's way of creating an opportunity for dismantling the false self so that true nature can shine through.

"Whether or not one is aware of it," Sister Rose Mary explains in her book *Group Spiritual Direction,* "God is constantly engaged with the human heart. God is present, inviting, cajoling, challenging, enabling, always loving persons to be who they are—lovers at home in Love. At some point in the spiritual journey we are awakened to this love affair and the subsequent choice to claim the primacy of love in our lives."[1]

"Our searching, our wanting, is reflective of God's seeking us," Sister Rose Mary explains. The longing we feel for orientation and guidance is a response to "God's prayer in us"—a call to mutual recognition and communion.

Sheikh Kabir Helminski expressed it this way: "The roles of lover and beloved switch between God and human being. The human is the beloved, and God is the lover—this gives you an idea of what worship is. Real worship only becomes possible when we realize that we're loved by something infinitely generous and beautiful."

It's just that realization that we heard over and over again as many of the Sages told their stories of how they understood the grace of being loved unconditionally by God or Ultimate Reality.

Joan: The thought that there might be a personal God—one who cares for us particularly—was especially poignant for me. Over the years, even though I had directly experienced the love of God in mystical states, somehow that relationship had become lost to me. This is the classic Dark Night of the Soul, where God disappears from sight and we feel alone and bereft.

Working on this book turned out to be spiritual guidance for me. I came out of the dark night—not back into the faith I once had, but into a deeper kind that had been maturing just under the surface all along. Moving beyond the surface stories of our lives and tapping into the vector of love changes the shine on everything.

Joan and Gordon: That essential shift in orientation from the surface (chronos) to the depth (kairos) is like the difference between eating the orange rind and tasting its fruit. Whenever a little leading, a stress, or a dark night knocks on the door of the heart, ask the simple question *Where is Spirit in this?* or *Where is the vector of love moving?* That straightforward inquiry allows your Soul's Compass to orient to a deeper truth.

In all situations you can take a few deep breaths and surrender to Spirit. Let it cradle you like the earth holds the roots of a tree. Trust it and take in the nourishment that's there. Even a moment of letting go can put you back into the flow, whether you're moving from Light to Light or breaking through the darkness like a seed beginning to germinate and move toward the sun. The secret of the spiritual journey is this: You are the same distance from home wherever you are—which, in the paradoxical language that describes the journey, is no distance at all. You're already there.

✸   ✸   ✸

Chapter Four

INTIMACY . . . SEEING WITH THE EYES OF THE HEART

"It is only with the heart that one can see rightly;
what is essential is invisible to the eye."
— Antoine de Saint-Exupéry

Regardless of the form that it might take, spiritual guidance is a process of knowing that's often paradoxical. We *know,* but we're not sure *how* we know, since our rational mind may not have weighed in on the matter at all.

For instance, when you meet a kindred spirit for the first time, there's a subtle but compelling sense of recognition. You don't know each other on an external level, yet your souls share a deep understanding. The metaphor most often used for this kind of meeting is that of a *heart-to-heart.* This type of intimate connection, where you move beyond the veil of superficial familiarity into an exquisite communion, is both the goal of the spiritual journey and its inherent bliss.

To see through the eyes of the heart means to look beneath surface appearances. The mind—whose function is to catalog, compare, judge, and codify experience—excels at the kind of knowing based on sensory input and memory. But there's another way of knowing so intimate and fresh that only poets dare to express it in words. It's so indescribably vivid and immediate that there's virtually no separation between the knower and the known. We become, or recognize that we already are, at one with a web of loving intelligence that's as close as our own hands and feet . . . yet as vast as the universe itself. In these experiences, the curtain of sleep parts and we find ourselves face-to-face with the Source of Guidance as it is manifesting freshly in this very moment.

When we asked one of the poets on our panel, Daniel Ladinsky, the question that informs this chapter: "How does the heart—the mystery of love—factor into what we understand as guidance?" he replied, "The heart having intelligence may seem something of an odd notion, but I feel that is where the deeper—the greater intelligence/guidance/wisdom—begins: in the heart. And to me, loving and intelligence is the same." It's this kind of intelligence, and the means to awakening it, that is the subject of this chapter.

The Intimate, Awakened Heart

"How do we know if our heart is awake, sensitive, and functioning, as opposed to contracted and numb?" mused Sufi Sheikh Kabir Helminski.

He continued:

> When the heart is not functioning as it's meant to, we perceive *things*. We even perceive people as things, and we treat them as such. To the extent that the heart is open and healthy, we perceive that we live in a very tender universe. We begin to see the tender aspects of human beings—a process in which wherever you look is the face of God. The face of God is everywhere. The whole universe is animate and conscious.
>
> The degree to which the heart is open is the degree to which we live in a loving universe. I suspect that there's no end to the dimensions of that experience.

Most of us have had glimpses of heart awakening that stay with us simply because they're "Aha" moments that feel like rousing from a deep sleep.

Gordon: Some 30 years ago, I was living on a ranch along the front range of the Colorado Rockies. It was broad daylight on a day like any other when—as I stepped off the porch onto the land—a sudden silence startled me into an acute awakening unlike anything I'd known before. An invisible curtain had lifted. All my thoughts had stopped, piercing the usual membrane between mental description and direct perception.

Ultimate Reality in its manifest, finely differentiated form had been there all along, right before my eyes. Now, in a moment of pure grace, it caught and held my rapt attention. A deeper and more immediate world revealed itself to all my senses and drew me into the silent luminosity of its being. The nearby elm trees, the towering cottonwoods farther to the west, and the snowcapped purple mountains beyond came vibrantly alive and present. Every living thing, including earth and sky, emerged from hiding like a theophany—an appearance of God. The conscious heartbeat of creation—its silent pulsing exquisitely alive with intelligence and love—was exposed and indistinguishable from my own heart's steady beat. In that moment, as time stood still and I prayed (unsuccessfully) never to fall asleep again, I had a taste of awakened heart.

Joan and Gordon: Such experiences are revelatory in the sense that they expose both our own true identity and the larger reality of which we're a part. When thought stops and ego stands aside, true Self is revealed in a way that is unique to us and is often purposeful in terms of our part in the overall scheme of things.

Hameed Ali described it in this way: "People who rely on texts believe the revelation already happened—to somebody else—and that it's encoded in a book. They just read it and believe it. With mystical experience, you don't rely on that kind of thing, even if you do believe it. You still need your own revelation, which is always a *new* revelation."

George Fox, the founder of the Quaker tradition, was asked how he could recognize guidance. His response, summarized for us by Quaker Deanne Butterfield, was similar to Hameed's. Guidance for Fox was characterized both by immediacy and by a sense of personal, fresh revelation that he challenged others to seek in their own lives. Deanne paraphrased his teaching: "The only way I know was that my experience was *real*. There's no point saying that Jesus said this or the apostles said that. *What canst thou say?*"

Spiritual Guidance as a Revelation of Love

The experience of guidance as revelation, as we heard from our Sages, is characterized by a profound sense of connection and intimate *knowing*—as when the once-hesitant climber comes to love the rock and the ascent reveals itself organically. The wisdom of the heart isn't a solo act. It requires both a lover and a beloved. The union of those two gives rise to a Third, the child of intimacy—an emergent property that is totally new and vital. It's a revelation because this is the first time it has ever come into existence.

Hameed continued his explanation of revelation:

> The guidance appears only as a response to the love of the heart. If the heart is involved—loving—if we're really curious about reality, want to see it, love to see it, and we love to see the truth more than any other agenda we have, then the guidance will manifest.
>
> The whole revelation becomes a love affair, just like wanting to know your beloved as much as possible. So we can't do it only as a mind thing. If it's a mind thing, the guidance doesn't show up. Without the heart being open and dynamically desiring truth for its own sake, the guidance won't operate.

"As *The Cloud of Unknowing* says," Father Thomas Keating echoed, referring to the 14th-century mystical text, "we can't know God by direct knowledge in this life, but only through love. And so love is a kind of knowledge, or a form of thinking."

Reb Zalman, never one to leave things vague or abstract, described the heart's intimate form of knowing in this way: "Imagine a point where the third eye is and the occiput [the bone at the base of the skull] at the back of the head. Now imagine a line between them and another line at the temple crossing the first line; then put yourself at that intersection. Then allow this point to sink into the heart—this spot," he said, tapping his chest.

He resumed his explanation:

46

From that place, look at the other person and there's already a different way of seeing than if you saw them through the two eyes alone. If you're a counselor, for instance, you'd normally see how they are in their body—what their complexion is saying and so forth. That renders the person an *it*. You see their shell. But if you go into the heart space, it's a different story. From the heart you see: *What are they longing for? What are they moving to? What's their purpose, their destiny?*

If I go only to my mind, I'll start working with reality—how they might be able to do something if they change this or that. But if I stay in the heart, I get an idea of who they are and what their destiny is. Different and sometimes surprising things come up in my mind when I ask a question, and that may be transformative.

The eyes of the heart are organs of divine perception. Only when we're present to the heart do we touch Ultimate Reality and experience it, penetrating surface reality with a kind of spiritual x-ray vision. The familiar world becomes *transparent,* revealing the luminous One beneath appearances.

When we asked how the mystery of love factors into spiritual guidance, Sufi teacher Taj Inayat described some of the subtleties of cherishing what's both concealed and yet also revealed as creation unfolding. For Sufis, God is a Hidden Treasure that's longing to be known—so just as we're trying to relate intimately to that mystery, it's also longing to reveal itself to us.

She explained:

Hazrat Inayat Khan [the founder of the Sufi Order International] said that the first and foremost object in the inner life is to make one's relationship to God more central than any other relationship. And there's a danger in that, because we can't help thinking of God as separate. In one sense God *is* separate—from our ego sense—but not ultimately, not truly, separate. It's a navigation to make that shift where we're relating to the center, to God, and then to see all beings and all relationships as expressions of that primary relationship. . . .

The deeper form of God [present in everything] can feel abstract. One of the teachings of the Sufi path is how to know the formless God without becoming abstract. So the same attachment, the same love and excitement that you have for the beauty of this world, the people, the presence of nature—how much it means to us that we can actually cultivate that for something that's formless!

There's definitely a way. It's like taking the essence, like a bee—taking the essence of the things of this world—feeling the quality within them, of which they're the manifestation, and then feeling into the invisible force that's even more subtle than the qualities themselves. It's following a trajectory without getting abstract.

Hazrat Inayat Khan said, "Well, you've heard the music. Are you interested in meeting the musician?" It's hard for some people to make those steps into the formless. But that's the teaching—how to become subtle. That's my own particular way, now, of receiving guidance . . .

"Oops!" she broke off. "There goes a little seal swimming by my window."

Joan: "You must have a window by the ocean," I observed, imagining how beautiful it must be on the California coast, where Taj lives.

Gordon: As we conversed a bit more about what Taj called "the in-between place where form and formlessness meet," I likened it to what the 13th-century Sufi saint Ibn al-'Arabi understood as *spiritual imagination*: our capacity to see both the manifest and the unmanifest creation with the eyes of the heart. When we see the unmanifest—like Michelangelo, who saw the form of his sculptures hidden within the raw marble—then we can bring it into being. That's spiritual guidance at work, manifesting the world of form.

"Definitely," Taj agreed, "and you have to learn to give yourself to it. It's an art."

"You were talking about meeting the musician through the music and following that subtle sense of God's presence," I observed with delight, "and then that seal appeared and so clearly touched your heart, like a theophany [an appearance of God]."

"Synchronistic guidance!" Taj concluded.

Joan and Gordon: We were left with a sense of how thin the veil is that separates the sacred from the familiar. The Sages were unified in a single voice when it came to what's necessary to pierce that veil and to see all of life as a continuously appearing manifestation of the Divine that's closer than our own hands and feet.

The secret to this alchemy lies in banishing the deadening sense of familiarity that covers the world. When something is familiar, we see it as a thing, as an object that's separate from us. And without curiosity about the deepest essence of what we perceive, there's no intimacy.

But when we know that the truth of a person, a flower, a sunset, or any "thing" is subtle and mysterious—that we can't know its essence through thinking alone—then the One can reveal itself through our own willingness to be open and present. We can see the shape of the sculpture in the marble of our life. The secret is to keep perception fresh—to allow the world to be a revelation that constantly changes—rather than thinking that we know everything about anything.

The Wisdom of Not Knowing

"Remember, this is a trip into the unknown," Father Thomas Keating remarked with a laugh when we asked him about his personal experience of spiritual guidance. "We don't know where we're going—or if we do, we're on the wrong road—so we stumble along and are constantly amazed by what God can do in the midst of our powerlessness to know what to do or how to do it. Maybe that's too personal an experience to be useful, but you asked me that."

The humility to realize that spiritual guidance isn't something that we can "think" our way to with our usual faculties for knowing was echoed by Hameed Ali: "The most important thing is humility. We don't really know what the right way to go is. We don't know the deeper truth. To allow ourselves to be in that helpless place without losing heart is what opens us up to guidance."

The intention to let go of the known is what the Sages returned to repeatedly in characterizing the mind-set that opens us to the wisdom of the heart—to the intimacy with life that is both the source of guidance and its destination. Rabbi Rami Shapiro tells a wonderful story about the wisdom of not knowing and how that relates to the willingness to give up cherished concepts. As background to his story, concerning the fabled Ark of the Covenant (which houses the tablets on which the Ten Commandments are inscribed), we need to appreciate how meticulous God was in specifying how it was to be built.

The acacia wood box that formed the body of the Ark was to be two-and-a-half cubits long and a cubit and a half wide. It was to be overlaid with pure gold and outfitted with carrying handles, since it would accompany the Israelites wherever they went. Two cherubim—the same order of angels whose flaming swords guarded the tree of life in the Garden of Eden—were to face each other atop the lid, or mercy seat. Their wings were to be outstretched toward the center without touching, creating an exquisite canopy: "There I will meet you, and from above the mercy-seat, from between the two cherubim that are on the ark of the covenant, I will deliver to you all my commands for the Israelites" (Exodus 25:22).[1]

When Moses needed guidance from God, he was to place his head between the angels' outstretched wings. When Rabbi Rami told us that story, his punch line—delivered with total delight—was: "So God is not in the box!" We're to look for him in the empty space between the angels' wings, the place of not knowing, where all our conditioning and old knowledge can be set aside and we can encounter the Mystery directly, face-to-face.

Don't look for the sacred in external forms or in what you think you know, Rabbi Rami advised. Revelation—the voice of guidance—can't be reduced to dogma, confined to houses of worship, or known by the rational mind alone. Guidance arises instead from an attitude of humble, curious attention—when you empty yourself of what you think you know and enter the same heartful state of receptivity that Moses must have had as he approached the Ark of the Covenant.

The role of spiritual guides or mentors, Rabbi Rami pointed out, isn't to help people *know* anything. It's to help them *not know*—to hold the space of not knowing so that the deeper wisdom of the heart has space to make itself felt. The late spiritual teacher Jiddu Krishnamurti said, "It is only when the mind is empty of everything that it has experienced, totally empty of the known—not blank, but empty, with a sense of complete unknowingness—it is only then that the real comes into being."

"In true recognition," Reverend Cynthia Bourgeault explained, "it's the heart that acts first, and the mind figures out what it's seeing later."

Reb Zalman Schachter-Shalomi persisted in trying to explain how the heart's knowing works:

> The problem is that it doesn't come in words, so by the time I put it into words, I've already made an overlay. . . . In the world of intuition, I don't have any words. But if I'm listening, I have to listen to the world of intuition, and I can't remember anything that I get in the world of intuition except when it falls down into the other world. *And so I say the soul knows so many things, but how come our mind can't wrap itself around it?*

Reb Zalman's good friend Father Thomas Keating expressed the same idea in different words: "When people think of being guided, of what they can rely on as direction, as authority—this not knowing, this subtler quality that seems to grow first out of the sincerity of one's practice and *the depth of one's opening to this relationship* to God—to some people this would feel not quite solid enough for that part of us that really seeks to have certitude."

He continued, clarifying what he means by "knowing":

Actually, it's not unknown, but it's known at a level beyond thinking or the usual rational apparatus. . . . There are forms of knowledge that are more direct, experiential—of a spiritual quality—that are unknown to us through the senses or through thinking but become more real by entering into the silence of God.

That's why meditation practice that's beyond concept [in other words, where you're not trying to experience anything, visualize anything, know anything, or achieve anything— you're simply open to whatever is] is so important. It habituates us to this level of knowledge. It can't necessarily provide it, but it reduces the obstacle to it—which is largely an overdependence on our present faculties—so that we can go to God in a way that's profound enough to thin out the veil behind which He hides.

We already have this capacity, so the journey is not a mad pursuit after something we don't have, but a peaceful awakening by its self-surrender to the life we already enjoy, but that's hidden from us by our illusory ideas of God, the self, and the adventure of life. It's a little hard to satisfy the theologians at this level, because they want to protect the distinction between God and ourselves. *Distinction, yes, but never any separation.* It's like the Hindus say, "Not one, not two." It's paradoxical because that's the way it is.

American philosopher Ken Wilber speaks about the tendency of love, as a universal principle of guidance, to function as progressively more inclusive circles of Self-revelation. Its momentum, if we're willing to follow it, draws us into participation in ever-larger wholes in which we don't lose our individuality, but gain meaning, significance, and depth. These are emergent qualities that arise when we let go of concept and follow our heart's leading beyond the edge of the known. That's when the Mysterious Other—which is closer to us than our own heart—emerges and we recognize it as a revelation of our own true Self.

Balancing Heart and Mind

If you've ever been close to a person with Alzheimer's disease, you recognize how important a healthy mind is. Without it, there's no way to navigate through this life or ultimately to tell if guidance is real or not. As Episcopal priest Suzanne Fageol told us, perceiving and following spiritual guidance is "a combination of head and heart."

Reverend Suzanne continued:

> The way that works for me has to do with my own personality makeup. The tricky thing about the heart is to factor in the wisdom it brings and not get left at the emotional level. What comes through as true heart wisdom is less intense than normal emotions—that's a clue.
>
> There's a calm, deep quality to it that encompasses a broader sense of myself. I feel like it's more attached to my soul than my personality. I wouldn't leave personality out, but I feel the soul's presence. There's a different sense—that sense of peace and integrity. Emotionality can be a real booby trap if you mistake it for guidance.
>
> One of the failures of New Age spirituality is that it mixes up heart with sentimentality. But St. Ignatius of Loyola [a Catholic priest who was the founder of the Jesuit order] was on to something with his description of consolation [the peace that comes from drawing closer to God] and desolation [the despondency of feeling separated from God]. The experience of consolation really does come from the heart.

When we first heard Suzanne lecture about consolation and desolation, this book was in its infancy, as was our Claritas Interspiritual Mentor Training Program. Her lecture was an "Aha" moment.

Joan: *I'm in a state of desolation,* I realized. The remembrance of times when I'd felt in communion with a larger Spirit—held and guided by it—came to mind with a rush of sweet tears. The longing for consolation was in itself a form of guidance, an invitation to return to a state of relaxed communion with life. The understanding that consolation is a natural expression of Spirit, rather than something to figure out intellectually, was a turning point on my journey of spiritual rediscovery.

Joan and Gordon: Receiving guidance and then acting on it requires a balance of head and heart, which would ideally be reflected in our educational systems. Fortunately, this idea is beginning to emerge in a variety of venues—secular as well as spiritual.

We took a trip to beautiful Vancouver, British Columbia, in the spring of 2004 to participate in an event called "Balancing Educating the Mind with Educating the Heart." Three Nobel Peace Prize laureates were honored at Vancouver's Simon Fraser University and presented with honorary doctoral degrees. They included His Holiness the Dalai Lama, who lives as a shining embodiment of humility and compassion; Shirin Ebadi, the intrepid human-rights-law professor from Iran, who courageously protects women and children; and Desmond Tutu, the bold yet gentle Anglican bishop who helped liberate the soul of South Africa from its apartheid past.

Top dignitaries from Simon Fraser University and from the University of British Columbia—the cosponsors of the event—came to the podium to make introductions and establish a context for the presentation of the honorary degrees. It was stunning to see these educators in their academic robes, representing the secular high church of the intellect, all bowing to what their noble guests represented—the wisdom of the heart.

Their message was that another century of educating the mind alone, without attending to the balance of the awakened heart, would lead only to chaos and catastrophe. Albert Einstein would surely have agreed with them. His fine mind helped develop the atomic bomb, but his equally fine heart understood the complex web of relationships that might hopefully prevent its deployment.

Ultimately, the reason why we seek spiritual guidance is that each of us, in coming home to our true Self, gains potential to act in a purposeful, compassionate way that can bring more clarity to our confused and troubled world. In one of his most frequently quoted statements, Einstein summarized the importance of recognizing the

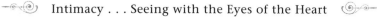

Oneness behind our apparent separateness and how that recognition can create a widening circle of wholeness and harmony that benefits all beings:

> A human being is a part of a Whole, called by us Universe, a part limited in time and space. He experiences himself, his thoughts and feelings, as something separated from the rest . . . a kind of optical delusion of his consciousness. This delusion is a kind of prison for us, restricting us to our personal desires and to affection for a few persons nearest to us.
>
> Our task must be to free ourselves from this prison by widening our circle of compassion to embrace all living creatures and the whole of nature in its beauty. Nobody is able to achieve this completely, but the striving for such achievement is in itself a part of the liberation and a foundation for inner security.[2]

Chapter Five

DOUBT . . . IS IT
GUIDANCE OR IS IT ME?

*"Doubt is not an enemy of faith. Doubt is the means by which
we scrape off the barnacles from the ship of faith."*
— Reb Zalman Schachter-Shalomi

Now that we've had a chance to listen to the Sages discuss their personal experiences of spiritual guidance and to consider some of the forms that it takes, our next topic is discernment.

How can you tell the difference between the ego's voice and that of Spirit? The spiritual journey, that shift in identity from ego to true nature, can be easily sidetracked. The false self is a Great Pretender—a master of clever disguises—whose objective is to keep its bottom firmly ensconced on the throne of our heart. That's why discernment is necessary. What if the voice that sounds like guidance is just the Great Pretender? With that idea in mind, we asked the Sages, "What's the role of doubt? Is it a help, a hindrance, or both?"

Reb Zalman began his answer with a caveat—a buyer-beware message. In his long experience, he was careful to point out, there's no recipe or formula that can indicate with absolute certainty if it's God or ego who's running the show. The proof is ultimately in the feedback (a subject that we'll consider in depth in the chapters that follow). "If you can give me an answer to this one [how to discern]," Reb Zalman said, laughing, "I'll become your disciple."

He brought his point home with a teaching story that took place at the deathbed of the enlightened Jewish mystic and founder of Hasidism, the *Baal Shem Tov,* or Master of the Good Name. His disciples, concerned about continuing on the spiritual journey once their master had passed over, asked him whom they should take as their next teacher.

Reb Zalman, delighted to act out the part, assumed the role of the Baal Shem Tov. "*Nu* [a Yiddish word conveying expectation, like *So?*]," he advised as if speaking to his intimate circle of disciples from his deathbed, "find out if he's any good. Ask him a question. Ask him what we should do with our thoughts that interrupt us in meditation, that drag us away. If he answers you, don't take him as a teacher. It's too facile to give such an answer."

The same is true with discernment, Reb Zalman continued. It's too facile to construct a process that will always, or even often, yield the "right" result. It's easy to go astray, since we all have our *meshugas* (a Yiddish word meaning "idiosyncratic craziness or nonsense"). Reb Zalman cited the example of people with bipolar disorder in their manic phase who think that they know the only answer in the world and are impervious to other feedback.

"Like some politicians," he added with a grimace. "They're the same in this way." Zalman stroked his beard reflectively. "They don't have doubt. I must always have doubt where the guidance comes from. Doubt is not an enemy of faith. Doubt is the means by which we scrape off the barnacles from the ship of faith."

The Two Faces of Doubt: Positive and Negative

"Can doubt be good?" Buddhist monk Ajahn Sona reflected in his clear, penetrating way. He answered himself:

> Yes, the Buddha says you have to doubt where there should be doubt. One thing that should be doubted is authority. Decisions shouldn't be made on the basis of authority, tradition, lineage, or pure logic—which is notorious for making mistakes. Authorities are in contention with each other, so you have to doubt them. The Buddha often repeats this in speaking to people who are try-ing to make their minds up about what they believe. He says the

only way to go is on the basis of your own personal experience. Which do you prefer in your own personal experience: miserliness or generosity, anger or kindness . . . in others and in yourself?

Sufi guide Taj Inayat spoke about the positive face of doubt in a very similar way:

> If we're questing for Source, finding the truth, we have to be open to revising our views and our ways and take in new information. I understand that the Dalai Lama once said that if science could prove something more real than the knowledge he has from Buddhism, then the tradition would have to change. It's a very rational point of view, being open to what's true and what's real. And so in that sense you question yourself. It's a positive or constructive questioning because it's in the service of knowing a greater truth, and it calls us to a deeper reflection.

Having made the point that doubt can be an important ally when it opens us to deeper levels of experience and reflection, Taj then took a look at the shadow side of this feeling: "The doubt that's a hindrance has a kind of paralyzing effect on our actions. We start doubting ourselves, or we doubt a project we started off with a lot of enthusiasm. We're afraid that if we make a move, we might make a mistake, so it keeps us in a state of anxiety."

There was universal understanding among the Sages that doubt has two faces: positive and negative—the face of inquiry and the face of anxiety. Inquiry, the love of the truth, brings us into connection with our true nature and with the Source of Guidance within. The face of anxiety is the ego, the false self, which creates the kind of unhealthy doubt that blocks openness to either hearing or acting upon guidance.

Reverend Suzanne Fageol made the distinction very clearly: "I think doubt is a help if you pay attention to it, if you make it an occasion for inquiry and ask what it's about. It may be a message that this discernment isn't done yet. Is there a red flag I need to look at more deeply? Where it becomes a hindrance is when you don't stop to identify it and [you] let it run rampant."

"So it's a friend," we summarized, "unless you don't inquire into it and it turns into its shadow—anxiety."

"Some people say, 'Just put it out of your mind and do what you're guided to,'" Reverend Suzanne continued. "Sometimes that's right. But the real question is: What's behind the doubt? It's like a yellow light. What's it pointing to underneath? Is it fear, loss of control, or a danger signal—'Don't go there'?"

Susan Baggett from the Center for Purposeful Living—always down-to-earth and matter-of-fact, even when she's discussing mysteries such as the nature of the soul—agreed that doubt can be both a help and a hindrance. "A healthy skepticism is about discernment," she began. "We can't be gullible. We think of common sense as a sense from the soul—an aspect of soul. But if doubt closes us down to possibilities, then it becomes a hindrance. One of the ideas we use in our work is that we're here to learn. This view gives us a way of staying open to ideas that we might never have thought of."

Peruvian educator and Incan shaman Cecilia Montero, demonstrating imagination worthy of her shamanic roots, reeled off a string of instructive metaphors for how doubt can block possibility. "Whenever I think of doubt, it's like a big closet," she said with a laugh, "in a bedroom that's more closet than bedroom. The bedroom activities are diminished by the closet, which is full of things taking up space. This is doubt."

Searching for other ways to explain what she calls "stale" or "unhealthy" doubt, she continued:

> It's like a seesaw that's always going up and down and never stops. It's like something we ate that didn't agree with us. I'm talking about the kind of doubt that makes you feel like you can't move—not doubts that are warnings that you may be making a mistake. This unhealthy doubt goes back and forth like a Ping-Pong match, and it's a waster of energy. It's stale. While you're in doubt, you're in the bedroom closet, not part of the world of possibilities. The rest of the room is filled with possibilities, but first you have to come out of the closet.

Coming out of the closet requires the willingness to let go of what you think you know, a vital role for healthy doubt according to Sister Rose Mary Dougherty, who's also a Zen teacher:

> When I ask, *Is this really so?* that kind of doubt's not restricting. In fact, it opens me to a deeper knowing or a deeper sense of mystery that's beyond what I can figure out rationally. There's another kind of doubt, though, that has more to do with self-doubt, in the sense of the "little self." That does become a hindrance for me. The first opens me to a confidence that there's something deeper than what I know right now; the second constricts me, closes me in.
>
> I like the phrase *cultivate the don't-know mind,* which is maybe not so much about doubt as recognizing that I just don't know the whole of it. I don't know your process. That's not even doubt, really, but a deep reverence. But if I think I have to know, then it becomes doubt. It becomes constricting and uncomfortable, and I begin pushing to find out.

Don't-know mind is rarely something we aspire to in this society, where we're taught that we should know—that we *absolutely* <u>must</u> know—to stay in the game.

With her dependable humility and honesty, Sister Rose Mary continued discussing the pressure to know and be "right": "There's a constriction and a kind of a manic effort to figure things out, to get it right for me—for you—to know the answers, to make them up if I don't know them. But the other kind of doubt, the not knowing, frees us to live into something so much bigger, so much more than we could ever ask for or imagine."

The founder of the Diamond Approach to Self-Realization, Hameed Ali, talked about doubt in much the same way as Sister Rose Mary did:

> When most people say they *doubt* something, they're not using the term philosophically; they're using it emotionally. Philosophical doubt is not the same thing as emotional doubt, so we need to make the distinction. Emotional doubt is destructive

to guidance. It's a hindrance because it closes the mind, closes the openness. Philosophical doubt is questioning—an inquiring attitude: *I don't know if this is true or not, but I want to find out.* Right? That's definitely a help, because it means you're moving toward not knowing.

Transforming Stale Doubt to Fresh Wisdom

Gordon: I had an experience that helped me transform a stale, sticky incidence of emotional doubt into wisdom that was fresh and open. Here's what happened:

My friend Paul and I shared a common interest in alternative visions of the future and had discussed them at length. On one occasion, he and I got together, and he announced that he was writing a major piece about this subject. Just a few days after that meeting, I was asked to author a piece on the same topic, which I'd been intensely engaged with at the level of both theory and practice for a long time.

It didn't seem to be anyone's exclusive domain. Regardless of who wrote about it, the future would definitely come and was always bound to attract a lot of interest from other thinkers. But because of the close timing, I felt awkward letting my friend know that I'd accepted the project, and I ended up with the nagging feeling that Paul felt cheated—as though I'd stolen his thunder.

That night, as I let my discomfort sink in, I was plunged into painful self-doubt. Had I jeopardized the friendship of this man who'd been so kind and helpful to me and with whom I'd loved to explore topics of mutual and passionate interest? Had I returned Paul's generosity of spirit with unkindness and proved myself a loathsome betrayer? Had I hurt someone I loved?

These were the questions that emotional doubt posed. Seeing myself through what I projected as Paul's suspicious eyes, I writhed under the possibility that I might in fact be at fault.

The pain, both that of hurting Paul and of worrying that somehow I was wrong, escalated to a full-blown superego attack. (The superego is the internalized critical voice of our parents that turns into harsh self-accusation. It's different from conscience, which is a form of inner guidance that lets us know whether our actions are bringing us closer to our divine nature or further away from it.) Under siege by a rabid superego, I felt as if everything anyone had ever accused me of had turned into a hungry lion that I'd loosed on myself.

The ego may be tricky, but the superego is downright cruel. I realized that I had to face Paul directly and clear things up. I was willing to see the full truth of the situation and let the chips fall where they may. If Paul could summon convincing evidence, I was willing to be hanged for my offense, so to speak. Emotional doubt gave way to curiosity about the truth—what Hameed Ali calls "philosophical doubt." No matter what the outcome, the important thing was obviously the truth. With the resolution to pursue it, I felt a deep sense of peace and finally got to sleep.

When we talked it through, Paul admitted that he'd felt as if the rug had been pulled out from under him, and that his own ego attachment had gotten in the way. We both agreed that I was already deeply involved with the topic, I had a perfect right to address it in print, and many more people were likely to join in the effort. The field between the two of us cleared, and unhealthy emotional doubt gave way to the kind of inquiry that results in clarity and peace. Curiosity, which is love of the truth for its own sake regardless of the results, converts negative doubt into the guardian of guidance, the "don't-know mind" that opens the door to fresh understanding.

Faith and Faithfulness: Beyond the Shadow of a Doubt

Joan and Gordon: In addition to faith in "don't-know mind" and our ability to inquire courageously into what's true, the Sages talked about a kind of faith that Sheikh Kabir Helminski called *faithfulness*. He explained: "Faith is understood in our tradition not as a theological belief, but as closer to faithfulness. The faithfulness is to—or the result of—our certainty that we live in a meaningful spiritual reality."

This certainty, which was shared by the Sages as a whole, refers to faith in the existence of a greater intelligence—a wisdom or Ultimate Reality—and our intimate, evolving connection to it. Our very existence, and the personal experiences we have of spiritual guidance, is what creates this bedrock of faith. Without the belief that some aspect of a higher intelligence reveals itself as guidance—wisdom that keeps us on track—the whole conversation about living a spiritually guided life would be nonsensical. Only the underlying conviction that we participate in a meaningful reality and can cooperate with it, whether we choose to think of that as following our dharma or carrying out our divine purpose, makes this conversation worth having.

We've decided to string together a few of the comments that the Sages made about faith as if they were having conversation together, rather than responding only to us—the hub of the wheel around which the invisible dialogue we're documenting flowed.

"From the Buddhist point of view, there's a great necessity for doubt," Rabbi Rami Shapiro began. "It's a substantial help. If I doubt, then I'm holding the world in a provisional manner. But for me the experience of the Absolute is sure and beyond doubt. My experience of being loved by G-d, and the love that overflows from it, is much too real to be doubted."

"And doubt, a hindrance?" continued Daniel Ladinsky. Invoking the pure faith that shines through his luminous translations of mystical poetry, he replied, "I could give that a big *Yep*—for I don't think anyone has ever gone swimming in God who was dressed in any serious doubts!"

"If we see reality as gracious," former Jesuit priest Wilkie Au added, "there's more of an ability to flow, surrender, and move with what happens in our life, trusting that in the end all will be well."

※

"Now faith is the assurance of things hoped for, the conviction of things not seen" (Hebrews 11:1) St. Paul told the Hebrews after his transformative epiphany on the road to Damascus. The very existence of spiritual guidance—which is the actual process of realizing true nature—is compelling evidence of "things not seen." Without being sure that there's a guiding wisdom greater than what we can see from our limited perspective, then we might be overcome with cynicism and nihilism. Those attitudes are so painful that, with the piercing irony of paradox, they give rise to rabid fundamentalist beliefs, which permit no doubt at all.

The distinction that the Sages helped us make between positive and negative doubt is eminently practical. Is the experience of doubt—as the late psychologist Abraham Maslow asked—a need to know, or is it a fear of knowing? The contrast between curiosity and fear shows up as a totally different felt sense. When you're experiencing negative doubt, the felt sense feels contracted—you're closed off and pulled in to protect yourself. But positive doubt—curiosity—is accompanied by a felt sense of expansion, spaciousness, and ease. The word *spaciousness* came up repeatedly in the interviews, so we'll take a moment to define it here. *It means, most basically, staying open to the moment, rather than being attached to a particular belief or agenda.*

The distinction between being open and closed—fresh or stale—both physically and mentally is at the heart of spiritual guidance. Opening (an attitude of welcoming and having trust in whatever will be revealed) expands your perspective and refreshes the body.

Gordon: As my story about an endangered friendship illustrated, positive doubt (the willingness to inquire into what's true, regardless of the consequences) feels like a relief. It's a transformative act akin to turning around to face a lion that's pursuing you in your dreams and boldly demanding a gift—a kind of dream practice shared by many cultures. The willingness to question transforms the energy wasted in fear and flight into a skillful means for awakening.

Joan and Gordon: We live in an age of competing fundamentalisms—religious and secular—each with rigid certainties that admit of no positive doubt. Religious fundamentalisms are reactions against what Rabbi Michael Lerner—a brilliant philosopher and futurist—calls the aggressive secular fundamentalism of modernity itself.

The three core tenets of secular fundamentalism are:

1. *Materialism*: the triumph of global capitalism

2. *Reductionism*: losing the emergent properties of the whole by reducing life to its component parts—the equivalent of diminishing the tree of life to a heap of carbon molecules

3. *Individualism*: the celebration of selfishness as the highest good

Materialism, reductionism, and individualism constitute a new orthodoxy that cloaks itself in science but, as religious historian Huston Smith puts it, is actually *scientism:* a belief system rather than a method of inquiry. There's no positive doubt—authentic curiosity—in either of these fundamentalisms.

The positive doubt that Dr. Wilkie Au calls "a hermeneutics of suspicion" rests upon the trust that a beneficent reality holds and defines us. That trust is the foundation for a culture where living faith based on the continuous, fresh revelation of spiritual guidance, coupled with a holistic type of scientific reason, can transcend fundamentalism and create the conditions for a more enlightened future.

In a *Time*-magazine feature article entitled "God vs. Science," Christian geneticist Francis Collins, the director of the Human Genome Project, put it this way in his debate with atheist biologist Richard Dawkins: "Faith is not the opposite of reason. Faith rests squarely upon reason, but with the added component of revelation."[1]

Chapter Six

THE ART OF DISCERNMENT

*"Who's making that decision: spacious
mind or narrow mind, me or God?"*
— Rabbi Rami Shapiro

Perhaps there ought to be the equivalent of a Richter scale, not to measure the strength of an earthquake, but to rate the intensity and clarity of revelations. They vary from the subtlest of leadings to earthshaking, world-changing experiences that allow the equivalent of spiritual lava to bubble up from the depths and transform the landscape.

We were on the phone with meditation teacher Sally Kempton when she brought up Saul of Tarsus. There he was on the road to Damascus, hurrying along to persecute some Christians, when he was knocked off his horse by a brilliant, blinding flash of light. He emerged from the experience a new person—a disciple of Jesus and the formative voice in Christian theology whom we know as St. Paul. But what if the revelation had been false or he'd decided to ignore it?

As Sally put it, "He's on the way to Damascus and suddenly the Divine shows up and says, 'No, go that way!' You can choose to follow guidance or not, and if you do, your whole life opens up. If not, you stay stuck. We're always looking for where the guidance is, and then there's the question of whether or not we'll make the decision to follow it. But learning to tell what real guidance feels like develops slowly over time."

Trial and Error: Discernment as a Learning Curve

"How does a baby learn to walk?" Medical intuitive Nina Zimbelman began her riff on how we learn the art of discernment. "Through trial and error," she continued, as we nodded our heads affirmatively into the telephone, her end of which was some 2,000 miles away in the mountains of North Carolina. She continued:

> Ninety-nine times out of a hundred there's a lot of ego in it and therefore a lot of pain. Being asked to step into an identity is very treacherous, but the gift is that you learn. All you can do is act as if what you're getting is guidance, and if ego's there, it will be exposed. If you set your intention to act on guidance—to follow Spirit—then if you do, you'll definitely learn if it's ego or not. Any slips along the way get dealt with as part of the growth process. All you can do is listen to the guidance and trust the process. It never looks like what you think it will.

Episcopal priest Cynthia Bourgeault heaved a sigh when we got around to the question of discerning whether or not guidance was authentic. It's clearly as big an issue for the clergy as it is for us ordinary folks. Reverend Cynthia called it the "most important question that has been asked in the Christian tradition from the get-go." She continued, "When you go back to the Desert Mothers and Fathers from the 3rd to the 5th centuries, they called this same question 'the discernment of spirits.' I think the reason that the journey exists for exactly the same length as our lifetime is because you need to learn to play your instrument—and you begin to recognize by trial and error the difference between ego and what's genuine."

Who's Running the Show—False Self or True Nature?

Discernment is a spiritual practice carried out in the ordinary process of daily life. It's concrete and practical because life is always giving you feedback about where you are on the journey.

Marrying a person who you know is a poor choice, for example, is a case where obvious guidance was ignored. But when positive doubt—questioning why you did what you did—is brought to bear on the situation, the experience is cast in a whole new light. Curiosity and love of the truth lead to clarity, resulting in illuminating inquiries such as: *What legitimate needs was I trying to meet? Where did my familiar ways of thinking and acting waylay common sense? Why did I betray myself? What can I learn through this experience?* In short, discernment asks, *Who's running the show here—false self or true nature?*

While the experience of making a poor choice can be a valuable part of the journey, without reflection and inquiry—the keys to the discernment process—the decision isn't spiritual. It's just an unconscious reaction that's likely to be repeated. Over time, the practice of discernment leads to choices that are more conscious and loving . . . that lead to less karma and drama and more clarity and peace. Because our primary identification is with ego, what Christian mystics Thomas Merton and Thomas Keating, among others, call the false self, the process of learning to attend to the true Self is bound to take both time and serious commitment.

While a few people, such as St. Paul, apparently get zapped with a lightning bolt that demolishes the false self and immediately reveals true nature within, instant enlightenment is rare—and often suspect. We're all enlightened occasionally for seconds, for minutes, or even for a day or two. But being established in that state permanently is another thing altogether. The program of transformation that's activated through the willingness to listen for guidance, to discern its veracity, and then to act on it is more akin to a gradual unfolding than to an instantaneous revelation. The old-time Quakers called this gradually unfolding process *perfection.*

In a pamphlet she wrote on spiritual discernment for Pendle Hill—a Quaker center for study, service, and spiritual growth—educator Patricia Loring wrote:

> Talk of perfection usually makes modern Friends uneasy. To go deeply into the writing of early Friends, however, is to glimpse humility rather than self-righteousness, deep willingness to

continue to change and be changed . . . a movement from false self to true Self. When we grope our way in search of reality, past easy definitions and conceptions of ourselves, we are graciously freed from the distortions imposed by "the world." One by one we move beyond conceptions of our selves, just as we pass beyond metaphors, symbols and conceptions of God on the way into unmediated, unknowing, intimate relationship with the Source of our being. . . . At the same time, we become more open to and aware of the intimations—the pure breathings, Friends used to say—of the Spirit in us.[1]

Perfection isn't about making the "right" choice in a particular circumstance—it's much more pervasive and radical than that. It's an unfolding process of transformation, a fundamental shift of identity out of the false self and into true nature, which brings about the intimate connection to Source that Patricia Loring was writing about.

While this is a spiritual process, it happens in the context of ordinary life. Everyday events, and our reactions to them, reveal the depth and breadth of the false self's grip and how it may be blocking the expression of true nature. Trying to discern something apparently secular—why we make certain choices even though we know they're not "good" ones, for example—is a powerful form of spiritual practice as long as we're asking the essential soul question: *Where is the vector of love moving in this situation?*

Love presupposes a gradual movement toward freedom that allows more appropriate and creative responses to the situation at hand. So discernment poses the question: *Am I acting with interior freedom, feeling the grain of the moment, or do I feel caught or trapped in some way?* This is an inner-soul inquiry that can't be judged from externals.

For example, perhaps you've been running the family business and it's brought you stunning financial success. If in the process you've become clearer and more loving, peaceful, and charitable, your discernment may be that you're on the right track spiritually. But if managing the business has resulted in burnout, irritability, cynicism, envy, or greed, where is Spirit moving in that picture? There's the discernment—what are the inner fruits, the soul fruits?

At the end of the day, all our external stories are simply containers for the inner narrative of the soul's journey home to Source. Each of us has places where we feel free, and others where we know that our perceptions are distorted and our actions afflicted.

Joan: For example, I'm highly conflict averse. My knee-jerk response to anger is to make it go away as soon as possible, which can lead to self-betrayal and self-deception. Penetrating these old patterns is at the heart of my spiritual growth.

Joan and Gordon: We all have distortions, which make up the body of the false self and result in loss of freedom. Buddhists call these distortions *poisons;* Hindus call them *kleshas;* Jews invoke the *yetzer ha-ra',* or evil urge; and Christians enumerate *seven deadly sins.* We think of them as the basic sources of magnetic deviance that throw the Soul's Compass off True North.

Encountering and recognizing these constrictions of freedom and then moving beyond them is the basic tension that the soul uses in order to grow toward true nature. The art of discernment, at its most mature and refined level, requires understanding how these obstructions work in us—which we'll undertake in more detail in a later chapter. For now, we'll look at some very basic metrics (that is, measuring tools) for discerning whether, in any situation, false self or true nature is being served by our choices.

The Golden Rule

While the external results of our actions don't tell the whole story, they can give us a good idea of which master we're serving—in the biblical sense, God or mammon (materialism, greed, and self-interest). Jesus spoke of discernment in this way:

> Beware of false prophets, who come to you in sheep's clothing
> but inwardly are ravenous wolves. You will know them by their

fruits. Are grapes gathered from thorns, or figs from thistles? In the same way, every good tree bears good fruit, but the bad tree bears bad fruit. A good tree cannot bear bad fruit, nor can a bad tree bear good fruit (Matthew 7: 15–18).

Evaluating the potential fruits of our actions and then pausing to make sure that they fulfill the Golden Rule, some version of which is stated in every world religion, is a time-honored way to guard against self-delusion and distortion that might hurt others. This most basic of all ethical teachings states that we shouldn't do anything to others that we wouldn't want done to us. But many acts of so-called spiritual guidance violate this rule. The inner meaning of *jihad,* for example, concerns vanquishing one's own false self. But if the Golden Rule is denied and jihad gets turned outward, then misguided violence that hurts innocent people is the result.

If discernment is based merely on subjective feelings, then any deluded act can be carried out—and perhaps even legitimized—under the rubric of spiritual guidance. Mountaineer and outdoor adventurer Jon Krakauer, whose ill-fated descent from Everest was told with riveting clarity in his *New York Times* bestseller *Into Thin Air,* wrote an even more intense account of rigid faith gone wrong.

In *Under the Banner of Heaven,* he told the story of Ron and Dan Lafferty, two fundamentalist Mormon brothers who believed that one of them was receiving a divine revelation to kill their sister-in-law and her 18-month-old daughter. The chronicle of how they acted on that "spiritual guidance," all the while convinced that they were doing God's will, was a tale as devastating to the mainstream LDS Church—which disavows fundamentalist, polygamist sects—as it was to the casual reader.

The problem was that the brothers weren't paying attention to that universal metric of discernment, the Golden Rule. While negotiating our own interior freedom and determining whether we're serving false self or true nature can be a subtle discernment, whether or not an act is compassionate is a clear indication of whether we're serving life or not. Killing a mother and a child fails—blatantly and indefensibly—the simple test of compassion and kindness.

Good and Evil

We've defined the Soul's Compass as an intelligence located in the heart that's capable of perceiving and responding to the good. In Hebrew there's a concept called *yetzer ha-tov*—the urge to good. Sometimes *yetzer ha-tov* is imagined sitting on one shoulder, and *yetzer ha-ra'*—the evil urge—on the other. We grow in wisdom through our attempts to inquire into, and ultimately transcend, the tension of those opposite impulses. The function of the evil urge is to clarify the good, the true, and the beautiful by motivating us to orient to the visible fruits of Spirit in our choices.

St. Ignatius of Loyola, the founder of the Jesuit order, was the Catholic dean of discernment. In the late 15th century, when he was born, discernment was indeed centered on distinguishing good from evil in the classic theological sense of whether a thought came from God or the devil. In the theology of Ignatius, which reflected the thinking of the time, the devil was thought to be a crafty creature intent on leading us astray who was separate from our own more primitive, instinctive desires and inclinations. But regardless of where the "evil urge" originates—most likely from our own inborn nature and conditioning—we can easily distinguish it from the action of our higher nature by the inner state it produces, which Ignatius described as desolation in contrast to consolation.

— **Consolation** is a feeling of inner warmth, of being loved by and loving the Creator. A state of interior joy, consolation is characterized by a quiet mind and an open heart. One feels inspired, confident, courageous . . . held and supported by unseen but beneficent forces.

— **Desolation** is a state of interior disturbance that Ignatius called "darkness of the soul." Sadness, sloth, and separation from God are its hallmarks. Today's common maladies of burnout, depression, despondency, addiction, and hopelessness are all symptoms of desolation.

Ignatius conceived of these negative inner states as a kind of vicious cycle. People leading sinful lives, he taught, are "treated very nicely" by the devil, who fills their imagination with all sorts of sensual desires. These temptations lead to more sin, which, in turn, leads to greater desolation.

A modern example might be getting a temporary buzz out of intemperate Internet shopping. The great mood you're left in doesn't last long, though—Ignatius calls it *false consolation.* Pretty soon you're back to feeling that hole in your soul that sent you and your wallet off hunting in cyberspace to begin with. And when the bills come, you might feel worse than before you started.

Another way of thinking about desolation (we're not including biochemical disturbances that lead to depression in this category) and consolation is that desolation is the fruit of the false self and consolation that of true nature. If you're happy and spacious—open to the moment, rather than attached to a particular agenda—in other words, you're on the right track. You feel free, and your choices are likely to be skillful and appropriate, rather than reactive and mistaken.

The Golden Rule and the felt sense of consolation are two very basic ways to discern where our impulses arise from and whether they serve love or fear. The nine fruits of the Spirit that St. Paul describes in the New Testament—which are similar to virtues listed in other world wisdom traditions—refine the art of discernment even further: "By contrast, the fruit of the Spirit is love, joy, peace, patience, kindness, generosity, faithfulness, gentleness, and self-control. . . . If we live by the Spirit, let us also be guided by the Spirit" (Galatians 5:22–23, 25).

The Fruits of the Spirit

The Christian fruits of the Spirit, taken together, are a summary of how to orient to true nature. The result of manifesting these fruits is the delight of consolation. Quaker educator Patricia Loring explained how they're used in a discernment process:

> Working with something as fallible as intuition requires some kind of touchstone for reality and truth. Some Christians use laws derived from Scripture. I work with the idea of the "fruit of the Spirit" mentioned in Paul's letter to the church in Galatia, in which he chides them for putting no boundaries on their behavior. He lists a number of willful and destructive behaviors that are marks of the failure to follow the guidance of the Spirit.

We looked these up and they include such things as adultery, lust, idolatry, witchcraft, hatred, lying, anger, envy, murder, drunken reveling, and the like.

Patricia continued:

> The fruits of the Spirit aren't a set of rules. It's a way of checking out where the impulse to action comes from: the Spirit, the ego, or more primitive impulses. Asking one's self, *Where's the love in this? . . . Where's the patient endurance? . . . The generosity? . . .* this provides a very rough boundary as to which of our intimations or inner nudges we'll honor as coming from the right place, as opposed to those that come from a spirit of revenge, greed, envy—all those other sources of our actions.
>
> The distinction between good and evil is the most elementary use of discernment. It helps distinguish spiritual guidance from impulses that spring from primitive instincts that may have had survival value in some earlier stage of human life but are no longer appropriate in the present situation of our species.

The nine fruits of the Spirit—without necessarily being identified as such—came up repeatedly in our conversations with Sages from most traditions. They're the subject of rich and practical teachings in every world religion, a guide to how an enlightened society—a civilization with a heart—might live. In brief, the fruits are the following.

Love

In its pure form, love is a radiant aspect of true nature that's projected unconditionally toward all people and things, rather than a program run by the false self to get its needs met. This distinction is made beautifully in the tiny pocket classic *The Way to Love: The Last Meditations of Anthony de Mello.* De Mello was a much-beloved Jesuit priest, universal spiritual being, and prodigious storyteller. In the chapter entitled "Love One Another," he distinguished four qualities of genuine love. These distinguish love from people pleasing, the desire to get something in return, or the need for self-aggrandizement.

First, genuine love is indiscriminate. The lamp shines on you whether you're kind or cranky. The rose spreads its fragrance to all. The sun shines on saints and sinners alike. *Second, it's gratuitous.* It gives without seeking anything in return. The sun isn't looking for praise or the rain for applause. *Third, it's unselfconscious.* The tree gives shade even if there's no one to receive it. The lamp shines whether or not someone needs its light.

"These things, like love," writes de Mello, "exist independently of persons. Love simply *is,* it has no object. They simply *are,* regardless of whether someone will benefit from them or not. So they have no consciousness of any merit or of doing good."

De Mello continues, "The final quality of love is its freedom. The moment coercion or control or conflict enters, love dies. Think how the rose, the tree, the lamp leave you completely free. The tree will make no effort to drag you into its shade if you are in danger of sunstroke. The lamp will not force its light on you lest you stumble in the dark. Think for a while of all the coercion and control that you submit to on the part of others when you so anxiously live up to their expectations in order to buy their love and approval or because you fear you will lose them."

De Mello suggests contemplating the control and coercion that you feel in your life so that you can drop them. If you don't, he maintains, then you'll never be able to love, since we do to others what we allow them to do to us. But when you can accomplish this, then you'll be free. "And freedom," he concludes, "is just another word for love."[2]

Joy

Reverend Cynthia Bourgeault quoted the early-17th-century German Christian mystic Jakob Böhme as saying, "I am a string in the concert of God's joy."

Rabbi Rami Shapiro made that quote real for us when he described his walking practice, which communicated the pure essence of joy:

> If I walk long enough, there's a rhythm that just lets me settle, and it becomes more of a dance than a trek. Something happens to the breath and the heart that opens my mind up. It has this erotic quality to it like dancing with a divine partner. I start to feel God's presence as this world. The birds, the trees, the cars—everything seems to resonate with the divine energy, and I become part of it.
>
> There's only this rhythm, this walking, and at this point I start to talk to God, giving thanks for what I have, asking for what I need. Mostly, I ask for the capacity to channel divine love. The practice is to get into that rhythm. It's like a domino effect: Everything comes through it. The body opens, the heart opens, my mind opens, and then I feel this connectedness with everything. Then I may stand stock-still or twirl like a dervish and feel the presence in, with, and as me. Then I come back and keep walking. Language simply fails at this point.

Words do fail, yet mystics from all traditions have tried to describe this ineffable joy. The bliss that arises from within—without dependence on anything external—is the most universal description of joy that we heard from the Sages. Like love that arises as an emanation from true nature, without need of an object to attach to, joy too is a state of internal freedom. It's another aspect of true nature that arises from connection to the Source of Being.

Peace

Peace is another aspect of true nature that's independent of external circumstances. Buddhist monk Ajahn Sona explained that the ability to be peaceful here and now, regardless of what's happening, is a sign of spiritual attainment. We can all aspire to "unshakable peace of mind right now in this very life," he summarized the essence of surrender with confident humility.

The idea that peace is conditional, depending on certain needs being met—being loved and appreciated, financially secure, well rested, having good work—is eventually replaced by *the realization* that the moment you're experiencing right now is the *only* one, and it can't be changed. In surrendering to the now, the clouds of want and fear part, revealing the radiant sun of true Self in union with the Source. Letting go to the now facilitates the shift out of clock time (chronos) into eternity or soul time (kairos). As Father Thomas Keating expressed it, "Eternity is not a long time. It's no time at all."

Episcopal priest Suzanne Fageol commented, "Consolation is a sense of deep peace, calmness, and tranquility—a joy that comes when you're moving closer to the Source. You can feel this peace even in chaos." Peace is a classic confirmation of discernment.

Joan: For example, at a point when I felt overcommitted and burned-out, I quit my monthly *Prevention*-magazine column and also returned a substantial advance on a book under contract. I had reason to feel financial anxiety, yet the overwhelming sense was peace and relief. That was confirmation that I was going in the right direction.

Joan and Gordon: In a similar spirit, geneticist Francis Collins described in his book *The Language of God* how he discerned that accepting the position as head of the Human Genome Project was in alignment with God's will: ". . . I spent a long afternoon praying in a little chapel, seeking guidance about this decision. I did not 'hear' God speak—in fact, I have never had that experience. But during those hours, ending in an evensong service that I had not expected, a peace settled over me. A few days later, I accepted the offer."[3]

Patience

Patience is another aspect of true nature. It's the capacity to wait while the mud of confusion settles, with curious interest in what's being revealed. Patricia Loring explained:

> One of the fruits of the Spirit that Friends rely on a great deal is patience so that you know what is coming from the ego or from what used to be called the id [instinctive drives and passions, many of which are repressed, either consciously or unconsciously, because they feel unacceptable], rather than from the movement of the Spirit in the heart. Both the controlling ego and the demanding id are impatient of waiting. They want to get it done, want satisfaction now, want to get on with things, make things happen.
>
> When something feels really important, the thing to do is wait and see what happens to that sense of importance. See how much duration, how much living, how much Life there is in it [Friends capitalize Life in this usage because it's a natural symbol of God, distinguishing it from the individual, historical life]. That was another thing that Friends used to say: "Is there Life in it? Where is the Life in it?"

Patience allows time to observe whether a leading is a flash in the pan or something more enduring, a process of discernment that Quakers refer to as "seasoning." To these masters of following spiritual guidance, hurry and urgency are an almost sure sign that something else is driving the action. Yesterday's great ideas often turn into today's *What was I thinking?* But when a leading persists, it's an invitation to keep the channels open.

This can be a slow process by Western, *I-want-it-yesterday* standards. What passes for patience in our culture often isn't patience at all—it's *im*patience taken to the limit. We *want* that business opportunity, house, or car. We don't have it in hand yet, so we have to wait, but we don't like doing so one bit. We feel tense and impatient, or excited and hyper, and we're prone to push our agenda—which may not be in our soul's best interest. This impatient *attachment to what we want*—even if we claim to be waiting patiently for it—makes it all but impossible for the mud to settle so that we can notice genuine guidance arising.

Kindness

When His Holiness the Dalai Lama was asked to define Buddhism, he replied simply, "My religion is kindness."

"In Buddhism, my understanding is discernment in the morning, discernment in the evening, discernment in the afternoon," Buddhist scholar Ed Bastian commented. "One is always in the process of discerning what is the compassionate way of acting and what is selfish. . . . Compassion is the sincere wish to remove suffering, and to achieve one's enlightenment in order to remove suffering and help others."

Kindness and compassion are also at the root of the Judeo-Christian tradition. When the 1st-century rabbi Hillel was asked to summarize the entire Torah while standing on one foot, he's rumored to have replied, "Love thy neighbor as thyself. The rest is commentary. Now go and study."

The skeptic who asked him this question, so the story goes, was so impressed with the rabbi's answer that he became a student of Torah. Jesus, another 1st-century rabbi, gave an answer similar to Hillel's when asked which commandment was the greatest: "'You shall love the Lord your God with all your heart, and with all your soul, and with all your mind.' This is the greatest and first commandment. And a second is like it: 'You shall love your neighbour as yourself'" (Matthew 22:37–39).

Rabbi Rami Shapiro, in his beautiful book *The Sacred Art of Lovingkindness,* writes about the Thirteen Attributes of Lovingkindness enumerated in a commentary on the Book of Exodus:

Moses asks to see God's glory, how godliness is manifest in the world (Exodus 33:18). God agrees, saying, "I will make all My goodness pass before you" (Exodus 33:19). God passes before Moses and calls out each aspect of goodness in turn: (1) realizing the divinity of self, (2) realizing the divinity of other, (3) cultivating creativity, (4) engendering compassion, (5) finding grace, (6) acting with equanimity, (7) creating kindness, (8) bringing forth truth, (9) preserving kindness, (10) forgiving iniquity, (11) forgiving willfulness, (12) forgiving error, and (13) cleansing yourself of delusion. Together these are called the Thirteen Attributes of Lovingkindness.[4]

When lovingkindness is cultivated and used as a means of discernment, your heart naturally overflows, which creates a condition of generosity, the sixth fruit of the Spirit.

Generosity

We had a deep lunchtime conversation with Yogi Mukunda Stiles about how to experience life as an overflowing cup so that generosity bubbles over as an attribute of true nature. Just as it's the nature of light to shine, after all, it's the nature of a full cup to overflow whether or not there's anyone there to receive the abundance.

Gordon: "When I was 18 years old, reading Nietzsche," I recalled, "I remember a chapter on the gift-giving virtue. If you're empty, you approach everything as a beggar, as a wanter; it's only when you're full within yourself that giving is pure overflow."

Joan and Gordon: Generosity, like love, is often misunderstood. Giving away money, time, and things because you want to be loved, be appreciated, or feel in charge is an activity of the false self. True nature radiates generosity from its fullness with no expectation of return or even the consciousness of being generous.

Like lovingkindness, generosity has many facets. The late Tibetan Buddhist teacher Chögyam Trungpa Rinpoche considered generosity to be the most important virtue of a bodhisattva—a compassionate being who remains on Earth to help others achieve enlightenment. He spoke of one facet of generosity as clear communication that's not for your own benefit, but to further the liberation of another. Good friends who can be truthful with you and let you know when you're acting as if you're off the mark are generous in that way.

Another aspect of generosity is the intention to see people through the eyes of the heart. Being with another person in the spacious, open fullness of the moment, without any agenda, creates the space for that individual's own true nature to show up. And when both of you move into that true identity, the Divine Presence emerges as the mysterious Third. This is the ultimate overflow of generosity.

Faithfulness

Yogi Mukunda Stiles spoke of faithfulness to the spiritual journey in this way: "Success in yoga is attained by two things: first, consistent, earnest practice over a long period of time; and second, dispassionate nonattachment from what happens in that practice."

Our friend and colleague Reverend Dr. Ruth Ragovin recalled taking her ordination vows. She was similarly reminded that her calling was to be faithful, not necessarily successful or effective. This stance of nonattachment moves the false self and its agendas to the side so that discernment can arise from a deeper place and faithfulness to spiritual guidance can continue to mature.

Attending to spiritual guidance is a lifelong practice, which rests on the faith that we're held by a larger mystery. Quaker Mary Hey described the self-reflective process of checking our alignment with purpose as a way of maintaining faithfulness to a spiritually guided life. A self-reflective review doesn't focus on our motives, Mary told us, "since any such exploration is likely to fall prey to our genius for rationalization and self-justification." Rather, the aim of a review is "looking out" to check for the "alignment" of our actions with the truths we're committed to upholding. *What are we actually doing here?* Do the fruits of our actions match our intention? That single question, pursued with faithfulness, can transform our lives.

Gentleness

Being gentle doesn't get much positive press in the modern world. But to be gentle doesn't mean to be a pushover; it signifies letting go of judgment and the urge to resolve difficult or angry feelings by acting them out. We need to feel what we feel but also to develop gentle restraint in how we express emotions before either letting them go or using them to come to a better understanding with others.

If you make decisions in the throes of fury or self-righteousness, or act toward others in this way, the fruits are rarely good. Things said in anger have a way of lodging in the brain's limbic system, where they create post-traumatic stress both for the enraged person and for the recipient of the anger.

Gentleness is a way of touching a living reality so sensitively that you can feel it responsively touching you back. It's literally "being in touch." Without it you can't have living contact with guiding presence in its exquisite subtlety. One way to cultivate gentleness is by cultivating spaciousness—the attitude of curiosity that is more interested in loving the truth than in controlling another person's behavior.

The Buddha taught that we all have suffering. If you compare yours to a cup of salt and then pour it into a bowl of water, the liquid will be undrinkable. But if you empty your cup of salt into a pond, the water will still be sweet. The difference between the bowl and the pond is in the attitude. Holding on to the need to be right puts you in the bowl. But when you're willing to give up ideas of right and wrong, seeking instead to see the other person's point of view—indeed, a larger perspective that views all situations as opportunities for growth and inquiry—then you're in the pond. There's a clarity and spaciousness to gentleness—a precision and a depth of understanding that leads to the ninth and final fruit of the Spirit, self-control.

Self-Control

Gordon: In my 20s, I was substitute teaching. One day I was called into a high school class on government, and as often happens when a substitute shows up, the kids were all but bouncing off the walls. I got their attention by naming how they were acting—that is, really restless—and then holding up my car keys.

"Who wants to drive a hot red Ferrari?" I asked. One young man stood up and reached eagerly for the keys. "There's one glitch, though," I added, dangling the keys over the teen's hand. "It has no brakes." When the young men's face fell, I inquired what the problem was.

"Well, it's useless if it has no brakes," he replied.

"Why is that?" I asked, and soon the class was engaged in a spirited conversation on how self-control—knowing how to use the brakes—is the flip side of freedom. That realization, and its relationship to government, was a breakthrough that some of the students probably still remember to this day.

Just as patience is often misunderstood as holding back from doing what you want, so is self-control. But knowing when to brake, when to shift, and when to accelerate is the skillful result of learning how to attend to guidance. The capacity to be still and wait for the right moment to accelerate is an expansion of possibility—not a contraction.

⁂

Joan and Gordon: Learning to use the nine fruits of the Spirit as a set of metrics for discernment doesn't mean that you'll be right in any given circumstance. At their heart, these fruits are invitations to self-reflection and experimentation—they're spiritual practices.

If you're an angry or stressed-out person, for example, what might it be like to choose gentleness and sit with yourself for a while rather than expressing those feelings—dumping your distress on others? If you're impatient and impulsive, what might it look like to give yourself breathing room when pressed for a decision? Working with even a single fruit of the Spirit can help you develop interior freedom, bringing you closer to your true Self. That's the gift of discernment and the reason why we call it an essential spiritual practice.

Shift Your Focus to the Ultimate Goal

With the clarity and brevity that characterize his teaching, Swami Adiswarananda shared five steps that he finds helpful in the practice of discernment. The steps, as you'll read, are delightfully circular, since you end up exactly where you started—at the very heart of the spiritual journey:

1. Shift your focus from immediate gain and loss to the "Ultimate Goal," the Swami advised, drawing out the *Ul* in a way that emphasized its importance, "which is union with the Divine. We have to subordinate all of our lesser goals to this ultimate one."

2. He continued in a very practical vein: "Then think of your responsibilities to others. You must think about family members and friends who are dependent on you for their subsistence.

3. "Recognize that in any decision there are four parts involving human will to one part involving divine intervention, or the wheel of Providence—this is the 80/20 rule. The art of making right effort and being physically and mentally disposed to do a good job aren't enough. There's also Providence. Therefore, in making a decision, you must take all five parts into

account. So if you're a farmer, do you have the right seeds, soil, and so forth? But the fifth part—whether there's rain, drought, or flood—is incalculable. You have to allow for that divine intervention in your deliberation.

4. "Meditate and consult your own conscience—and not just in one sitting, but repeatedly. Tell the mind the pros and cons and then let it simmer for a while." This is the seasoning step: waiting to see whether the leading persists or evaporates.

5. "Remember the Ultimate Goal, which is Self-knowledge and union with the divine. And when in doubt," ended the Swami, "go to the nearest sage." Since the nearest sage is inside of you, perhaps talking with a spiritual friend or mentor can help you find the wisdom within.

Paying attention to consolation and desolation, using the Golden Rule as the most basic ethical guideline, and attending to the nine fruits of the Spirit—perhaps by choosing one or two that speak most clearly to the distortions of your false self—are also ways to locate your own inner sage. As the original Quakers said, discernment is a process of perfection that is a *gradual unfolding*. Faithfulness to the process leads to a greater awareness of the false self and its distortions—which, in turn, removes sources of magnetic deviance that turn the heart away from the true Self that is the Ultimate Goal.

Chapter Seven

THE PRACTICE OF DISCERNMENT

"In the realm of spiritual development and learning," shaman/ poet Oriah Mountain Dreamer told us, "almost everyone goes through the phase of thinking that they have a direct line to God. A woman I know attended a workshop and came back with messages for everyone—she was just full of stuff. But that's just a phase she eventually came through. When we first touch the excitement of being able to connect with a deep place, the ego is thrilled. There are lots of goodies there, and it's much more fun than some of daily life is."

It's the "direct line to God" problem that threatens to make spiritual guidance suspect and potentially dangerous. Politicians and religious figures frequently pass along what they believe to be spiritual guidance to others. Even when it turns out to be wrong or profoundly damaging, other believers often continue to support these self-styled prophets. When people are in positions of power—such as clergy, politicians, therapists, or even those who claim psychic gifts—practicing due diligence about the veracity of their claims in relationship to your own life is a personal responsibility. Secondhand "messages from God" don't relieve you of accountability for the choices you make.

Regardless of the source of so-called spiritual guidance, there are six distinct types of wisdom that can help you practice discernment:

common sense, head wisdom, heart wisdom, body wisdom, reflective wisdom, and the wisdom of transcending opposites. In this chapter, we'll consider how these ways of knowing can aid you in evaluating guidance that comes through any channel.

The First Wisdom: Common Sense

Joan: I was once contacted by a woman who had a clear and urgent message: "You have three alien implants in your brain, and I've been guided to tell you that you must remove them." The procedure, she hastened to add, was quite simple: Drinking three vials of specially treated water (which she happened to have on hand) at the bargain price of only $200 each would do the trick. Although her cure was infinitely preferable to brain surgery, making a discernment in this case was—pardon the pun—a "no-brainer." The woman was either totally credulous, certifiably insane, or a crook. In any case, my answer was a testimony to common sense: "Thanks, but no thanks."

While the bizarre case of the alien implants—which were in vogue in certain circles at the time—was easy to dismiss, sometimes the guidance that people have for us requires more careful discernment. Oriah Mountain Dreamer explained:

> We sometimes get guidance that's not for us. It's never just for us, since we're all interdependent. Sometimes we get a dream for another person, and it's risky to share that because the possibility of self-importance is enormous. The role of community reminds us that there is no *them* and *us*—just *us* and *us*. We all have our own subjective reality, however, and we need to respect that. If I get guidance for another person, I'm aware that it may really be for me. It has to be repeated, and relentlessly so, in order for me to take it seriously.

Joan and Gordon: Oriah uses her common sense very clearly when it comes to guidance. Over a long period of time, she's made particular observations about when it may be for her or for someone else. These observations have led to rules of thumb about sharing information that comes to her. One way that she gets guidance is through what she calls "advertisements," which emerge in the dream state. She described them in this way:

> The quality is a non sequitur—a cutaway to a flash of an image of someone I know—and then back to the dream. This sometimes happens in meditation as well. This "advertisement" quality marks it as something that *may* not be simply for me.
>
> One of these was about a woman considering other work possibilities. In this case it was easy to decide whether or not to share it with her. I could just say, "I had a flash of you doing this." I didn't have to invoke authority, like saying that "the Grandmothers [a group of women elders who appear to her in the dream state] told me."

Joan: I experienced firsthand my friend Oriah's common-sense approach about when to share her guidance. After advertisements concerning me had persisted in dreams for several nights, Oriah consulted the Grandmothers: Should she tell me about the visions or not? While they had the potential to change my opinion of a person I was close to, they also had the potential to ward off serious harm. The Grandmothers—who usually answer Oriah's questions by posing ones of their own—asked her to consider how she'd feel if the visions came to pass and she hadn't given me the information. This was an appeal to the wisdom of common sense.

"I'm very careful about sharing these things," Oriah explained. "If you do share, then the person you give your guidance to needs to sit with it. What does it mean to them right now?" The recipient of prophecy, in other words, has to take the same care with discernment as does the prophet. In my case, the information proved important and spoke very clearly to an important discernment I was already making.

"Timing is also important," Oriah added. "Is it a useful thing to share, and how and when do I do that? People will sometimes come up to me with a message from the Grandmothers, and I'll say, 'No, thank you.'"

Susan Baggett reminds her students at the Center for Purpose-ful Living that common sense is an attribute of the soul that's overlooked at our peril. It may not be the only way of knowing, but it's still an important starting point for the discernment process that leads to the second form of wisdom—linear logic or head wisdom.

The Second Wisdom: The Head

Joan and Gordon: Once you've evaluated a situation using common sense, then a more careful accounting is in order. St. Ignatius, like a modern-day coach, suggested making lists of pros and cons. *Should I take that job or not?* You might make a list with columns of pros and cons evaluating things such as how much you'd enjoy the work, what the pay is like, how the job might impact family time, what the prospects for advancement are, and how it fits into your overall vision of life.

Making lists, said Ignatius, should be a prayerful thing, under-taken as a sacred act. Asking for guidance before you begin creates an open, inquisitive mind-set. Once you've studied and evaluated your lists, he advised, the next step is to make a provisional decision and offer it to God, asking Spirit to confirm it.

Then you go about your day as usual. In the evening, during a period of retrospection, the decision is revisited using the fruits of the Spirit to discern whether or not your decision feels right. Do you still feel good about it or not? Is there a felt sense of peace surrounding it? Does it evoke love? Or perhaps you notice irritation, fear, or distress, which indicate a need to go back to the drawing board.

Another of St. Ignatius's guidelines concerns the time needed for discernment, which will obviously vary. As you might guess, he suggests taking more time when the stakes are higher. Big decisions such as marriage, joining a religious community, having children, and the like may take weeks, months, or even years of serious contemplation.

Letting go of hurry and urgency, and giving things the time they need to season, is—hearkening back to the first wisdom—

a matter of common sense. Many of us could profit from taking time with discernment and telling people who ask us for things that we'll think about it and get back to them later.

The Third Wisdom: The Heart

After you've used common sense and logic, the wisdom of the heart can act as a confirmation of your decision. The fruits of the Spirit that we considered in the last chapter are largely tests of the heart: *Is my response to this situation loving? Is it patient? Is it generous? Is it kind?*

As an example, perhaps you've studied your list of pros and cons and decided to accept the job you were offered, even though the commute is very long and will take up time you'd rather spend with your family. But when evening comes and you sit with the question of whether or not taking the job is a loving choice, memories of being a child and almost never getting to share dinner or talk informally with your father come to mind. You wonder and inquire honestly, *Do I want to repeat this pattern of parental absence with my own kids?* It feels familiar, so you're comfortable with it—drawn to it, even. But reluctantly, you realize that trading better pay for less family time feels like a poor choice to you.

"We can observe the tangible results of what we're doing," Susan Baggett from the Center for Purposeful Living told us. She explained:

> *Would I do it for free? Was the action inspiring to others? Was it inspiring to me? Inspiration* is a word we use frequently, and we think that inspiration is clearly and definitely of the soul.
>
> We can also look at attachments: *Was I attached to the outcome? What was my intention? To feel good, or to think of myself as a good person? Was this action soulfully or personally motivated?* We realize, of course, that most of us have mixed motives, but we aspire to selflessness. We look at Mother Teresa as an example of doing something not from her separated self, but out of soul.

Susan's colleague Thomas White continued: "We can look at the quality of the choices we make. If we make the hard choice, it's more likely to be of the soul. But there's another aspect: Not everybody has a real strong connection with their heart. So even if we make decisions that are ego based, if the choice is more selfless than it was earlier, it can still be a response to guidance. Getting less selfish than before is an important part of spiritual growth."

Gordon: "Some psychologists believe that behavioral change precedes attitudinal change," I offered, "and if you make different external choices, over time that will affect you at a deeper, more internal level."

"I want to paraphrase a quote from Henri Nouwen," Thomas added in agreement. "We don't think our way into a new way of living; we live our way into a new way of thinking."

Joan and Gordon: Those new ways of acting and thinking gradually refine the ego and make room for the wisdom of the heart. "I don't know," began Daniel Ladinsky. He pondered:

> I think we're stuck with the ego till the very end, though I do believe the curtain between ourselves and God [the curtain being the ego], if you will, can become thinner and more transparent. And thus, that which we then perceive as guidance—when acted upon—will have a greater potential to benefit others. To me that is always a reliable gauge of being in touch with one's spirit: how one's life affects for the better their immediate family, neighbors, community, and then for some, their country and even the world.

Because we're all interconnected, what we do to any one person affects us all. When we're altruistic, the act changes both the external world and our own internal one, releasing hormones that create health and well-being. If you recall an altruistic act, chances are that you'll feel warm and peaceful. Perhaps an expansive sensation will suffuse your heart. That's consolation—which, when you think about it, is reward enough for any good deed. His Holiness the Dalai Lama calls empathetic acts of kindness "wise selfishness," since they're the best gift we can give to ourselves.

Perhaps the deepest wisdom of the heart is compassion toward ourselves, even when we're looking outward to helping others. Rabbi Tirzah Firestone put it so well:

> The one rule that I've come up with is that in discerning the voice that tells you it's time to rest or work or that the tide is turning, that voice should engender self-love. It may be a harsh voice that tells you to gather your energies and move out, but it's always going to be self-loving, as opposed to the ego-ridden or straining voice that's saying the same thing but leaves you with a film of self-chastisement or self-diminishment. It won't be like the voice of a rebbe [a teacher or wise guide] that's loving, even when being truthfully harsh. It will be more like a truthful, inspiring updraft of love and encouragement—"You can do this."

Joan: "Like a cheering section," I agreed.

"I use this discernment in working with others," Reb Tirzah continued. "I listen to voice tone. Are they speaking in a kvetching, nagging, self-hating tone or a 'Yes, you can do this' tone—which is more important than the message itself and is the voice of the true Self. This encouragement is life giving. There's an energy and a self-love that's engendered, and that's the most important thing of all."

The Fourth Wisdom: The Body

Gordon: I remember hearing sociologist and peace activist Elise Boulding compare making a discernment to eating a particular food. That's an interesting notion to consider. If you ate your decision, what would it feel like in your body? Hot peppers or hot chocolate? Sour milk or a fine Stilton cheese? Which choices energize and nourish you, and which ones are depleting? Do you really want to plan lunch with a friend when you routinely feel drained and empty every time you spend time together?

Yogi Mukunda Stiles, an expert in the mind/body connection, spoke about body wisdom as an assessment technique for discernment: "We could see if stress is dropping down." He spoke with the authority of a person who has taught yoga for decades and can assess the relative state of tension in his students with a practiced gaze:

> The tensions in the neck should be less. The restrictions and unevenness of the breath will open and become smooth. Prolonged and subtle breathing begins to happen. In the mind, the experience would be what I like to call "mind-pause." The space between thoughts increases and the mind quiets down.
>
> Are you happier? It's not about material things, your relationship, or anything external. The gauge is whether happiness arises within you of its own accord. There's a teaching in the Shiva Sutras [a central text in Kashmir Shaivism, the form of Advaita Vedanta that Mukunda practices] that says: "For those who sit in the presence, bliss spontaneously arises from the heart of its own accord."

Rabbi Rami Shapiro also talked about physical correlates to discernment:

> If it comes from the ego, I get exhausted; I feel wasted at the end. But if it's coming from a larger Source, I don't feel wasted. I may be tired, but there's no sense of having wasted anything. There's a fullness, a completeness, that suffuses me. Also, there's no aftertaste—like aspartame. When ego's involved, it may taste sweet for a moment, but there's a definite bitter aftertaste.
>
> When it's a pure act of grace, there's a wonderful sense of emptiness. Nothing's left over. In the Bible, the Jews are wandering in the desert after the exodus from Egypt. G-d sends manna to sustain them, and they can only collect enough for one meal. If you store it, it rots. Jesus talks about this same concept with his teaching about the lilies of the field. There's a radical sense of trust in following guidance. There's no use hoarding, because the necessities are all provided.

Joan and Gordon: The ease of letting go and trusting creates a profound state of relaxation. When there's no hoarding, grasping, or attempt to control, the brain and nervous system produce what Harvard cardiologist Herbert Benson, M.D., calls *the relaxation response*. If you practice yoga or meditation, you're familiar with this state. The mind is calm, the body comfortable, and the heart feels suffused with warmth.

Sister Rose Mary Dougherty described guidance as a "full-body experience" that involves an expansion of heart that can be easily noticed and recalled. Over the years she has learned the difference between the feeling of interior freedom, a characteristic of the true Self, and "un-freedom," the feeling of constriction that follows when the ego is trying to take control.

She explained:

> It's getting to know what un-freedom feels like in me. I can feel the constriction almost. And as we come to know ourselves, we begin to recognize those patterns of un-freedom that dictate our actions. And it may be that in a particular case we know that we're choosing from a place of un-freedom, but that's the best we can do now.
>
> I think of it like a seesaw that goes back and forth. We begin to notice what freedom and un-freedom feel like in us. Sometimes we might not know about an action itself, but if we stay with it long enough, we begin to notice what direction it's taking us in. Is the choice leading to a greater expansiveness and freedom for love, or is it closing us in on ourselves?

Both Sister Rose Mary and Reverend Suzanne Fageol, along with Professor Wilkie Au, commented on the importance of the felt sense to discernment. The late American philosopher and psychotherapist Dr. Eugene Gendlin devised a system of tuning in to felt sense called *focusing*. It's based on the idea that we're always in intimate connection with everything within and around us, rather than separate from it.

If you eat an apple, for example, the process involves chewing, swallowing, digestion, metabolism, elimination, and all the other intricate complexities bound up in extracting energy from food. Focusing is a way of sensing the entire process. It brings the hidden landscape of interconnections into view—the implicate world beneath the surface of explicate reality.

Felt sense is a way of grasping this implicate order—a holistic way of knowing that might be called intuitive or guided. Dr. Gendlin came to an understanding of focusing when he and his students at the University of Chicago reviewed hundreds of hours of taped psychotherapy sessions conducted by different practitioners, trying to see which were most effective. They sampled psychotherapists from diverse schools of thought—from Freudians to Reichians—and the results were surprising.

The effectiveness of a session had relatively little to do with what the therapist was doing—it had more to do with what the *client* was doing. Successful clients had the ability to locate and name the felt sense of what it was they were dealing with. When they could do this, they gained a measure of freedom from it . . . of objectivity. They could make what was an unconscious "knowing" more conscious, and this ability—as Sister Rose Mary explained when she contrasted the feeling of inner freedom with that of being caught or constricted—is a great help to discernment.

Felt sense is a special category of a larger form of wisdom: self-reflection. Wisdom researchers suggest that this is the most important type, since it provides valuable feedback about what's happening both moment to moment and over time. It also affords us the opportunity to correct our course and make amends for mistakes before small things blow up into major problems.

The Fifth Wisdom: Self-Reflection

Reb Zalman Schachter-Shalomi explained, "I was harsh to a person once, and that night I sat down and thought about it—and the next time I saw the opportunity to make a public apology, I did so. If I didn't do the right thing, how do I fix it? These are things that are easy to forget, so it's important to write them down." That, continued Reb Zalman, is why observant Jews practice retrospection each night before going to sleep. Without it, harvesting the wisdom from errors is a much more haphazard undertaking. Retrospection is a commitment to daily self-reflection that keeps the decks clear and invites right action and spiritual guidance.

"At night before sleep," Reb Zalman continued, "you review the day and examine your conscience. Then there are forgiveness prayers said to clear karma in this and all other incarnations." The resultant clarity and willingness to look at one's behavior cultivates discernment and realigns the practitioner back to the Source of Being. This daily reflective practice in Judaism—called the "Bedtime Sh'ma"—begins with the recitation of a prayerful affirmation of faith that translates: "Hear, Oh Israel, the Lord our God, the Lord is One." After this affirmation of unity comes:

- Retrospection of the day, beginning with the last thing that happened and going back to the moment of awakening

- Reflection on what needs repair

- Prayers for forgiveness

- An invocation of the four archangels and the *Shechinah,* the feminine face of God

St. Ignatius suggested a similar reflective exercise as a form of ongoing discernment. Called the *examen of conscience,* it can be done daily, weekly, at the end of a year, or anytime when reflection is called for. The Examen has five steps:

1. A short meditation to quiet down and shift into a mode of appreciation for the gift of life itself and the specific blessings of the day

2. A prayer for the grace of being able to see clearly— and understand accurately—divine guidance

3. Retrospection of the day (week, month, year), with attention to consolation and desolation: Where were the fruits of the Spirit present, and where was the ego—or in classic Ignatian theology, evil—active?

4. Reflection on how you either gave in to ego or followed divine guidance, expressing regret or giving thanks in light of your actions

5. Reflection on what might be required to follow guidance more adroitly in the future, by recognizing and hopefully avoiding the pitfalls of ego

In spite of the best intentions to make the practice of discernment into a measured process with specific wisdoms and competencies that can be identified and developed, the truth is that we keep bumping up against seemingly irreconcilable differences. A man wants to accept a job offer because it's in the field he loves and the pay is good. On the other hand, the hours are very long and it will be disruptive to his family life. A woman wants to be compassionate to others and care for them, but in the process she isn't taking care of herself. The bind she finds herself in seems to be that if she takes care of her own needs, then she's selfish.

The sixth wisdom addresses this paradox: The world is comprised of opposites—so how can we make choices that take both poles of a situation into account while allowing a new perspective to emerge?

The Sixth Wisdom: Transcending the Opposites

When the great inventor Johannes Gutenberg's attention was torn—divided between his preoccupation with his work problem (how to mass-produce books) and his enjoyment of new wine at the local Oktoberfest—he found himself staring at the wine press in an intoxicated reverie. Suddenly, the two opposing poles of his attention merged into an "Aha" that became the inspiration for the printing press.

This invention, which revolutionized Western civilization, included but was far greater than the inventor's opposing preoccupations with work and wine. Something new had emerged that was qualitatively different from its constituent parts. Journalist, novelist, and social philosopher Arthur Koestler called this function of creativity "bisociation," a one-plus-one-equals-three kind of math that transforms a tension between opposites into a breakthrough.

"Without Contraries is no progression," declared the poet William Blake in *The Marriage of Heaven and Hell*. "Opposition," he added to the paradox, "is true Friendship." Although it can be uncomfortable to have our habits, prejudices, or partial identities (who we take ourselves to be) challenged and disrupted, it's those very pattern disruptions—those messengers of guidance disguised as irreconcilable contradictions—that have the potential to wake us up to greater possibilities.

Resistance—choosing sides and fighting protracted win-lose battles to preserve our preferred position—is rarely if ever a wise response to the tension of opposites. It almost always keeps us stuck in repeating patterns of action and reaction. By feeling antagonistic or defensive rather than curious about "the other side," we become dissociated (rather than *bi*sociated) from the rich stream of life that seeks to flow into new harmonies through the integrative process of creative emergence.

The tension of opposites, rightly interpreted, is an invitation to include and transcend opposing views and interests. The 19th-century philosopher Hegel's dialectic does this with thesis and antithesis, bringing them into a higher-level unity—a synthesis—that embraces but is greater than the sum of its differing parts. One of the ways to create the space for synthesis is to relax into the tension between the opposites. The history of creativity is rich with examples of people who puzzle and puzzle and then when they go on vacation—or drink wine at the Oktoberfest—something new clicks.

Father Thomas Keating talks about synthesis in this way: The false self, in his experience, has a genius for reducing the mystery of life to its preconceptions and to the habitual patterns for getting love that we developed in childhood. Meditation, on the other hand—the unstructured ascent into mystery that accompanies contemplative practice (just sitting in silence and experiencing what is)—doesn't try to undo all that conditioning or to get in there and wrestle with it. Instead, it invites us to share a different state of being that is entirely beyond the opposites that the ego constructs.

When we enter silence, none of our energy goes to maintaining the false self anymore and suddenly we're free, living at the threshold of the Universe revealing itself and standing there in the most welcoming way. That's why silence, the letting go that can happen in meditation, an afternoon in nature to put the dilemma aside, or a reverie such as Gutenberg's can open the door to a transcendent wisdom beyond the opposites.

The six wisdoms that we've discussed here are a rudimentary menu for the practice of discernment. Common sense, rational logic, the wisdom of the heart, the wisdom of the body, self-reflection, and reconciling the opposites are all aspects of attention and awareness. But only when we're willing to use them all—and then to let go of them altogether—can we come to that place at the threshold of the known where authentic guidance can break through our constructs and show itself to us. The Universe is in a state of continuous emergence, and only when we let go of our ideas and preconceptions can we hear the voice of Spirit as it's revealing itself in this very moment.

Chapter Eight

DO NOT TRAVEL ALONE: WHEN TWO OR MORE ARE GATHERED

"A hunting party sometimes has a greater chance of flushing love and God out into the open than the warrior all alone."
— Hafiz, translated by Daniel Ladinsky

As we've seen, discerning whether guidance is real or not can be a tricky business. It's particularly easy to fool ourselves when we're left to our own devices, since our blind spots are, by definition, blind. That's why physicians don't treat themselves and therapists look to others for help when it comes to understanding their own minds. The same thing holds true for matters of the soul. It's best not to travel alone, but rather to look for healthy, authentic communities of trusted others—even if that consists of a friend or two—who can point out what we can't see for ourselves.

In answering our question "Is there a particular role for community in helping us come to right action?" Quaker educator Patricia Loring commented that while there's undoubtedly "that of God" in all of us, there's "a lot of other stuff as well." Primitive, instinctive drives and unconscious social conditioning, particularly when combined with the reactivity and desire-nature of the false self, create a dazzling array of distortions that obscure guidance. The problem is that when left exclusively to our own devices, we fall prey to our almost boundless capacity for self-deception. What may look like an altruistic impulse, for instance, often reveals itself in retrospect as egoic desire—the need for admiration or affirmation.

The best remedy for self-deception is the clear mirror of spiritual friendship, either in a formal or informal context—in community with a few friends, a spiritual mentor or guide, or as part of a spiritual community, or *sangha.* The function of authentic community is neither to create conformity nor to reinforce egoic competitiveness. Its aim is to orient us to the higher ground of true nature by providing clarity and supporting our best self. One of the reasons for the human proclivity to repeat the same mistakes over and over again is that we have so few occasions for assisted reflection—and so few people capable of rendering skillful assistance.

The bond that gives coherence to spiritual friendship, as Sister Rose Mary Dougherty wrote in her book *Group Spiritual Direction,* is a common desire to do the will of God. In other words, what defines this type of relationship is a shared *orientation* toward the Inner Light or truth.

Gordon: Consider the art of Japanese flower arranging, in which I had the privilege of taking a course. I learned the importance of two things: (1) the magnificent diversity of flora, and (2) how they harmonize when they're in alignment.

Perhaps an arrangement began with three stems of wild iris. The first was placed in the vase at its full length. The second was cut to two-thirds that length and placed at a different angle. The last was cut to one-half the length of the first and placed at its own unique angle. This invisible geometry was repeated with other leaves and flowers until the arrangement was nearly complete. But the final step created ultimate harmony: All the blooms were turned to face a common source of light.

Spiritual community thrives on the balance of these two invisible principles of order—the irreducible value of our individual uniqueness and the harmonization of our differences through a shared orientation to the Source from which illumination flows.

An Authentic We: The Positive Face of Community

Joan and Gordon: Poet Daniel Ladinsky responded to our question about the role of the community in this way:

"A hunting party sometimes has a greater chance of flushing love and God out into the open than the warrior all alone." That is a Hafiz line I carry around in my memory. I bet the Beloved misses the beautiful, beautiful American Indian tribes that once roamed this earth. Noncommunity to them was unthinkable. It is as vital to most humans as the sun to this world. We die without healthy interaction with each other, though perhaps for some very rare spiritually advanced people that interaction can take place in ways that most of us could not comprehend and surely should not try to imitate. Just this morning I was reading a Nicholson translation of Rumi. The title of that Rumi poem is "Do Not Travel Alone."

Buddhist monk Ajahn Sona agreed with Daniel that community is an essential part of spiritual practice. Referring to this group as *sangha* (the spiritual community of people who practice the *dhamma*), he told us:

It's one of the Three Jewels—as we call it in Buddhism—the Buddha, the dhamma, and the sangha. The latter is your living example and is invaluable. It's only the rarest individual who finds their way without the sangha; it's almost unknown.

Humans, of course, are socially dependent and learn at the school of example. As a musician—I was trained as a classical musician—I learned by playing with individuals who were more skilled than me. It's not really possible to develop more refinement without profound interaction with people who have spent decades cultivating these sensitivities and passed them on generation after generation. So that's what the sangha is.

It's the same as any worldly art. We learn spiritual arts the same way, through close and continuing interaction. So why not spend time with those who've spent years cultivating the way? We start by playing the notes, and then eventually we make music—and then we've joined the sangha. The kind of music that comes out of the orchestra when the sangha is practicing well together is beautiful.

Father Thomas Keating continued on a similar tack: "This is why you apprentice yourself—if you can find such a person—to one who has experience of the journey or to a *community* of people committed to the transformational purpose of life. And so it's subtle—it's very clear if you're in that space, but very unapproachable if you're not. And so the means for doing so (classically) has been a qualified teacher or community, as the case may be, trusting in common discernment or the common sense of a group of people over one's own."

The community's function, as Patricia Loring reminded us in the Quaker context, is to *"listen one another toward wholeness"* by helping each other transcend restricted, partial, or distorted viewpoints. Father Thomas is clear that the condition for meaningful participation in such a forum is to move from egocentric willfulness to a sincere and humble willingness to wake up to the divine impulse already present in our hearts.

"The difficulty in waking up," he clarified with a smile in his voice, "which could happen in an instant—is that our will to do so is overlaid and distorted by what William James called *willfulness*. Willfulness is the pursuit of desires, most of which are irrational and are begun in early childhood. They are fossilized into energy centers around which our thoughts, behaviors, feelings, and evaluations, entering our little sphere of gravity, are going all the time. They are like planets circling the sun. *So that level of gravity, or that magnetic field, needs to be changed.*"

The shift from willfulness to willingness—which is opening oneself to spiritual guidance—is the condition for that magnetic change. We've been using the metaphor of the Soul's Compass. Its needle points in the direction of the truth of the moment, to our own true nature, and to Ultimate Reality itself—in order for us to align ourselves with a course of right action. Spiritual community is a means of consciously identifying and correcting for magnetic fields that distort perception so that we can regain accurate direction for our lives.

But willingness is not the same thing as mindlessness. It's not an abdication of inner authority or personal responsibility. In fact, one of the most obvious forms of magnetic deviance is what Father Thomas refers to as "over-identification with one's group."

"This taking refuge in the sangha," according to Sister Rose Mary Dougherty, "isn't a replacement of personal responsibility. Instead, its purpose is to give us the support we need to travel alone with our own 'Inner Teacher.'" Sister Rose Mary makes the vital distinction between a true community, an "authentic we" that furthers discernment, versus a web of conformity, an "inauthentic we" that extinguishes the very possibility of discernment.

An Inauthentic We: The Plural of Egoic Is Wegoic

Buddhist monk Ajahn Sona defines the plural of *egoic* as *wegoic*. Sometimes a group isn't a real sangha. Rather than helping members realize their inner wisdom and move toward it for the good of the whole, it functions like a communal false self with a set of shared beliefs. This type of collective may be benign, but sometimes such groups can be as malignant as life-threatening cancers.

Cult leader Jim Jones, founder of the Peoples Temple in California, moved his congregation of true believers to the rain forest in the northeast corner of South America in the mid-1970s. There, in a remote jungle settlement in Guyana called Jonestown, just a few years later he commanded them to swallow cyanide-laced Kool-Aid. More than 900 people died in this famous mass murder/suicide that made the world wonder how people can lose their senses and follow someone who's obviously insane.

Then there was David Koresh, a charismatic young man who changed his name from Vernon Wayne Howell. He assumed leadership of a cult called the Branch Davidians and proclaimed himself the Messiah—which was, in part, a license for what authorities suspect was murder, rape, and polygamy. In 1993, an ill-fated raid by the U.S. Bureau of Alcohol, Tobacco and Firearms turned his Waco, Texas, compound into a flaming inferno, killing Koresh, most of his followers, and their families. Seventy-six people died in all, including 17 children under the age of 12.

In 1995, members of a Japanese cult—Aum Shinrikyo—released neurotoxic Sarin gas at rush hour in a Tokyo subway, killing 12 people and sickening more than a thousand others. The leader of the Aum Shinrikyo (Supreme Truth sect) believed that the world was coming to an end and succumbed to apocalyptic madness.

"I have a friend who says that you can't trust anybody spiritually until you've been part of a cult," Oriah Mountain Dreamer told us. She continued:

> At that phase we don't realize that we can't dedicate ourselves unquestioningly to a belief system, that we need to question. From the teacher's side—the perspective of people wanting to guide someone—genuinely seeing what a person is missing can result in too much of a desire to get people to where you think they should be.
>
> This is an issue of where authority resides. When you offer guidance with the understanding "if it fits," you hand authority back to the person. But think about terrorists who are prepared for missions in a way that overrides their conscience and inner spiritual authority. It's given the semblance of a call to martyrdom, but it's really just brainwashing.

"Who are you choosing as a community of discernment?" Suzanne Fageol considered. "Who forms your spiritual community? Ultimately, this relies on your own checking of feedback for resonance. Following spiritual guidance isn't about giving away your decision making to others rather than relying on yourself. You have to know yourself well enough to know whether the support you've sought out confirms your true Self or supports you in your distortions."

An authentic spiritual community "has to be a specific kind of community dedicated to conscious living," Rabbi Rami Shapiro told us.

> The role of the community is to challenge one another so that you maintain doubt and open-mindedness. When a community tries to fix things for its members, it's a disaster. The individual has to work through their own life experiences with the support of the group—but it has to be their own authentic inner work. You can bring your brokenness to a group, and then you realize that it's

part of you, but not all of you. The group acts like a witness—no one judges, helps, or damns. There's no egoic chaos. You become a witness to your own craziness, and that's healing—12-step programs, for example, are powerful spiritual-growth programs outside of a religious context.

"Group mind is not group think," Susan Baggett from the Center for Purposeful Living explained.

"So how do you distinguish group mind from group think?" we wanted to know.

In group think, Susan explained, a leader tells you what to believe. At the Center for Purposeful Living "an idea or thought is put out into the center of the circle, and if there are 35 people here, there may be 35 ideas. We consider how closely the ideas align with our purpose. The ideas that don't align stick out like sore thumbs. So it's easy to tell."

Susan's colleague Thomas White picked up on the conversation: "Once a decision has been made, then we all buy into it. Sometimes we've made very mediocre decisions that have turned out well because we've all bought into it. But we've made a lot of mistakes as well."

"Do you ever have dissenters who can't go along?" we inquired.

"Believe it or not, it's never arisen," Susan told us. "We've never seen it happen."

"We have a trust in the group wisdom that's evolved over time," Thomas explained. "And even when we make mistakes, no one says 'I told you so.'"

"We've always approached this as an experiment," Susan continued. "So we support things until they don't work, and then we do something else. It's not like we're all going to go down with a burning ship—we change directions. We don't take a position and hold on to it, so we trust the wisdom of the group to tell us when we're off course, and then we'll adjust."

In inauthentic community, the entire group may be off course, but dissent isn't welcome. A blind adherence to a course of action can result in chaos and destruction. Jesus's parable of the Gadarene swine is often used to illuminate how this happens.

Gadara was an ancient city of Palestine that was the site of a miracle where Jesus cast out demons into a herd of swine, which then ran headlong into the sea and perished. The swine, en route to drowning, appeared to be "in formation," as the late psychiatrist R. D. Laing explained in his book *The Politics of Experience*. Laing used the example of one plane in a group flying out of formation. *But is that plane off course, or is the rest of the group headed in the wrong direction?* By assuming either that the planes in formation are on course because they're the majority or that the one out of formation is off course, we're in danger of making a serious logical error called the *Gadarene swine fallacy.*

Knowing the difference between being in formation with others and being on course with our own inner guidance is vital to a sense of spiritual direction. Spiritual relationship paradoxically requires our willingness to abide in the purity of our own sacred aloneness. This means that there's no clinging, suffocation, or enmeshment—no agendas or attachments to force us into formation. We're as beautifully alone as a star in the night sky, with our own center of gravity. And yet, the space of mutual reverence that holds us allows each person to shine like a jewel in the bosom of the infinite. Together, we form beautiful constellations. This sacred form of relationship is what Quaker educator Parker Palmer characterizes as "intimacy without impingement"—respecting each person's sacred otherness.

An authentic community knows more, feels more, imagines more, and intuits more than its members, because the members don't reduce who they are to a lowest common denominator. Instead, they expand by reaching with others toward what writer and philosopher Aldous Huxley called their "Highest Common Factor"—knowledge of ultimate truth. The creative field that emerges from an "authentic I" relating soul to soul with other "authentic I's" amplifies the light that each member brings. As Jesus taught, "For where two or three are gathered in my name, I am there among them" (Matthew 18:20).

An inauthentic community, on the other hand, knows less, feels less, and cares less than its individual members. Group think, mob mentality, or any type of conformity that represents a surrender of individual responsibility reduces collective intelligence. The result is one dumb, lockstep, stock response in the face of a changing reality.

Loss of differentiation is devolution, not transcendence. Imagine your body if you tried to move as one rigid lump instead of with the supple bends and turns that allow you to dance or play the piano. In any group, as in any individual, a diverse range of capacities fosters creativity. The difference between the graceful and *appropriate response* that typifies an authentic *we* and the clumsy *stock response* of an inauthentic we is the difference between freedom and its absence.

The psychologist Erich Fromm described the inauthentic we in his account of how collective madness overtook some of the German public who were "only following orders" during the Third Reich. Then, as now, there was one thing people feared more than death: being alone.

In order to save ourselves from this peril, from being ostracized or publicly humiliated, we may willingly blind ourselves to our own truth when it conflicts with the "formation" that our group is flying in. Then we forget our own orientation and enter what Fromm called "the social unconscious." In the film *The Matrix*, some people chose to take "the blue pill" and became part of a somnambulistic mob—docile and complacent. Those were the cowards who chose the comfort of conformity over the uncertainty of being themselves.

Solomon Asch, one of the founders of social psychology, performed a famous series of experiments to demonstrate the pressure of conformity. He brought together a group of research subjects, only one of whom was left in the dark about the real purpose of the experiment. Asch showed the group a drawing of three vertical lines of differing lengths: long, medium, and short. All but the uninformed subject had been coached to insist that a shorter line was indeed the longest. Despite what their eyes saw, one-third of the uninformed subjects consistently agreed with the majority. This self-blinding confirms Fromm's observation of how powerful the desire is to be enfolded in belonging, secure in a group identity. But whenever we retreat into mindless obedience or its mirror image—

the need to maintain absolute control—we're fleeing freedom. And what is freedom, other than the courageous participation in, and creative interaction with, the Unknown—the only condition for being on course with our true nature?

Individualism, as opposed to individuality, however, is another form of un-freedom. The armor around our hearts, when we're fearful of dissolving and losing ourselves in relationships, precludes the Self-to-Self intimacy that's at the heart of spiritual growth. Americans, in particular, have suffered from prolonged ambivalence about community and the insistence that individual gratification at any price is the highest good. This fearful individualism has left an aching spiritual void at the heart of American life.

Much of the modern world shares this dilemma. The challenge of the 21st century, according to systems theorist and futurist Ervin Laszlo, is to transcend the extremes of individualism and collectivism that clashed in the ideological wars of the preceding century. Neither the *laissez-faire* free-market capitalism that has exploited the planet, nor the totalitarianism that sought to vanquish human freedom—what Laszlo dubs the Lone Ranger or the Collective Farm—are adequate expressions of what it means to become fully human and responsible in an interdependent global community.

Spiritual community transcends the dichotomy between individualism and conformity through a soul-to-soul, center-to-center encounter that invites the presence of a higher intelligence—one that we need desperately at this pivotal moment in world history. The late humanistic psychologist Carl Rogers called that higher intelligence "the wisdom of the group."

Gordon: In the Rogerian groups I facilitated in the early 1980s as part of the La Jolla Program at the University of California, I noticed that as each person let down his or her guard and moved toward a more "authentic I," it was like placing another bulb into a string of Christmas-tree lights: Only when the last person in the group showed up in a real and present way did the whole string light up. Group intelligence flowered and the participants became more than the sum of the individuals present—an emergent, creative, and delighted "we."

Communities for Discernment

Joan and Gordon: Authentic communities, like sanghas, are places where we can learn, grow, and create. Community also amplifies Light and facilitates the shift of its members toward true nature, which is the ultimate purpose of discernment and their best hope.

Reverend Suzanne Fageol, who's a member of several groups dedicated to spiritual growth and mentoring, commented, "There's a quality of listening, a holding of me in my best self that they have a picture of, and the ability to make inquiries that open my experience and help me shift out of ego or move into Spirit. Then I'm in a position to check in with my own experience, because ultimately I'm the one who has to say yes or no to what the community is feeding back to me. So, in this way, the community acts as a discernment container."

Oriah Mountain Dreamer also spoke to discernment as an important role of community. While the community can be a spiritual or religious group, sometimes it's a community of friends who know you well and can tell when you seem off: "There was a time when a man was trying to con me out of money," Oriah shared with us. She explained:

> In the middle of this situation I had a flash to call a friend who just said, "You know, Oriah, you just don't sound like yourself." That was enough to get me to slow down. My own discernment was out of commission, but I trusted her and told the man that I needed to wait 24 hours, take a breath, and regain my own sense of discernment.
>
> There are times when we can lose that connection with discernment and we don't really know this, but others can tell. That's invaluable. We can't always trust our own discernment, so it's good to ask others, "How do I seem to you about this?"

"We need to put support in place," Oriah continued. "When I was younger, I thought I could fix some basic things about myself—like my tendency to take on too much work. My hubris was, 'Now that I know this about myself, I'll fix it.' I know now that I might have a blind spot forever, so who are the people—my advisory group—who have the *acuity* and vision about how much energy it takes to do certain things?"

The acuity Oriah was talking about has to do with clear-sightedness. We should note that the human eye has two features designed for seeing: (1) First, there are the cones of the eye, which are good for focusing on a single target in our line of sight; (2) then there are the rods of the eye, which give us less acute, but more encompassing, peripheral vision. A good spiritual community can act as our rods so that we not only see what's right in front of us, but also what the larger context is.

Quaker Thinking on Communities

Quaker Patricia Loring told us:

> Part of the function of the community is to discern—as a community—the rightness of things. We may provide Clearness Committees, small-group experiences in which people may discern things that pertain to their particular lives. Once a month we come together to consider matters that affect the community as a whole. The formal name for that is a "Meeting for Worship with Attention to Business." Once again we're sitting in a kind of open contemplative prayer, bringing with us questions, situations, and possibilities for illumination and discernment.

> Friends will make no move unless everybody assents. There is no tyranny of the majority. If we're divided, we may hold it over for some months, allowing time for prayerful reflection and for emotions to settle before we examine it again.

Boulder Meeting member Deanne Butterfield spoke about a meeting for worship as a kind of collective phone booth for listening to God—a coming together in the space of receptive unknowing:

What's the role of the group? If one trusts this process [speaking in a meeting], then one has to be open that a message that's spoken out of the silence is truly a message from the Divine. And it may not be, but we have this obligation to each other in our seeking to listen deeply and to hold that insight and test it.

What if this is a message from God? What would it mean for me? It's not an intellectual "Should we add this to our creed?" kind of thing. It's an invitation to inquire within oneself whether this is something I can add to my spiritual reservoir. Sometimes a message isn't from God, but we don't judge. Sometimes it's so far out of our experience that we just don't know what to do with it and have to keep sitting with it and talking about it outside of the worship setting.

If you assume that people in this worship are grounded and seeking, then you have to listen to them. The guidance isn't between me and Spirit alone. It's also about weighing what someone else got. Maybe their message was intended for me and I wasn't able to get it any other way.

The collective coming together in a meeting also amplifies the Light that comes through. "Because there is that of God in each of us, we each experience and can access different parts of the Divine," Deanne explained. "We can each experience subparts— different parts. So when we sit together seeking access, then the presence of Spirit is amplified," which is exactly what we experienced while interviewing Deanne Butterfield, Denny Webster, and Mary Hey, our three Quaker Sages from our local Boulder Meeting. The field that held us seemed to grow increasingly clear, bright, and expansive.

That sense of expansive communion, what the Quakers call a *gathered* meeting, where the Divine Presence becomes palpable, probably saved the lives of a Meeting in colonial days. Denny Webster told a story about how the Quakers became friendly with the Native Americans in Pennsylvania: "We still have a strong connection to Indians. A group of Indians came into a meeting and were going to kill and scalp the people, but the meeting was gathered. You could feel it. The Indians just sat down and joined the Quakers, because they didn't respond with fear in the ordinary way. They were greeted by people who recognized something that *they* did as well."

In terms of discernment, "The committee is a mirror, and hopefully a clean one," Mary Hey told us. She continued:

> Oftentimes a person's discernment affects the whole Meeting, as when we declared the Meeting as a sanctuary for Salvadorans. We were funneling people through our Meeting, so that involved all of us. It took time to reach the clearness to do that. Right now the Meeting as a whole has a member who's going to prison for an act of civil disobedience. When somebody has a leading that they carry through with the support of a Meeting, then the Meeting takes the responsibility for caring for her external life while that member goes to prison. She's "acting under the care" of the Meeting.

While many churches, temples, and mosques create communities of care and support, some, like the unprogrammed Quaker Meetings, seem more like a sangha of musicians learning the subtleties of spiritual practice. These kinds of open communities are marked by a spirit of experimentation, rather than a commitment to dogma or group think. The latter type of community may not only block spiritual guidance, but also in some cases endanger both group members and the world at large. Religion gone wrong and reified—turned into a dead husk, devoid of life—can be one of the greatest threats to spiritual discernment and inner freedom.

Solomon Asch, the social psychologist who studied group think, identified—as antidotes—four components of successful collaboration:

1. *Mutual respect,* a level playing field where there's no dominance hierarchy

2. *Openness,* which entails being open not only to one another, but to new ideas, new thinking, and new inspiration—and to feedback and correction

3. *Trust,* which ripens over time as people gain experience with one another

4. *Shared vision* or purpose

After she'd read a draft of this chapter, Patricia Loring suggested a fifth antidote from the Quaker perspective:

5. The "additional dimension of the *felt presence,* movement and guidance of the Spirit of God, in and on which Friends feel our interactions rely. I love the image of a sangha of musicians. I see them as jazz musicians, responding sensitively to one another even as they listen intently to the deeper patterns and possibilities of the music in which they are held."

We're social animals who need one another to grow physically, emotionally, and spiritually. When communities can help us abide with curiosity and patience in the magically pregnant space of not knowing, then they point us to the inner voice—the Inner Light—that dwells in our own wise hearts.

Chapter Nine

PRACTICES FOR ALIGNING
WITH THE SPIRIT OF GUIDANCE

"The wind of divine grace is always blowing.
You just need to spread your sail."
— Swami Vivekananda

An attitude is a posture or position in which we hold ourselves. The red-tailed hawks that ride the thermals outside our mountain home hold their wings in an attitude that invites the wind to lift and carry them. In relation to spiritual guidance, the attitude for aligning with the Spirit of Guidance is humility—an open-minded curiosity and unconditional surrender to life as it's unfolding—coupled with the faith that all situations, even those that appear dire on the surface, carry the potential for awakening.

Spiritual practice is a way to develop and maintain attitudes of receptivity to guidance. Hindu Swami Adiswarananda counseled that there's a time factor inherent in awakening to our true nature. "Who knows when it might happen," he observed, "in a moment or in many lifetimes? But we must be prepared for the recognition, and you can't hurry it."

In this chapter, we'll explore how to stay awake and prepared so that when guidance and revelation come, you'll notice what's happening. Jesus explained the attitude of watchful receptivity in a parable related in the Gospel of Matthew. He compared entering the Kingdom of Heaven to ten maidens waiting for the arrival of a bridegroom. Half remembered to take flasks of oil for their lamps; the other five forgot. They waited so long for the bridegroom that eventually they all fell asleep. But finally, at midnight, the cry went up that he had arrived. The wise ones lit their lamps and entered the bridal chamber, but by the time the foolish ones had procured oil and found their way there, the door was shut. Keep awake, Jesus finished the teaching, because you don't know the day or the hour when the Lord will come.

Keeping watch for the bridegroom is a metaphor for being receptive to the Spirit of Guidance that brings you home to the Kingdom of Heaven—the recognition of who you are and why you're here. The oil in the lamp that provides light for the journey includes a variety of spiritual practices that we'll explore in this chapter. These maintain and develop the essential attitude of humility—the spacious receptivity to what is that keeps us vigilant through all the watches of the night.

Understanding Spiritual Practice

The Sages identified a variety of actions that foster the attitude of wakefulness, which is part of the purpose of spiritual practice. There are many other aims: developing compassion, training equanimity, drawing closer to God or Ultimate Reality, and inquiring into the nature of reality, to name just a few. Since we're all different, a spiritual practice suitable for one person may not work for another.

Joan: It's not everyone, for instance, who could spend seven years meditating in a cave like my friend Tibetan Buddhist teacher Lama Surya Das, who started out his life as an American Jew.

Reverend Suzanne Fageol commented: "Practice is personality specific, and its choice ideally rests on your *spiritual typology*—what sorts of threads draw you and make your connection to the Divine stronger. Certain portals work best for people, depending on their inclination—like the four different Hindu yogas. There's a path of devotion, action, contemplation, and intellect. It's a matter of knowing who you are and what works for you. . . . Whatever that is, the idea is to take time for practice and do it regularly."

Buddhist monk Ajahn Sona also discussed spiritual practice as a continued effort:

> Of all the religions, Buddhism is probably the preeminent one that insists upon personal effort as a means to salvation. The teaching most emphasized in the Pali canon is effort. The Buddha said, "Monks, make effort. If you could not make effort, I would not tell you to make effort, but since you can make effort, therefore I say make effort. . . ."
>
> Look at this like an Olympic athlete. They do hard things and make the report that there's a breakthrough after a long time of practice. But they practiced. It looks effortless, but it flows out of preparation. In Buddhism, there's a faith in causality. If you plant a cherry seed, you never get an apple tree. The causes are put in and the results follow. If you put in skillful efforts, you must come out with skillful results. That's the single principle that the Buddha gives. This is something you can do and confirm for yourself.

What Is My Spiritual Path?

Joan and Gordon: People often wonder what their path might be, and there's no lack of them. The Dalai Lama wrote, with some delight, about the wondrous "spiritual supermarket" that Americans have to choose from. Check out the Internet and you can find information that was once the province of the mystic elite. Now it's there for the asking—including, in many cases, information about local groups.

There's tremendous diversity in spiritual practice because there are so many different human dispositions. Just because your parents were nurtured by a certain religious tradition or by particular practices, it may not follow that they're equally suitable for you. And just because you hold Mother Teresa in a special place of reverence doesn't mean that, like her, your path is karma yoga—selfless service.

Swami Adiswarananda offered a very concise teaching about how you might discern whether or not a particular spiritual path is your dharma—the innate course that your soul takes to Self-realization. If it is, he explained, then it should feel *natural, efficient,* and *graceful.*

Natural

An action is natural, according to the Swami, when it's spontaneous and lacking in self-consciousness. You claim no special credit for what you're doing; instead, it flows from your own natural disposition of mind. "Birds don't brag that they can fly," he said in his lilting, musical accent. "It's a natural function." For a person whose dharma is prayer and contemplation, sitting in a cave for several years might take fortitude, but it's in accord with a natural disposition.

Joan: My book *7 Paths to God* outlines seven basic spiritual typologies. Some people are contemplatives; others are nature mystics. The practices of the latter draw on the natural world and its cycles and seasons. Some people's dharma is creative. The harmony and beauty revealed in their poetry, architecture, music, or writing *is* their spiritual path. Others, like Susan Baggett and Thomas White from the Center for Purposeful Living, are karma yogis. Meditation teacher Sally Kempton, Rabbi Rami Shapiro, Sheikh Kabir Helminski, Sufi guide Taj Inayat, and others are deeply devotional—worship of a personal God as the Divine Beloved is their dharma. Some of the Sages are more intellectual—their natural path is knowledge.

Whatever your own dharma is, the important thing is to accept it gracefully. If you're a nature mystic, don't force yourself to follow the path of knowledge or imitate someone else who has taken up prayer and fasting. In the past, teachers often tried to make left-handed students into "righties," which isn't a good idea. Your brain knows what it was made for—and so does your heart.

Efficient

"Don't take your actions in the world personally," the Swami counseled, "because it's not you working—it's God working through the particular vessel that you provide. You can do your dharma easily and naturally because you have the appropriate skill and level of mastery to accomplish the tasks required; therefore, your actions are efficient and don't take undue energy." Instead, they bring what he calls "the joy of spiritual creativity."

I know a man named Jake who's a concert violinist. Although he attended medical school because his parents demanded it of him, he never went into practice. "I just wasn't any good at it," he explained. He achieved a certain level of proficiency, but his heart wasn't in it, and he felt as if it was always a struggle that left him stressed-out and exhausted. But making music? It's efficient . . . it just falls from his fingers because he was born for it.

Although Jake was finally able to realize his dream of becoming a concert violinist, a natural and efficient function for him, it took years of practice to get to that point. Playing the violin requires effort—but not undue effort, as medicine did, because the gift for it is an innate capacity.

Graceful

The third and final way to discern dharma is that it's graceful. We're like actors on a stage, Swami Adiswarananda explained, and as such, we need to play our roles with beauty and balance: "A graceful performance is marked by proportionality, discrimination, rhythm, and harmony—your dharma fulfills the law of aesthetics and beauty."

Like the concert violinist, there's an innate gracefulness in performance. If your attempts at writing poetry are tortured, in other words, it's probably wise to look elsewhere for your life's purpose and spiritual path. Nonetheless, gracefulness—like efficiency—takes time and perseverance to manifest. A virtuoso violin performance touched by the Spirit of Divine Beauty may look effortless, but it rests on a foundation of skillful practice. The same is true of any spiritual exercise.

Whatever your particular path may be, it's important to recognize that all are like rivers that flow to the same sea. The purpose of every path is the same: to bring us into communion with our own true Self and the Spirit of Guidance.

Essential Spiritual Practices

Joan and Gordon: Contemporary philosopher Ken Wilber, the founder of the Integral Institute, is widely regarded as an interspiritual genius. He's deeply concerned with identifying basic, foundational, spiritual practices that transcend external religious differences—what he refers to as *essential spirituality.*

Gratitude, for example, requires no particular ideology, yet it trains spaciousness and receptivity—that I-Thou attitude that cuts through judgment and preference and invites the presence of a Third. Concentration is likewise an essential skill because without it we can't sustain watchfulness. Mindfulness practice trains awareness, as well as leading to the core insight that *we're* not our thoughts: Thoughts come and go, evanescent as bubbles, but the ground from which they arise and to which they return is constant—it's the Ground of Being itself.

In this section, we'll consider several essential spiritual practices that are useful for all people, regardless of whether they're religious, spiritual, or both.

Praying for Help

Joan: We arrived at Reb Zalman Schachter-Shalomi's home in Boulder, Colorado, early in the interviewing process. We were armed with our brand-new Olympus digital recorder, my trusty Mac laptop, and a number of assumptions that turned out to be wrong. One of them concerned prayer.

Settling down in soft, easy chairs on either side of Reb Zalman—who looks every bit the archetypal sage that he is—we asked him about the *sh'ma,* a Hebrew prayer that translates: "Hear, Oh Israel, the Lord our God, the Lord is One."

I thought—quite naïvely—that because the *sh'ma* relates to listening, it might yield insight into receiving guidance. As my opening salvo, I referred to it as the most important prayer in Judaism, to which Reb Zalman shook his head kindly in the negative and responded: "The *sh'ma* is really an affirmation, rather than a prayer. We're not addressing the *sh'ma* to G-d; we're addressing it to ourselves. Moses was addressing it to the people of Israel, the same as when Muslims say, *La ilaha illallah*—'There is no God but Allah.' It's a statement of faith. When you say, 'What's the most important prayer in Judaism?' it's *Ana Adonai hoshiya na*—'Please God help us.' It's like the *Kyrie Eleison*—'Lord have mercy.'"

Reb Zalman's explanation struck a very personal chord for me. In the past, when I'd heard the common translation of the Kyrie Eleison: "Lord have mercy on me, a sinner," the word *sinner* was off-putting. But we're all sinners in the sense of its Hebrew root, which means "to miss the mark." Still cycling out of my Dark Night of the Soul, I recognized that all my knowledge and practice of positive psychology were not, and never had been, enough to help me hit the mark. The distance between where I was as a human being and where I hoped to be—braver, more truthful, more patient, and compassionate—was daunting. Perhaps prayer was, indeed, part of the answer.

And, truly, it has been. The Joan who's writing today is a far different person from the one who sat with tears in her eyes as Reb Zalman suggested that prayers for help were the most important in the Jewish tradition.

Joan and Gordon: Meditation teacher Sally Kempton talked about praying for help in a way that we both—as writers—could definitely relate to. She told us:

> I'd worked out a kind of bargain with the Divine, where it was okay to pray for qualities like surrender, unselfishness, humility;

for the greater good; for my teacher's work, et cetera. Then I got into the habit of asking for grace and guidance when I was writing or preparing a workshop. I tend to be a perfectionist, and when it wasn't "right" or flowing, the whole process would become torturous. So I learned to sit beforehand with a prayer for help, quite formal, saying, "I don't get what to write, how to write it." I would offer up this prayer with a real sense that I couldn't do it myself, asking, "What do *You* want to say?" It was all highly pragmatic for me at first—I needed help; I turned to God. I felt incapable of producing on the level I wanted, so I would turn it over to a higher power and that would bypass my self-confidence issues.

Then, in time, the prayer became much less of a desperate request for help, and more of a surrender to letting the deepest possible truth be spoken.

There's a practice I teach that you can find versions of in many traditions. You write down the question or problem, then you download everything your mind has to say about it. At that point, you go into meditation, or chant, and when your state has shifted into a deeper awareness, you ask for guidance. Then you just write what comes up. The answer arises from whomever you think you're accessing—God, your higher self, your intuitive self. . . . I'm devotional, so I like to invoke a personal presence, but it works just as well to tune in to the spaciousness.

The intention to remain awake and spacious and to orient to the true Self rather than to the ego is an attitude: a specific orientation in which we hold ourselves so that the wind can lift our wings. That essential shift in orientation from closed to open—being aware that you don't know the whole truth of anything, but staying curious and open to being shown—has the power to bring you directly into the *now*. Being present in the now is simple enough in concept, but quite demanding in practice . . . which is exactly *why* we practice and why two people from fundamentally different traditions—a Jew and a Vedantist—have a similar habit of praying for help.

Stillness: Cultivating a Quiet Mind

"If we're living a life governed by ego and acquisition," mused Sheikh Kabir Helminski, "how can we possibly listen to guidance? By the time it comes, it will be a pretty heavy message. It won't be subtle with all its beauty and grace—it will be a hammer over the head. . . . We have to open the inner space of silence and stillness to listen to the guidance."

That space can be opened in a variety of ways: meditation practice; harmonious and beautiful surroundings; walking and other forms of movement; music; chanting; and simplifying life so that we're not incessantly eaten up by the demands of getting, spending, and then maintaining a variety of things we could live more peacefully without.

While you can think of silence as an attribute of remote locations, it's mainly a state of mind. Anyone who has ever tried to meditate knows how many thoughts interrupt. In a mere 20 minutes, it may seem as though you can review a lifetime of hopes and fears . . . to-do's and to-don'ts. Whenever the mind isn't otherwise occupied, it tends to latch onto one thing after another. This habitual chewing of the mental cud—which goes on relentlessly for most people—produces interior noise, whether you're sitting alone in a pristine forest or walking along a busy city street.

One of the results of steady meditation practice is a gradual stabilization of attention so that the mind becomes quieter and more settled. The experience of that is the arising of a peaceful, receptive interior silence. The inner dialogue may not stop entirely, but we "dis-identify" from it, recognizing that we're not our thoughts, but something deeper. As Father Thomas Keating teaches, meditation is a fundamental shift in attention away from thoughts—which are like boats that float down the river of consciousness—to the river itself, which is our participation in Ultimate Reality.

The peace and contentment that accompany this insight gradually transform your way of being in daily life. External circumstances don't ruffle you so much, and it's easier to stay centered, like a top with a low center of gravity. Furthermore, guidance arises spontaneously from the level of consciousness that isn't limited by the usual faculties of knowing.

Ajahn Sona described how that occurs:

> Most problems are not to be solved, but dissolved by silence and clarity. Those that remain afterwards we can use discursive means to solve. But the clear thinking that follows silence is what we want.
>
> In the West we've forgotten the genius of intuition, which is chased away by this agitated, desperate thought that we have. So what we've lost is our trust and folk knowledge of the value of silently waiting and listening. We jump right in because of our training in our educational institutions to begin discursive thinking. They show us the "on" switch, but they never show us the "off" switch. And so you're left, especially at the end of a university degree, as a thinking machine at the mercy of only one faculty in the way of getting knowledge. The other faculty, that quiet listening and the trust that out of the deeper mind profound answers come, is not taught.
>
> So that's one of the things I specialize in—telling people there's another way of coming to an understanding of things. What I usually say is that 95 percent of your problems are not going to be solved; they're going to be dissolved when your mind becomes quiet. You'll come out of that quiet state and you'll realize that *95 percent of my problems weren't real*. If they are, the 5 percent—if there are 5 percent—can now be dealt with by clear thinking. So for most people, a great deal of confusion and what seem to be overwhelming difficulties are dissolved rather than solved.

But meditation isn't the only way to cut through the mental thicket of discursive thinking. Walking into Mukunda Stiles's home or yoga studio invites clarity and quietness of mind. Not only are the spaces simple, harmonious, and entirely free of clutter . . . they're also beautiful. Spiritual art—Tibetan thangkas, statues of various deities, and skillfully rendered mandalas—creates an atmosphere of peaceful stillness.

Both of us are yoga-therapy clients of Mukunda's, and we've noticed that our bodies begin to relax and our minds to slow down before the sessions even begin. The peaceful presence so easily felt in his studio also suffuses his meditation room, or his "cave," as he calls it. We sit in front of his altar—which displays sacred objects ranging from a woolen cap once worn by his guru, the late Swami Muktananda, to various images of the Divine Mother. Candles that symbolize the Inner Light and its union with the Divine Light complete what's surely a deluxe cave, even in its simplicity.

Psychologist Linda Backman, who specializes in regressing her clients to what she and they believe is the life between lives, spoke of a number of different practices that could lead to a clear and quiet mind. When listening for guidance, she told us:

> . . . quiet helps—not just in terms of sound, but also in terms of physical space. You need some solitude to step away from everyday demands. Being with yourself without intrusion is crucial. I do believe that some people gain their guidance from literal quiet and stillness. For other people, like me, that's not always the most efficient way. Some people need to be outside moving or need sound.
>
> Shamanic journeying to the accompaniment of a drum is a practice that works well for me. I also like staring into a candle at night and listening to the sound of running water. Being in the shower is a great place for me to get guidance. Some of the efficacy may be due to the water, literally to being cleansed. But some of it is about removing the trappings of "me" in the outside world: being unclothed . . . being removed . . . not having my contacts in so that I can't see that well.
>
> And, of course, I have to mention music. Certain kinds of music instantly galvanize spiritual connection. Piano music is a favorite of mine—I suspect that it shifts my energy. Night or early morning, when the veil is thin, is when I connect most easily to guidance. It's quieter then on the earth.

Taking even a few minutes to quiet your mind when you wake up in the morning can make the entire day flow much more smoothly. It also sets the stage for being more conscious and wakeful. But perhaps the most unexpected and gratuitous result of taking time for inner silence is that it encourages gratitude, another facet of humility that's a universal spiritual practice. The Christian mystic Meister Eckhart once said that if *Thank You* were the only prayer you ever said, it would be enough. Scientists agree, since gratitude is currently one of the hottest research areas in mind/body medicine and positive psychology.

Gratitude

"I'm thinking of this statement that comes from a Zen koan or Zen poem: 'I meet Him, but I do not know His name,'" Father Thomas Keating mused, searching his prodigious memory for the exact source of the quote. Then he continued with it: "'In gratitude here is all.' Now, is that a personal experience or not? It seems to me incredibly personal and advanced—in other words, it's a relationship with an Unknown Presence that inspires gratitude, and this is one of the fundamental responses in growth toward the Divine Presence. But whether you consider it personal or impersonal, I think that's a matter of cultural understanding."

Sheikh Kabir Helminski, a translator of Rumi, delights in how the 13th-century Sufi poet-saint communicates "above all his own sense of awe and appreciation for the dimension of divine abundance." *Gratitude* and *gratuitous* share the same root—the divine abundance that Father Thomas is always invoking as God's unlimited gift of "hospitality." We're at a banquet here on planet Earth despite all the problems that confront us, and our job is to receive the abundance that's set in front of us. Gratitude is precisely that—the capacity to receive and to be present to life in its awesome, changing display of beauty, terror, creation, and destruction.

Joan: When we're children, receiving comes naturally. As a baby, my grandson Alex used to get so excited when he looked around that he'd actually shake with delight. He was a natural teacher of *Kabbalah*—which means "the receiving." But drinking up the world with the innocent excitement of a child is short-lived. As we get older, some of that receptivity shuts down as the ego comes into play, with its judgments, wants, and fears. Life starts to lose its luster, and in taking it for granted, we develop a more superficial, reified connection to things—what philosopher Martin Buber characterized as an I-It relationship, rather than the intimate I-Thou relationship that invites guidance. It's easy for an adult to walk past a beautiful pond hosting a flock of geese and see little more than the piles of bird poop on the shore.

Joan and Gordon: One of the great contemporary teachers of gratefulness is the Benedictine monk Brother David Steindl-Rast. A senior member of Mount Saviour Monastery in Elmira, New York, Brother David is a Catholic theologian with a doctorate from the University of Vienna. Like many of the contemporary mystics we've met, he's fun, funny, down-to-earth, and deeply interspiritual.

Brother David was sent to a Buddhist-Christian dialogue in 1967 and began to receive extensive training in Zen practice. Alternating periods of retreat with lecture tours around the world, he is a global spokesperson for what he calls gratefulness—the Great Fullness. Gratefulness is a natural practice of mindfulness, he teaches, a way to come into the present moment, regardless of your belief system. His Website (**www.gratefulness.org**) has an extensive and frequently updated section on practices that support this attitude. One of the simplest and most effective examples is to retrospect your day before bed and choose one thing to be thankful for that you've never expressed appreciation for previously. The result is increased mindfulness throughout the day, since you're continuously on the lookout for something new to be grateful for.

Gratitude isn't limited to thanksgiving for the good things, though. It encompasses the wholeness of life—what we usually categorize as "bad" and "good," neither of which may be as it initially appears. There's a famous Taoist teaching tale about a poor Chinese farmer who seems to be having bad luck when his only plow horse runs off during planting season. But then his fortunes appear to change dramatically for the better when the horse returns, leading a herd of wild mustangs. However, "good" turns "bad" again when the farmer's only son tries to break a mustang, is bucked off, and breaks his leg instead.

In the next verse of this long tale, the Emperor's soldiers arrive in town to conscript all the young men for a hopeless war in which they will most likely perish, but the wounded son can't go. The story continues, illustrating the fact that since everything is inter-related, we can't so easily decide what's good or bad. We may, for example, experience gratitude down the road for something we learned during an episode that we'd first thought of as "bad."

But why not be grateful now? Brother David suggests that you can identify the skills you need to cope with current problems, imagine yourself using them, and be appreciative of what you're learning in the process. The culture of modern medicine has fallen in love with the practice of gratitude—which, it turns out, is a vir-tual panacea for our ills. Writing out a daily list (or even a weekly one) of things you're grateful for increases energy, motivation for carrying through projects, and well-being. It reduces anxiety, depression, stress, anger, pain, and physical symptoms.

One study found that women who had lived with abusive men but who could identify positive things they'd learned had fewer symptoms of post-traumatic stress disorder than those who didn't find a silver lining. Since gratitude is a practice that cultivates acceptance of what is, even as it encourages more positive choices, it's intimately related to the development of another attitude con-ducive to guidance—surrender.

Surrender

"Learn the alchemy True Human Beings know," wrote Rumi. "The moment you accept what troubles you've been given, the door opens." Cultivating the ability to "be here now" and to accept your situation is an attitude that's easily misunderstood. It doesn't mean abandoning the effort to improve your personal life or the world—but it *does* mean that you'd be a lot more comfortable and efficient if you stopped resisting the reality of the moment. The past and the present can't be changed—they are what they are, so there's no point wasting energy in the wish that they were different.

That's what Buddhist monk Ajahn Sona calls bad hope. Resisting

what is only creates mental agitation that muddies the waters and obscures guidance that might lead to more skillful means for creating a better future. Ajahn Sona explained:

> All conflict with reality as it is must be overcome—in other words, our irrational and neurotic objections to things as they are. We have to surrender our wishing things would be some other way in the past or in the present. The final acceptance and reconciliation of well-being in the midst of the way things are right now—not to wait—that's the key, the sign that someone has achieved some high vision of *dhamma*. They are well now even while these tragedies go on around us. We are well. So that has to do with the personal will and the universal will. You have to be at one with it. I'm sure, in the theological kind of language, one would not be arguing with God.

Joan: "So you don't argue with reality," I remarked, laughing, "and others don't argue with God."

Ajahn Sona transcended the linguistic split between reality and God by putting surrender in universal terms: "We don't argue with the Universe, because we always lose."

Joan and Gordon: Metaphysician Nina Zimbelman expanded on this theme. She talked about a transformational experience in which she felt surrounded by the Presence of Love, which told her: "To live from wholeness, you just have to pass one exam. It only has one question—I'll even give you the question. To live from wholeness, accept what is. *So the question is, 'Do you accept what is?'*"

Nina explained, "The more you accept this, the more at peace you are. If the river turns and you don't turn, you end up on dry land."

Nina is a petite but seemingly fearless woman who appears to be the very archetype of surrender. She's a warrior, with the radical trust that every life experience comes in the service of wisdom. At one point she was living in Egypt, with a successful career as a metaphysical teacher. Then she received guidance to move to a small town in North Carolina without any clear idea why. Such a monumental upheaval would scare the average person silly. But Nina accepts change the way that a Fortune 100 executive or a religious missionary might accept reassignment.

"I was living in a villa in Egypt. I had a great life," she told us. "Then I was assigned to Appalachia. Why here? It turned out that it was the best place for me. I had to learn how to be nobody. I was an incognito person, with a $9-an-hour job, learning how to be ordinary. I came in yesterday from painting a building I was guided to build, and there was your phone call requesting an interview, to access another dimension of me. One part of me is the house-painter. Another part is the metaphysical teacher. They're all me, all one. There's no difference between them."

It's a big deal to move across the globe, especially when you have no idea why. What if you make a mistake and that wasn't guidance calling after all, but just a wrong number? Nina has a fundamental trust that there are no wrong numbers. In her understanding, you're just as close to waking up—whether you define that as enlightenment, God-realization, or becoming fully human—working a low-paying job in Appalachia as you are being rich and famous. The key is to surrender to whatever condition you find yourself in by finding the wisdom in it.

Peruvian shaman Cecilia Montero, another model for the fearless trust that is the heart of surrender, told us: "I have dared myself to take the wrong path along the years—and then make it an exercise of will to find the right choice within it."

The human ability to discover life-affirming choices even in less-than-optimal situations is the foundation of fearlessness and surrender. The essential spiritual questions *Who are you?* and *Why are you here?* aren't about getting your own way or manifesting material desires. There's no end to desire and no permanence to material possessions. In the blink of an eye everything can be taken from you—health, wealth, vocation, and even your loved ones.

Psychiatrist Viktor Frankl survived four Nazi death camps during the Holocaust. Out of that experience the inspiring book *Man's Search for Meaning* was born. Perhaps Dr. Frankl's most famous quote is: "Everything can be taken from a man [or woman] but one thing: the last of human freedoms—to choose one's attitude in any given set of circumstances."

In fearlessly relinquishing our narrow self-concerns and choosing surrender, we become less preoccupied with our own misery. That leaves us available to encounter reality without blinking and see where it's open to the best expression of ourselves and our interactions with others.

When we think about the attitudes that reveal progress on the spiritual journey, empathy and kindness to others are at the top of the list. Near the end of his life, writer and philosopher Aldous Huxley—an expert on the essential spirituality present in all traditions, which he called *The Perennial Philosophy*—was giving a lecture at MIT. The escort who squired him around was none other than the young Huston Smith, who later became a noted writer on world religion. When Smith asked Huxley what spiritual advice he had for us, the elder replied simply, "Try to be a little kinder." This wisdom is at the heart of forgiveness—both for oneself and others—which is an essential spiritual practice, because it sets the forgiver free.

Forgiveness: Putting Down the Knife

When we asked poet Daniel Ladinsky what spiritual practices were particularly important for developing the capacity to listen for and act on spiritual guidance, he e-mailed us this response:

> *There is a wonderful little Hafiz story (as you know I am a big Hafiz fan) that I feel encapsulates the beginning of spirituality (or guidance, and listening) and is probably a profound and simple how-to manual, if one is looking for that. Not to say it will be easy to act on this story, but here it is: Once a young woman came to the great 14th-century Persian poet Hafiz and said, "What is the sign of someone who knows God?" And Hafiz then became very quiet, and looked deep into this young person's eyes, and said, "My dear, they have dropped the knife, they have dropped the cruel knife they so often use upon their tender self—and others." Yes, to the degree that we can drop the knife, and no longer harm ourselves—or others—physically, emotionally, psychologically, spiritually is the degree to which we awake the needed intelligence and strength to allow ourselves to be guided by all the forces around us that I feel are always trying to help.*

Letting go of the past and forgiving yourself is fundamental to making the shift from false self to true nature. Otherwise you continue to accumulate karma. Swami Adiswarananda commented, "Karma is not fatalistic, and not relevant or binding to the true Self. When you see your karma, you can't see this part of your experience as good and that part as bad. Both of those aspects of experience are paths to liberation. You can't split your experience into black and white. What makes the difference between the saint and the sinner is that the saint sees his own holiness, while the sinner is focused on his own sins."

The Swami considers self-blame a spiritual roadblock and suggests adjusting your attitude through *repentance*—which means literally to *think again:* "Instead, regard the pain and suffering that show up in your life as symptoms of the neglect of your soul and as calls to renew and reinvigorate your spiritual quest. You're like a plant in the soil, and the water of repentance will help that plant to grow and flower. The flower is emblematic of kindness, love for all beings, and Self-knowledge."

Repentance is not just about you. Rethinking the past includes people who may have hurt you. The Buddha compared resentment to a hot coal you pick up to throw at someone else, while *you're* the one who gets burned. Dropping the coal—or the knife, as in Daniel's telling of the Hafiz story—isn't about condoning someone else's bad behavior or waiting for an apology. It's unilateral disarmament. Forgiveness is entirely about you, a radical commitment to reclaiming your peace of mind and to extending empathy and kindness to other human beings regardless of what they've done to you.

The John Templeton Foundation, which supports research in spirituality and healing, has funded dozens of scientific studies concerning the effects of forgiveness on health and well-being. It also supports the Stanford Forgiveness Project, which was first directed by psychologist Frederic Luskin. One of the most moving of Luskin's projects was the Stanford–Northern Ireland HOPE Project, in which 17 men and women from Northern Ireland, all with family members murdered in the violence there, went to Stanford for forgiveness training. After just a week, these men and women who'd lost parents, children, spouses, or siblings reported a 35 percent decline in head-aches, stomachaches, and other symptoms of stress and a 20 percent drop in symptoms of depression. Unforgiving people in general are more stressed, depressed, narcissistic, angry, and paranoid; are less likely to help others; and have more physical symptoms than those who have managed to drop the knife.

Forgiveness is a potent form of surrender to what is . . . coupled, perhaps, with gratefulness for what has been learned. The result is that we realize we're nothing and nobody special. Everybody suffers and makes mistakes. Everybody just wants to be happy, and kindness goes a long way toward making that so, as does the universal spiritual practice based on the attitude—or orientation—to loving the truth.

Loving the Truth

"Guidance has to do with the development of attitude, the right kind of attitude," Hameed Ali explained. "One is openness to the truth, *openness* in the sense that I'm open to see whatever the truth is, regardless of consequences. That openness implies not knowing—recognizing the importance of, and getting comfortable with, not knowing what the situation is, what's going to happen."

We've all had moments of inquiry and loving the truth without calling it that. Maybe your nemesis at work falls off the curb in front of your office building. You instinctively jump into the street to help him and a speeding car narrowly misses mowing both of you down. Later, over coffee, the two of you talk with an intimacy that wasn't possible before. As you describe your experience of nearly being killed, you're in touch with your body, in real time, reporting what you're actually feeling. The energetic field between you and your former enemy noticeably shifts: It's intimate and clear. The old hostility is gone, and it's as if you're seeing each other for the first time. When preconceptions melt away, it can seem as though the moon has risen and the landscape is suddenly revealed in all its magic.

While Hameed Ali focuses on personal or interpersonal inquiry as a path to truth, the Quakers add practices of group inquiry. Truth is a sacred principle to the Religious Society of Friends, and its practice infuses every aspect of life. Boulder Quaker Meeting member Deanne Butterfield told us:

> We raise our kids with the notion of genuine honesty being one of the highest values. That's generally not true in our culture. We don't just do it because it's one of the six major things we're supposed to do, but because of the fragility of our ability to know the truth. We don't want to jeopardize our relationship with truth by violating it in little ways, since we need it for the big stuff.
>
> What the Quakers have learned is that truth has to be addressed humbly and without self-righteousness. So it shouldn't be humiliating to other people or coercive. The truth is told out of a humility that's bold. It sometimes shocks non-Quakers that we're so direct in our speech. Because acting out of what's true is so important, we try to practice that everywhere in our life.

"We're called to live our life in ethical ways," fellow Meeting member Mary Hey picked up when Deanne was finished. "Peace, simplicity, integrity, equality, and community are the guiding principles; and they're almost invisible. You also see the terms *veracity* and *authenticity* a lot. In terms of the 21st century, this means having your words match your life—living up to your Light. So we have queries in our meetings that regularly address whether we're living up to these principles. There's no national Quaker organization that tells you what to do. The monthly meeting is our basis, and every Meeting has its own queries so that we can be accountable."

Examples of queries might concern whether meetings for worship are held in expectant waiting for divine guidance, whether people feel encouraged to share their spiritual insights, and whether one arrives at a meeting with heart and mind prepared. Queries are an example of how Quakers use inquiry as a way of loving the truth. As well as being an individual practice and a group practice within meetings, inquiry extends into every relationship.

Deanne Butterfield explained:

If Mary and I don't see something the same way, rather than trying to tell each other what to do, the tradition says that we need to inquire closely so that we understand each other: "Mary—tell me more about whatever." That's how we come one-on-one to understand the other.

We also have a process called a Clearness Committee, which is convened to help a person get clear. We do it before marriage, for example, or for other important life transitions and decisions. But even if I go in because I need an answer like "Should I be divorced?" the committee never gives advice. The clearness has to be mine. The committee only asks questions. It's an exercise so that people can ask questions for themselves. They then report on what they've discovered to the larger Meeting (the whole church), which has the opportunity for further questioning. The committee is a mirror, and hopefully a clean one.

All of the practices we've discussed—praying for help, stillness, gratitude, surrender, forgiveness, and loving the truth—are all facets of a single jewel: humility. It's that basic attitude of not knowing—but being willing to be shown—that allows the ego to step aside so that true nature can emerge. The willingness to let go of the known is the oil for the lamp of awakening . . . our readiness for the unexpected moment when the divine bridegroom will appear. Awakening can happen anytime. Why, as Father Thomas Keating suggests, not now?

※　※　※

Chapter Ten

OVERCOMING EGO . . .
THE BIGGEST BLOCK TO GUIDANCE

When we asked the redoubtable Reb Zalman Schachter-Shalomi what blocks spiritual guidance, he responded—as he often does—with a story. Painting the kind of lively mental picture that makes him such a beloved teacher, Reb Zalman explained the origin of our most basic *introjects,* the beliefs we import from our family and culture, which make up the invisible lens through which we see the world. In other words, what we "believe" we now know, what we've even been carefully "taught" to know, is precisely what keeps us trapped in ignorance. He told us:

> Every mother does this to her kids. The kid says, "I don't like Uncle Hymie. He stinks." The mother says, "He loves you. You're wrong—that's not the way he is." So she talks the kid out of his own shit detector. That's what happens to us when we're bent out of shape by an introject. Our shit detector is broken, and that's when we can't listen to divine guidance. The best way to clean that up is to use the internal workings of moral husbandry, if you will. To take care of your own behavior, do a nightly examination of conscience to figure out how to do things better and to work with other people who can give you feedback. Without feedback, you're lost.

Between *Rosh Hashanah,* the Jewish New Year, and *Yom Kippur,* the Day of Atonement, come the ten Days of Awe. This is a time for introspection and retrospection so that you can examine yourself and get beyond some of the blocks that separate you from a truer knowing. Every year before these High Holy Days, Reb Zalman explained, he asks two or three good friends to point out the things that may be obstructing his way that he can't see himself.

Other wisdom traditions are equally keen on removing what we call sources of magnetic deviance. The Buddhists focus on the most central distortions of ignorance, desire, and anger or aversion, which they call the *Three Poisons.* Ignorance is the most basic in all traditions. If you don't know that you live in a meaningful spiritual reality and that there's a way to wake up and realize your true nature, you're lost. Then you believe that your ego is the answer to the question *Who am I?* Since the ego maintains its identity by splitting reality into what it either craves or rejects, these poisons are what keep the wheel of *samsara,* or illusion, spinning.

The Hindus enumerate *five kleshas,* or obstacles to the spiritual journey, that expand on the three poisons by adding pride and fear. The Catholics match those five distortions and raise them two—adding gluttony and sloth, for a total of *seven deadly sins.* These are all facets of ego, the separate sense of self that believes it's the "doer," the ultimate shaper of your life, rather than a partner in a bigger story.

As Rabbi Rami Shapiro put it, "There's only one block to guidance: me. If I get in the way and try to hear what I want to hear, whenever my ego gets into the process, that's the only block. Fear, anxiety, and lack of self-esteem are all derivative of the ego."

Psychologists think of the ego as a central identity—a *Who am I?* that needs to be strong and coherent, lest it fall apart during stress, leaving a black hole of emptiness and despair. The word *ego* comes from Latin and means simply "I am." It's a necessary center of what psychologists call *agency*—the healthy ability to think and act in an autonomous way. But in spiritual parlance, the ego refers to a different kind of critter entirely: the separate, prideful "doer" who wants to control the universe rather than catching the winds of wisdom and guidance. This smaller sense of self that lives in separation from a larger whole is intrinsically fearful and attached to getting its desires met or avoiding threats in order to feel secure.

In this chapter, we'll consider how the ego separates us from guidance, and how, when we shift our sense of gravity out of its fearfulness, a larger intelligence can be expressed through us.

Domesticating Our Fear

"Attention is the first preparatory work for being guidable," said Reverend Cynthia Bourgeault. "And then along the way what blocks that integral motion of recognition/action, the ability to put into effect what we hear, is fear. We need to be constantly domesticating, taming, gentling our own fear."

The fear that drives people is twofold: (1) fear that we won't get what we want, and (2) fear that we'll get what we *don't* want. If we follow our guidance to write this book, for example, what if it turns out poorly? If fear is in charge, then we'll feel like failures, which would be a serious blow to our ego identities. Fear leads to unpleasant trains of thought that extend far beyond present circumstances: *What if this book doesn't sell? What if no one reads it? What if—because we put aside other projects to complete this one—we end up living in the basement of one of our kids' houses or dining on cat food in our old age?* Fear doesn't even consider the possibility that the book is an authentic expression of listening to guidance and that regardless of its apparent success, or lack thereof, it's our dharma—that place where the inner spiritual journey and one's purpose converge.

Rather than staying peacefully present to what's unfolding, when fear runs wild, we're trapped in horror movies of our own making. None of the things we're worried about are happening, yet our minds and bodies react to them as if they were real. Furthermore, fear blocks skillful action. On the one hand, it can lead to hasty, ill-considered decisions. On the other, it can be paralyzing.

"I find that the deepest threat on the spiritual path," said Reverend Cynthia Bourgeault, "is any sense of urgency of 'I have to have . . .' or 'I need . . .' When this urgency enters your life, the rest is going to be correspondingly distorted. So, if you start out with

'I need a group' or 'I have to have a group,' or 'I need a teacher' or 'I have to have a teacher'—'I can't do anything until I find them,' with this sense of squeezing the cactus—as long as you have this urgency, you're going to get into trouble. You're not in a state to recognize what you need."

"You wait out the instinct," Quaker educator Patricia Loring added. "You wait out the rush of being in charge of doing whatever it is that you're going to carry out. The bad word here is *haste;* nothing is done in a hasty manner, so that there's a chance for all of the emotion and instinctual drive to dissipate. Then the clarity of what's there and where the motion of the heart is coming from emerges. Time seasons things and refines whatever is pure from all the other things that will inevitably be in there that are cultural or instinctual or whatever."

Patient waiting in the now, rather than making up stories about the future, domesticates fear. That requires the humility that we keep coming back to. Humility—the antidote to fear—is the admission that we don't really know what will happen or what direction to go in, but we're open to following guidance and being shown. This requires willingness to live in the unknown, which scares the pants off the ego, even if we *are* committed to a spiritual journey.

Buddhist monk Ajahn Sona agreed that the most common block to guidance is sheer fear of the unknown: "This is why we stay in bad relationships or bad jobs. You will get continuous advice by your teacher to go into the unknown. What does ignorance present itself as? *As knowledge.* It seems to be the known. Real knowledge appears as the unknown. This is the paradox. That deep ignorance is the hardest thing to remove." Anger and greed are visible, he continued—referring to two of the three Buddhist poisons—but ignorance, the third and most subtle, is hidden.

Listening to Sister Rose Mary Dougherty talking about domesticating fear of the unknown was also very helpful. For most of us, the deep-seated fear of the ego doesn't just give up and go away. Working with it is a continuing challenge that's part of the journey: "And for me fear is also a factor that gets in the way of acting on guidance. I can see something clearly, and yet there is this terrible fear of—I don't want to say of not being successful, but whatever it is, of moving out into the deep, moving out into the unknown, that kind of paralyzes me for a while and keeps me from acting upon the guidance that I see.

"I would just add one more thing," Sister Rose Mary continued in her patient, down-to-earth way. "Another thing that gets in my way, maybe it's related to the fear, is that I might see this piece very clearly, but then I take it and begin to run into the future with it. What I imagine may be totally unrelated to what I'm seeing now, but that contributes to the fear. If I take this first step, maybe this [imagined future] is where it's going to lead. And I don't know that. So it's second-guessing or judging or adding my own spin to something."

When we asked Sister Rose Mary to give us an example of what she meant, she related a delightful story of synchronicity, where one thing led to another in a way that no one could imagine or predict. The range of possibilities in any situation is so much greater than anything our small egoic self could possibly conjure up. She told us:

I was in a Zen retreat, and my job was to attend to the person who was going to be made a teacher. In the middle of the retreat, I asked her whether she wanted a foot massage, and she said yes. Well, after I asked her, I thought, *Why in God's name did I ever do that? I've never given a foot massage before in my life.* Well, that led to my getting into studying foot reflexology, which led me to the hospice where I am now. The director thought I wanted to come there to work, and I was just trying to get information on certification to do reflexology.

But sometimes instead of just moving from Light to Light, I say, *Okay, I'm giving a foot massage—oh, this must mean that.* And I'm guessing what the next step is. If I had foreseen any of these steps, I probably wouldn't have made a move. I just would have canceled out the whole thing. When we begin to impose our own sense of what's coming next before we really know, then we begin living a scenario that's not real. And of course, we don't want to go there.

Domesticating our fear and learning to live in the present requires two things: (1) the humility to let go of fantasies about the future, and (2) the courage to let go of the past. The latter requirement means that we have to give up one of the ego's most cherished possessions—the story of who it thinks it is.

The Story of Me, Writ Large

Pride is one of the seven deadly sins. One way to define that is as an addiction to our story and what we think we know about ourselves: *I'm a Christian, I'm a Muslim, I'm a Jew, and we're always persecuted; I was an abused child; I'm unlucky at love; I'm a winner . . . or a loser. I* is both the central letter in the word *pride,* as well as the compelling subject of our life stories. Reverend Cynthia Bourgeault, eloquent as always, calls this form of egoic pride *The Story of Me, Writ Large.*

Reverend Cynthia told us a story about going to a spiritual intensive to do the work of George Ivanovitch Gurdjieff, a Greek-Armenian mystic who attained notoriety as a crazy wisdom teacher and master of sacred dance. While Gurdjieff died in 1949, his techniques for awakening to the sacred and moving beyond conditioned patterns of ego are still widely used and were an important part of Reverend Cynthia's early spiritual work.

"It was the first time I ever went to a Gurdjieff work intensive," she began.

> We were about a hundred of us at our little place, and I was assigned to the kitchen for our work intensive. The pressure was relentless. We had to make three meals a day for 100 people, and I was with people who were whizzes in the kitchen.
>
> For three days I was in misery, and then on the fourth day I was told, "You're joining the music group." Well, this was great news, as though finally they'd affirmed my true talent. Then, on the last day, just as we were showing up for the final appearance of the week, someone came and said, "You're going back in the kitchen." They set me down with a large bowl of beans to chop;

and I was sitting there weeping as the sound of my musical group was wafting over the balcony, and the lady who was our team leader, with this sphinxlike presence, said, "You can use this moment to see something, or you can waste it in self-pity."

And, bingo, it was a wake-up call that changed my whole life. I saw that what was happening in the music group was merely affirming and stroking all my previous talents, and I saw that what was going on was just self-pity at having my ego dislodged. The kitchen was exactly the right place if what I said I wanted—an increase in consciousness—was what I *really* wanted. Disciplined spiritual work does this; it goes right for the jugular where we're pinned by our conditioning. It's experiences like this that began to free my consciousness from its absolute slavery to its conditioning and its story.

Reverend Cynthia continued:

Ego grandiosity can get in the way big time, and it's an almost inevitable learning curve because when many of us enter the journey, the egoic self is the only self we know. But it will obscure the journey if you don't manage to swing out of it. Thomas Keating said, "The notion that God is absent is the biggest illusion on the spiritual path." My way of saying it is that God is always present, and we're the ones who are absent. Guidance is always present, and it's we who are absent. Usually the reason we're absent is because we're hanging out in our noise or we're hanging out in the ego.

When we hang out in the depths of ourselves, guidance is merely joining the track of the story of our life as it's already being authentically lived. You can't separate yourself from it. The major problem is to turn down the background noise that comes from the story of yourself—thinking that you are your egoic self—separating from the fear that comes from living trapped in that smaller self.

I want to quote from a brilliant teacher, one of the most brilliant underground healers of the 20th century, Beatrice Bruteau, who is both a Vedantist and a Christian contemplative. She wrote an article called "Prayer and Identity," which absolutely galvanized me. Her idea was that who we are when we say "I" doesn't stay at a fixed place, but shifts along a spectrum from the most bound and neurotic, like who you are when all your buttons are pushed, to the most spacious and nondual. Where we are in any moment will determine how we see and think about God.

I found this amazingly freeing—that our sense of selfhood slides along a moving scale. Normally I talk about myself and live in the high egoic level. I have a sense of the personal, and my life has a history to it. But actually the center of selfhood needs to be held a little more nonpersonally. The self needs to be more in the "I am" place.

"The great Christian mystics like Thomas Merton, Meister Eckhart, Bernadette Roberts, Wayne Teasdale, and Thomas Keating have known that," Reverend Cynthia explained. She continued:

If you can notch that center of your selfhood, that deep feeling of where you live from and speak from, into that "I am" place, then you don't leave the personal behind—and I think this is the genius of Christianity—rather, the personal becomes the violin upon which you play the music of God. So it becomes beautiful and useful: how to live in that personal selfhood wisely to the glory of God without getting stuck in that as ego validation—because we already are the glory and the shining, and it flows through our finite form. It's just not all we are, and it's not the Source of who we are.

I think this is a real growing edge for Christian metaphysics in the 21st century. It's very reluctant to lose the egoic because it confuses the egoic with the personal and knows it's a religion of the personal. These two levels can coexist and integrate beautifully, but we need to repatriate our mystics [bring them back from the margins to the very center of our awareness] who point the way into which Christianity can move into its true Self.

Just as human beings have egos, so do institutions. Whether civic, religious, or political, they evolve by moving out of more limited identities into greater states of freedom. As our personal center of gravity slides from the lower reaches of egoic fear, through higher egoic levels of identity, and ultimately into the "I am" place of true nature, we get wiser. It's hopeful to think that our institutions can do the same.

"In our mainline Christian churches," Professor Wilkie Au, a former Jesuit priest, explained, "there has been a developmental lag." He went on:

> They've stayed with the institutional learning that was mainly directed by authority figures while they were growing up. But part of the shadow dimension of our institutional leadership is that they've never really wanted us to develop into autonomous, functioning people who would be inner directed.
>
> Inner authority is the wisdom that comes from our own personal experience and reflection. I try to validate that as a source of divine guidance so that people can balance their looking upward and outward by looking inward and deeper—strike the balance—glean the wisdom that comes through a tradition-bearing community, but yet not abandon their own experience and the inner voice, the inner compass. The two have to be held in a creative tension.
>
> [New Testament scholar] Marcus Borg talks about the historic paradigm and the emerging paradigm—they're almost like two traditions mainly based on their interpretations of biblical authorities. The earlier paradigm was more concerned with facts, and the emerging paradigm is more concerned with meaning—it's more metaphoric. The earlier paradigm is concerned with *Did it happen?* while the emerging paradigm is concerned with meaning—*How does it contribute to human life?*

The ways in which spiritual guidance might contribute to human life as a whole are limitless. But to enter the arena of expanded possibility that guidance provides, both as individuals and as part of institutions, we have to stay vigilant and curious—to become lovers of the truth rather than slaves to cherished identities, opinions, and beliefs. That essential curiosity is what lifts the veil of ignorance, fear, and attachment that obscures spiritual guidance.

The curiosity needed to lift the veil that separates us from a direct perception of possibility is a very personal ongoing inquiry. We need to ask regularly and with true interest, *Where is egoic pride and attachment at work here?* Reverend Cynthia gave us a valuable way of doing that. She explained that if we could replace just one letter in the ego's personal drama—*My Story*—we could experience *Mystery* instead. And it's mystery, the discipline of knowing that we *cannot* know the whole story—and the willingness to let go of the starring role in our own drama and the roles of writer and director—that overcomes all the blocks to guidance.

The next time you feel caught in fear, desire, or anger—or immobilized by sloth—try paying attention to the story that you're telling yourself. Is it one of pride? Of cherished self-definition? What would it be like if you could drop the story and engage the mystery instead?

Maybe your story is that you're a person whose identity is bound up in being the perfect leader, parent, caretaker, writer, teacher, businessperson, man, or woman. What would it feel like to challenge that story when you noticed it coming up? What would it be like to take a breath, let go, and ask, *What is true in this moment, right now?* The answer, of course, won't come from your mind. But it's there in your body, your felt sense, and your willingness to let go of the known and connect intimately with the Spirit of Guidance as it's arising freshly in this moment, here and now.

When we can do that—even at a rudimentary level—then our being, what Reverend Cynthia calls the greater *I Am,* forms a conduit for wisdom and skillful action to manifest in the world . . . as you'll appreciate in the following chapters:

1. Contemplation (that *I Am* presence) flows seamlessly into action.

2. The divine DNA that is that seed of human evolution germinates in ways entirely beyond our limited understanding.

3. Leadership and guidance merge and move us toward a culture of wisdom—a civilization with a heart.

UNFOLDING THE HEART
OF SPIRIT IN ACTION

"Contemplation," mused poet Daniel Ladinsky. "I wonder if the average person really knows the main definition of that word."

If you look it up in the dictionary, you'll find two different meanings: (1) The more common one is to think about something deeply; and (2) the less common is prayer or meditation that facilitates a direct experience of God or the Inner Light—a listening to the heart. That was the definition we had in mind when we asked our Sages to reflect on the question: "How do you understand the relationship between contemplation and action?"

The story of the 18th-century Quaker preacher John Woolman is a good introduction to how enlightened action flows from a deep connection to Inner Light. In his early 20s, Woolman became a strong voice of conscience opposing slavery. But it was a painful experience in his youth that enabled him to unfold the heart of Spirit in action so steadfastly in his later years.

In his journal he recounts the story of being a small boy on his way to a neighbor's house and coming upon a mother robin sitting on her nest. Without thinking, he picked up a stone and threw it at her. She fell dead, and after a few minutes he was "seized with horror at having, in a sportive way, killed an innocent creature while she was careful for her young." As he explains, "I beheld her lying dead and thought those young ones, for which she was so careful, must now perish for want of their dam to nourish them. After some painful considerations on the subject, I climbed up the tree, took all the young birds, and killed them, supposing that better than to leave them to pine away and die miserably."[1]

This painful experience helped Woolman internalize his family's Quaker teachings about love and reverence for life in a profound way. He became a persuasive witness to kindness, and although slavery wouldn't end until the Emancipation Proclamation of 1863, in 1790 his antislavery efforts culminated in the Society of Friends petitioning the U.S. Congress for abolition. His inner beliefs and their seamless flow into outward action were visible proof of Woolman's integrity.

Integrity, from the Latin root *integritas,* means "wholeness." That quality is what's so inspirational about Woolman's life. His inner realization and outer actions were complementary sides of a single, unified movement of Spirit. As we'll consider in this chapter, *spiritual guidance is a movement of Spirit that flows naturally from contemplation to action, neither of which is fully true or complete until met by the other.*

Doing What You <u>Can't</u> Not Do

"'The way will open' is a traditional saying," Boulder Quaker Denny Webster told us about the relation of contemplation to action. "If you sit in expectant waiting, the way will open. You can trust that it will."

"Opening in general is not about doing; it's about seeing what comes from sitting in silence," her colleague Mary Hey added. "The only thing in the way of seeing is *me.* A related concept is that of leadings. The Holy Spirit does intervene in some way and actually points in a direction. *A leading comes upon you and asks you to do something that you can't really shake.*"

She continued:

One of the heroes of our tradition is John Woolman, who had an insight about slavery in the 1700s. He was able to read and write and had to write a bill of sale for a slave, which made him very uncomfortable. He developed a belief in the wrongness of slavery that he just couldn't shake.

At that time many Quakers held slaves, and this was a source of sadness for him. He became more and more uncomfortable, so he'd speak to people about their slaves in a quiet way. He went from Meeting to Meeting registering his protest gently by refusing to be served by slaves. He wore white because slaves made indigo and other dyes. He never humiliated or coerced anyone, just went about in white and asked questions about slavery. This behavior wasn't welcomed in his own Meeting, but the leading he had was so powerful and compelling that it simply took over his life. . . .

We love the story of how Woolman refused to draw up a will for an elderly man because it involved the transfer of his slaves as property. Some time elapsed, and then the man returned to Woolman, this time asking that his slaves be freed upon his death. Eventually whole Meetings moved to the North and gave up their slaves. The truth of what he was saying became obvious to people, and the whole Society of Friends shifted because of his leading. He didn't bludgeon people; he just shared his feelings.

Woolman worked within the traditions of the Friends, whose practice of seeking and following guidance flows naturally—beginning with *silence* and patient humility—from *seeking, waiting, listening,* and *opening;* through *leadings,* the *discernment* of leadings, and *confirmation;* and finally, when called for in a way one "can't shake," to *witnessing* peacefully in word and deed that which one feels truly led to. This entire progression from contemplation to action is what the Quakers recognize as spiritual guidance.

The Dynamic Face of Spirituality

Spirituality is often thought of as passive—a form of supremely inner-directed navel gazing that avoids contact with the outer world. Swami Adiswarananda, in his usual clear and cogent way, debunked that myth, describing the seamless flow of inner truth into outer action that's the natural, unobstructed movement of spiritual guidance. He expressed this natural flow succinctly in his book *The Four Yogas:*

> Karma-yoga does not make a distinction between meditation and action. . . . Self-realization is not a state of inertness but the blossoming forth of spirituality in a dynamic way. It is not passively seeing one's own Self in beings and things. One who really sees the Self in all and all in the Self feels the joys and sufferings of all beings as his or her own. Seeing God within and serving all beings as God's various transfigurations are two aspects of the same experience.[2]

"I think that contemplation and action are two sides of the same coin," agreed Rabbi Rami Shapiro. He explained:

> Deep sensitive experience leads to engaging the world; contemplation leads to action. But a contemplative practice that removes us from the world is only half a practice. The more inward I go with contemplative practice, the more outward I can go, and the more constructive I am. I think that when you root your actions in contemplation, there's a lot less to do. Too often we mistake busyness for effectiveness, and then we burn out. Social activists rooted in contemplative practice may be less likely to burn out, since their action is more effortless and cuts with the grain.

Shaman/writer Oriah Mountain Dreamer had a similar thought. She was in New York on a book tour shortly after 9/11, and many people asked her what they should do. She described her response:

> I said I had faith that if we could sit in silence with what had happened and what was happening inside of us right now, then right action would emerge. People were hungry for a way to be with what was happening. But if you don't have a practice, it's

hard to access this kind of mindfulness and presence when you need it.

The first step to action has to be a deep, shared contemplation in silence with what is—a listening to the stories of what is and what that stirs in us. I have enormous faith that right action would flow from that place in everyone. I think of social-activist groups flying in with the best of intentions but no ability to sit in shared silence. They often end up, as [author and spiritual teacher] Wayne Muller says, "doing good badly."

Sheikh Kabir Helminski commented: "Going inward is not a pulling back from life. You can see that by going into the center, we also gain the ability and presence to go outward appropriately, creatively, and dynamically. To go out only, without inner counterbalance, is to go outward into a disordered or chaotic and lost state of being."

"Contemplation and action are really the same," Reverend Cynthia Bourgeault spoke to that counterbalance, "and as one meditates deeply, contemplation narrows the distance between prayer and life because your action is always an immediate and integral response to what's in your heart."

"I see [the flow from contemplation into action] as a circle or the infinity symbol," said Susan Baggett from the Center for Purposeful Living. "We contemplate a spiritual principle, and then part of that contemplation is about how we put this into action. Then we contemplate the action—the result—of what we've learned. So it becomes an ever-expanding circle of contemplation, action, contemplation, action. That's practical spirituality to us."

"I think contemplation and action come out of each other like a figure eight—an infinity symbol," Reverend Suzanne Fageol commented in a similar spirit. "They create a natural rhythm like breathing: contemplation, in breath; action, out breath. Each movement changes the other. It's like a dance—*rhythm without monotony*—where each, contemplation and action, changes the other."

Joan: I added, "It's the difference between a dance that's mechanical and one that's alive—like lovemaking."

Contemplation and the Conversion of Consciousness

Joan and Gordon: Our friend Robin Casarjian is the founder of the Lionheart Foundation, which has liberated inmates in prisons from the solitary confinement of their own self-hatred. Her Houses of Healing program succeeds by first teaching the prisoners to extend forgiveness and compassion to themselves. Through meditation and group work, they come to new understandings of who they are in essence, at the deepest core of their being. Only this changed sense of inner identity—a contemplative connection to the true Self—Robin told us, leads to fundamental changes in external behavior.

Sister Rose Mary Dougherty shared a similar understanding of contemplation as a *conversion* of the experience of self—a fundamental shift in identity from the false self to true nature. That shift of identity has the power, she believes, to reconnect doing with being. She explained it in this way:

> Going back to the practices for seeking spiritual guidance, I believe in the saying of Lao-tzu, quoted in the Tao Te Ching: "Search your heart and see . . . the way to do is to be." Ultimately, when we really come to that place of fully living who we are, right action just flows, and we don't even recognize the separation. The being becomes the action; the action becomes the being.
>
> I think the truth is that there are things that keep us from living in that deeper place of being, which contemplation is. I forget the name of the man who said: "Jesus was much more interested in a conversion of consciousness than in importing information to deluded minds." I love that, because for me contemplation is about the conversion of consciousness that then allows us to see and to do from that place.

The integration of heart, mind, and life that describes the spontaneous flow from contemplation into action is the *subjective* experience of wholeness. The external result—a more compassionate, harmonious world—is *objective* wholeness. The *integral* wholeness of inner and outer reality—of ourselves and of the world—

is the innate potential inherent within creation that's the basis of real faith.

"Faith," said Sheikh Kabir Helminski, "is always alive with and balanced by action and works. We have a word in Arabic, *salahaddi*—those who keep the faith and perform the actions of reconciliation." He related this to the Jewish concept of *tikkun olam*—to heal the world. Reconciling the broken parts of our still-fragmented world is, he emphasized, the intended result of spiritual guidance. He stressed that it takes trust and faith in the impulse of Spirit toward ever-greater wholeness for us to come into partnership with it. That partnership is what he means by "contemplation."

"To contemplate is to act," was Daniel Ladinsky's concise equation, "though this may be an internal movement of thought or will or feelings. I have never really considered this before, but I think all we ever do is act, though at some point our actions become smarter and thus the results are *less of a drag on our wings,* less painful, and we can . . . find a greater sense of well-being, longer durations of peace, expanded moments of happiness."

Neutralizing Karma Through Selfless Action

The "drag on our wings" is what Swami Adiswarananda understands as *karma*—the loss of interior freedom that occurs when the motives for our actions are selfish ones. "Each selfish action forges a chain of bondage—of the body in the form of addictions, of the mind in the form of delusion and dependence, and of the soul in the form of spiritual blindness."

"All the maladies of life have their roots in the loss of yoga, which is the loss of contact with the Self, the Ultimate Reality," the Swami writes. And from diagnosis he moves immediately to treatment: *The separative walls of past karma can only be demolished by karma-yoga, or selfless action.*

Selfless action may sound like bad-tasting medicine—certainly to our frightened egos—until we realize that it means acting from the ground of *wholeness* that is the basis for wisdom and compassion. The chief cognitive and perceptual difficulties with selfishness are that they provide such a narrow view of reality that we're effectively blinded and misled, as well as far less effective than we might otherwise be.

The late Trappist monk Thomas Merton put it this way in his famous *Letter to a Young Activist:*

> You are probably striving to build yourself an identity in your work, out of your work and your witness. . . . That is not the right use of your work. All the good that you will do will come not from you but from the fact that you have allowed yourself, in the obedience of faith, to be used by God's love. Think of this more, and gradually you will be free from the need to prove yourself, and you can be more open to the power that will work through you without your knowing it.[3]

The Right Use of Will

Changing your motive for action from selfishness to service means using your free will for the benefit of something higher—unfolding the heart of Spirit in action. Such right use of will creates the kind of graceful, natural, efficient performance that Swami Adiswarananda considers evidence of living one's dharma, the outer path of action that leads simultaneously to inner illumination. When you're steadfast in living your Light, as the Quakers told us repeatedly, then that Light grows.

Spiritual teacher Hameed Ali describes the capacity to maintain contact with the Inner Light and express it outwardly as *the will in service to the truth.* We're all human and subject to numerous distracting influences and mistaken identifications, but "one learns," Hameed says, "usually through the difficulties of trial and error, that one cannot continue to experience Being if one lives his life according to the belief that he is the ego individuality. One's action, behavior, style of life (all manifestations of Will) must be in harmony with the Truth of Being. This quality of will is what's needed to support and sustain a life lived as a faithful embodiment of one's own true nature."[4]

Live your Light, in other words, not your lampshade.[5] And that means not only loving, but actively willing, the truth. Father Thomas Keating told us that purification of motive, of will, is relatively easy. It's habit that trips us up, because it's unconscious, automatic, and taken for granted.

Gordon: The late philosopher and writer Arthur Koestler treated this subject brilliantly by identifying two vectors of learning that move in opposite directions. The first vector is what an industrial engineer I once knew described as *"reducing mystery to method."* When we're first learning to drive a car, for example, it's still a mystery, but by the time we're proficient in the method, we don't have to think about it anymore. Driving has become automatic and therefore unconscious. Our "robot" or habitual mind can drive for miles on a crowded freeway at high speeds while we're planning tonight's dinner.

But sometimes the pattern is disrupted. A deer jumps out in front of us as we near the exit and suddenly we're called back to attention. This override of the robot by the conscious mind—which restores choice about what to do next—is what Koestler viewed as the opposing vector of learning: *the recovery of mindfulness.* That recovery brings us back to what Peruvian shaman Cecilia Montero calls "the realm of possibility."

Both vectors are useful. We don't want to have to keep relearning how to drive a car; nor do we want to give up the ability, when the situation is changing, to respond by aligning with and choosing a new direction.

Joan and Gordon: But do we have to wait for a deer to jump out in the road or for any habitual pattern to be disrupted by external forces? Our conversations with the Sages suggest that freedom can be reclaimed by *willingly* participating as unique individuals in the greater movement of life's flow that we're calling spiritual guidance. Willingness—the will to selfless action that isn't a negation, but an affirmation, of the desire to allow and serve the greater good—is immensely freeing.

Willing the Good

How often have you sat in your home and listened to bad news, feeling helpless. There are wars and genocide, but what can a single person do to help?

The thought that we're just one and can't make much of a difference can undermine the will to make the world a better place. When Boulder Quaker Mary Hey described their process of witnessing, however, something clicked: We don't always have to change a situation; sometimes all we can do is to bear witness, trusting that our simple act of compassionate presence can help change the world. Through witnessing, our contemplation *becomes* our action.

We'd seen groups of people on Boulder's outdoor Pearl Street Mall with signs witnessing for peace. They stood still and quiet, without talking or approaching anyone. But we'd never stopped to appreciate, and experience, what they were actually doing.

Mary Hey told us:

> We just stand with a sign that says we believe that war is wrong. It says, "We believe that there are nonviolent ways to deal with conflict. We believe it is possible to live the kind of life that takes away the occasion of war. We believe that love is the most powerful force on Earth."
>
> It sounds a bit like a creed, but that's not the intent. We stand on the Common with small gray cards that say these things. We offer the card but don't approach anyone. People have to decide to come to us to get the card. We started this in the 1980s and have done it off and on, and more recently on a weekly basis, since 9/11. It's a witness, a vigil.

She continued:

> The word *vigil* is a religious term as well as a mariners' term. It means "standing watch." When we give out a card, we get an astounding range of responses. We're a blank slate, standing silently, and people project on us. We're the essence of nonviolence.

They can take the card or not. For me this kind of witness is the greatest practice of nonaggression. But it's not just the absence of aggression, it's the presence of love, it's disarmament—being totally vulnerable. . . .

A guy came up to me and said, "You're not getting anywhere doing this." We're not *trying* to get anywhere. The majority of people who say anything say thank you or dance or tell you that you need to smile more. You're like a guard at Buckingham Palace. If we're called to speak to someone, we step out of the vigil. So that's a witnessing. I have strong beliefs about war, and this is a way to honor them. We've handed out 10- or 12,000 of these cards.

Witnessing, we learned from Mary, is a form of action. She and her fellow Quakers try to be as truly present as possible, centered in their Inner Light, to witness for the possibility of a better world. "Quakers are sometimes called practical mystics," Mary continued her explanation of the peace vigils and the will for the good that they embody. "I've had amazing experiences in the vigils where the world's just melted, but the witness is what we are, not trying to get somebody to vote differently or trying to do something."

When Professor Jacob Needleman asked groups of his philosophy students to list what they considered to be the virtues of a morally or psychologically developed person, he was surprised that none of them even mentioned the word *will*. Needleman agrees with Benjamin Franklin, one of the heroes in his brilliant work of moral philosophy *The American Soul: Rediscovering the Wisdom of the Founders,* that our world's entire history of war and violence can be traced to a general inability to *will* the common good.

Needleman makes an eloquent and persuasive case for this very capacity being what motivated the founders of American democracy—Washington, Franklin, and Jefferson. Their enlightened view of patriotism "meant service to God through love of mankind."[6] All of them, and many of their contemporaries, had designed rigorous programs of moral self-improvement against which they measured their daily shortcomings through self-reflection and retrospection. This is reminiscent of the Ignatian practice of "examen of conscience," or what Reb Zalman Schachter-Shalomi described as becoming naked before God in order to flush out any impulse to hide the truth, even from himself.

George Washington—as described by Needleman—willingly renounced his position as President at the height of his power and went home peacefully to Mount Vernon. He was a man who had struggled to perfect himself and was perhaps our greatest hero and example of enlightened will. "The most influential actions of the most influential man in American history," Needleman wrote, "are movements of stepping back and the surrender of personal power. The most decisive actions of America's great symbol of will are actions of letting go."[7]

Washington stepped back in order to let his newly freed fellow citizens—as the test of democracy—follow their own spiritual guidance, or as he put it in his Farewell Address, the inner authority of "above all, the pure and benign light of Revelation."[8] As Needleman explains, "Washington steps back in order to *allow* what is good to act, in order to allow that which is greater than human pride to act in the life of mankind."[9]

"Washington, then," writes Needleman in conclusion, "is the hero of will and self-struggle; but it is a will and self-struggle that does not affirm the ego or destroy its opposite. It is a will and self-struggle that *steps back*—that yields, mysteriously, not like a storm, but like a prayer."[10]

It would be difficult to find better words, in ending, to describe the marriage of contemplation and action that is the working of spiritual guidance—unfolding the heart of Spirit in action.

✹   ✹   ✹

Chapter Twelve

SPIRITUAL DNA: MAPPING THE GENOME OF TRANSFORMATION

You may have seen *Schindler's List,* the fact-based movie directed by Steven Spielberg. The story is about the industrialist Oskar Schindler and his day-to-day complicity in the brutal forced labor of a Nazi concentration camp, even as inmates deemed unfit for work were being taken away daily for extermination. Ultimately sickened in his soul by this demonic situation, Schindler compiled a list of those he claimed were necessary to his wartime production efforts—including some who were too weak to stand or walk—in order to save them from the gas chamber.

The miracle so powerfully conveyed in this movie was that the flower of human goodness and kindness could suddenly bloom and flourish in such unlikely soil—and in a person who until then had seemed utterly callous but became willing to risk his life for strangers. The significance of this redemptive story was not lost on the German public, who flocked to the film in unprecedented droves, hungry for a mirror in which they could see the depth and purity of their own essential humanity reflected at last. It was as though a pearl beyond price had been *recognized* and plucked from the foul mud in which it had been obscured for years, its purity and value undiminished.

Schindler's List leaves the audience with an unspoken question: *Is there something irreducibly good, true, and beautiful in the human soul—our essential nature?* If there is, then what is the Soul's Compass that guides us to it? Is the freedom to transcend selfishness that Father Thomas Keating refers to as our "capacity for God" and the Buddhists call our "Buddha nature" already at work in us? And can it possibly be that the ability to begin the world anew from what's best in us—even as the daily headlines tempt us to lose heart—is an innate potential?

We invited the Sages to reflect on the question of human evolution with an aim toward getting practical answers relevant to our lives today. If there is a subtle force pulling us toward full realization of our human potential—a positive direction in which evolution is inviting us to move—then aligning our human intentions and actions with that movement would be a way to participate actively as partners in the evolutionary process.

Specifically, we asked them three overlapping questions:

1. Is there something within your tradition that corresponds on the individual and collective levels to an entelechy or principle of becoming, a force that drives evolution into a form like an acorn becoming an oak?

2. If so, what is a human being—and creation at large—evolving toward?

3. What's the ultimate goal or possibility to keep in mind?

"Now there's a Harvard word for us, *entelechy*," responded the poet Daniel Ladinsky. "I had never seen it before. First, I want to give you my dictionary take on that word, which is 'the realization of potential, the supposed essential nature or guiding principle of a living thing.'" He went on to recount a dialogue he'd had with a young priest from "one of the finest seminaries and theological schools in the world."

"Do you think that God could give you His own experience," Daniel asked the priest, "and if so, what would you then know?

162

If you had that experience, who would you then *be?* I know that when I die, and maybe even at some point before that, the husk will completely fall from my soul's eye and I will find myself: a Magnificent, Luminous, Divine Sovereignty that is so perfect in itself that I could never, ever desire anything more than to just be alone and forever explore the Immaculate Quintessence of Self that God knows."

Daniel is describing the convergence of two trajectories—or movements of Spirit—one personal and one cosmic. They're advancing toward each other through mutual attraction into a state of conscious enlightenment that is at once our own personal, individualized, human awakening ("the husk will completely fall from my soul's eye and I will find myself") and the self-recognition of God ("His own experience . . . the Immaculate Quintessence of Self that God knows"). The turning point in the human story—a tragic plot based on mistaken identity and its complications—may be precisely this moment Daniel describes: the Universe consciously awakening through us, the enlightening flash of *Self-recognition* that is at once our own and God's. Few, if any, of us—even with our poet's best effort to convey it—can relate this description of evolution's ultimate direction and fulfillment to our own experience.

A Hidden Treasure Desiring to Be Known

Daniel Ladinsky is articulating a classic spiritual understanding of the ultimate intention that gives evolution both its dynamism and its directionality: "It's a dying to our false self and a rising to the true Self that is God's will manifesting in our uniqueness"—in Father Thomas Keating's words, "the possibility that we have of living each moment in a divine way: that is, to allow God to experience being human in our particular uniqueness."

Hameed Ali put it this way: "The universe is developing in such a way that it becomes more conscious and more aware of its totality, and it can only do that by developing organs of consciousness by which it can perceive and see and experience that. These organs are the individual souls, and these organs can see and experience more fully the more they are developed." Our personal spiritual development—in other words, the refining of our own subtle capacities—and the creative unfolding of the infinite Universe are interdependent dimensions of the same emerging consciousness.

This account of evolution corresponds with what the angel of revelation, Gabriel, told Mohammed in the Hadith—a book of the sayings of the prophet and the early history of what became Islam: "I was a hidden treasure, desiring to be known, and so I created the world in order to be known." The awakening of the creation to the Divine Artist alive in it, in us, *through us,* thus becomes the aim—the intention—of it all. The divine and infinite Unmanifest One, nameless and unfathomable, out of a profoundly compassionate desire to be known—to be *recognized*—created the world and all of its creatures.

The late Jesuit priest and paleontologist Pierre Teilhard de Chardin called this cosmically realized state toward which evolution is heading "divinization." And this is perhaps what we see foreshadowed on the ceiling of the Sistine Chapel, where the finger of Michelangelo's God reaching toward the equally outstretched finger of Adam suggests an impending touch and shock of recognition—a flash of cosmic light far greater than what's released in an atomic explosion.

To find the locus of that touch where the divine and human sides of our living nature make contact, perhaps we need look no further than the spontaneous and compassionate impulses of our own wise hearts when they make contact with those of others. "There is that of God in every person," Quaker educator Patricia Loring reminded us, "and the connecting point is in the human heart. That's the point of change and the point of possibility, the point of invitation, and probably the only place where we can meet the cosmic and know how to change things, how to make it better."

"Ultimately," said the Quaker Mary Hey about our evolutionary potential to become fully human, "it means to become more loving." She continued:

> But there's too much I don't understand—why people do what they do to each other, why there's so much suffering. But

my job isn't to speculate about what I don't know. It's like talking about the afterlife. All I can really summon on this topic is humility and compassion. Reach out and do what you can to relieve suffering. I've pretty much stopped asking why it exists. You can be asking why while you're standing right next to someone who needs your help. There are all these confusions when somebody begs: Are they lazy? Do they want alcohol? These days I just give to anyone who asks. It's not my job to find out why they're asking. And sometimes when they thank me, I feel like I'm being touched by an angel.

Many of us have had a similar experience, the healing power of *recognition* that is the dignity bestowed on human suffering—sometimes our own—by any act of true compassion. Mary *recognized* the person begging, who in turn became the angel who *recognized* her—a *Namaste* moment. It's interesting that in his book *The End of History and the Last Man,* American philosopher and political economist Francis Fukayama argues that the driving force of human history is neither reason (which today is embodied in science) nor desire (embodied in free-market consumer capitalism). Rather, the driving force of our collective human story over all these many generations is what Plato called *thymos* and Hegel later translated as *recognition*—the striving by each of us for our essential value to be seen and known in this world. Throughout history, one unrecognized class or group after another has risen up, willing to sacrifice their very lives, in order to be accorded that indispensable dignity that we cherish more than life itself: to be recognized with respect as humans, intrinsically valuable by virtue of our very being.

Fukayama thought that the advent of modern democracy, once universalized, would bring about an end to history as the struggle of one class or group against another, because all persons would finally be recognized by one another as equal, and peace would prevail at last. But even this great advance would still be an external form of recognition only—humanization, certainly, but not yet divinization. We might all gain a seat at the table of consumption, but we would not yet have fully recognized the Inner Light, the divine nature that is the One Spirit of all that lives. We would not yet have fully recognized *ourselves*.

Recognition implies revelation. The ways in which our evolutionary potential—or "God's presence at work in us," as Father Thomas Keating says—is revealed *through* us in ways that are concrete, specific, and well known. The fruits and gifts of the spirit, the virtues as described by all faiths, such as charity, peace, kindness, joy, generosity, faithfulness, and gentleness, are concrete and specific revelations of aspects of our true nature in particular situations. We can immediately recognize and appreciate them when they appear because of some innate faculty in us that knows the good when we see it. That intelligence is lodged where our own innate goodness resides: in our hearts.

Quaker Mary Hey's compassionate charity for a person who is begging, the sincerely grateful response by the begging individual who sees and acknowledges her kindness—in that exchange there's a revelation and mutual *recognition* of the Inner Light that they both share. Enlightened lives such as Christ's or Buddha's, as well as the kindnesses and other virtues of ordinary people we've seen or known, are inspiring to us precisely because we see our own best selves, our noblest possibilities, reflected in them—and that is of evolutionary significance. These revelatory lives, by mirroring our own true nature, awaken us to its presence and encourage its further realization. This is why, as our Quaker friends told us, "When we live our Light, the Light increases."

Living our Light is conscious evolution, but what does that entail? "We have within us, if at least we have the state of Grace going, *the whole program of transformation—in other words, the kind of Divine DNA* the Holy Spirit is that calls each one of us to a particular function or vocation or place" in a living Universe that Father Thomas went on to describe for us in its entirety as "the body of Christ."

"So it's a Divine Seed," he continued. "If we really are the children of God, there must be something of God in us, meaning that the deepest truth about us is the fact that our very being is the image and likeness of God. But it has been distorted by human freedom and human conditioning so that it's hard to realize as we grow in self-consciousness. And so the spiritual journey addresses the human condition head-on, with its need for purification of our mistaken ideas and behavior, but also the empowerment of our unconscious to allow the gifts we've received to manifest."

Now this latent capacity we all have, according to Father Thomas—ultimately to see beneath the veil of familiarity that hides our own divine nature and to "allow the gifts we've received to manifest"—suggests the existence of a driving force behind evolution that's different from what strictly reductionist biologists claim. That force is a creative impulse toward the transformation of consciousness in all that lives, rather than a mechanical drive toward basic survival for its own sake. Survival to what end? If we can't answer that—if we can't feel into our deepest longing—then life becomes meaningless, and this precious incarnation is wasted.

The "selfish gene" theory of the British biologist Richard Dawkins—an ardent materialist—tells us that the master motive of evolution is a strictly biological repetition compulsion on the part of our genes to be endlessly replicated through our progeny and/or that of our kin. Survival, and that alone, is the name of the game. But this theory doesn't explain altruistic acts such as Oskar Schindler's deliberately risking his life for people completely unlike himself, as another great scientist, Francis Collins—head of the Human Genome Project—has pointed out in his rebuttal of Dawkins. Something nobler in Schindler's nature trumps the merely mechanical demands of his own biology. That nobler something is what Father Thomas calls "the whole program of transformation" and "something of God in us." He's suggesting that we have altruistic or "unselfish genes" that can unfold not just more of the same, but something emergent and evolutionary—"the gifts we've received," or the virtues of our true nature.

This theory squares with what another biologist and philosopher, Rupert Sheldrake, sees as the other half of the story that Dawkins leaves out. Nature, according to Sheldrake, is a dynamic balancing act between two forces: (1) *habit,* the repetition of form or pattern; and (2) *creativity,* the emergence of ever-new forms. The complexity scientists at the Santa Fe Institute and elsewhere agree with Sheldrake, seeing creative emergence as an innate and ubiquitous quality of nature.

H_2O, for example, has "emergent properties" such as the ability to flow, freeze, and vaporize that can't be deduced by examining a single molecule in isolation. Only when there are a sufficient number accumulated do the properties we associate with water emerge. Similarly, there are qualities of Being latent in our humanness that, as we move beyond the molecular boundaries of our separate "false self" toward greater wholeness and communion, begin to manifest as godlike virtues, all of which are creative.

"We call it Shakti," said Sally Kempton, the former Swami Durgananda. She explained:

> It's that dynamic, dancing force that's moving as the Universe. In our tradition, one of the goals is for an individual to recognize his or her Godness, recognize the unity, and then to live as an individual with the full moment-to-moment awareness of that unity. There's a concept in Kashmir Shaivism that I find resonant: the idea that God becomes an individual partly in order to experience individual uniqueness. There's a profound deliciousness in experiencing yourself and others as divine expressions, which are also unique. A couple can embody this perspective in a really great way. I believe that this is what we're evolving towards—to live in that amazing space where you experience fully both difference and unity—moving between the two without being stuck in either. That's the Universe recognizing itself through all these eyes and minds, through every living being. I believe that's where it all wants to go—that God became the world for the sake of knowing Itself in a dance of love.

"That's the whole messianic aspect of Judaism," said Rabbi Rami Shapiro, "the hope that we're going to go from the infantilization in the Garden of Eden to higher consciousness, where we have internalized the Divine and bring it forth into the world. It's true for individuals and for society as a whole."

That hope is not an empty wish, but an actual perception of concrete possibility—here and now. Most of us get only glimpses of that possibility, if we do at all. We catch subtle intimations of higher consciousness . . . of that harmony within wholeness, of that mystic dance of love that Sally describes so ecstatically. Meanwhile, the idea that there's a positive evolutionary invitation exerting its pull on us may seem to be as fictitious as a pie in the sky. But we know that the capacity for love, truth, and beauty—what the pioneering psychologist of human potential the late Abraham Maslow referred to as our higher nature—exists, at least in potential form, within all human beings. Capacities, Maslow demonstrated, are also needs, so there's a drive inherent within them to express themselves.

But where does all this theorizing about the spiritual intention of evolution leave us in terms of how we participate in a practical way in the evolutionary process? The late futurist and social theorist Robert Theobald once identified three basic approaches to the future:

1. The first was to forecast it by projecting today's dominant trends forward. At this point, these are largely negative futures featuring overpopulation, terrorism, and global warming.

2. The second approach was to assume the existence of a benign trend such as the inevitable emergence of a New Age. Both of these approaches have the fact that they're deterministic in common. The events they forecast will occur whether or not we do anything about them.

3. Finally, Theobald said, there's a third, nondeterministic approach to the future, which he favored. That future rests on being able to imagine or perceive existing potential and take action to realize it.

We Are Part of the Creative Apparatus of God

We'd like to offer a fourth approach to the future that we infer from what the Sages have told us. The future, they and we agree, is not yet determined, and the present is indeed pregnant with rich and varied possibility. But the creative action to be taken in any given instance ought not be unilateral on our parts. Seeing our-selves as separate and controlling is where humans have gotten into the most trouble in the first place—like the mythical Prometheus who stole fire from the gods and was condemned to endless suffer-ing as a result. Rather, our panelists told us, our human role is to humbly yet boldly participate in a *co-creative* process by cooperating with what spiritual teacher Hameed Ali calls "the optimizing force," which we'll describe more fully in the following section.

The late English mystic Evelyn Underhill, in a similar vein, devoted a good part of her book *The Spiritual Life* to cooperation with God. She wrote: "Our place is not the auditorium but the stage—or, as the case may be, the field, workshop, study, labora-tory—because we ourselves form part of the creative apparatus of God."[1] When the words "Thy Will be *done*—Thy Kingdom *come!*" are sincerely uttered, she continues, "[t]here is energy, drive, pur-pose in those words; an intensity of desire for the coming of perfec-tion into life."

Is there, for example, a quality of love, harmony, or beauty missing from the current situation we find ourselves in—those attributes or forms of perfection that the Sufis equate with the "the Spirit of Guidance"? And do we see a practical way to introduce those transformative qualities into what's unfolding in our lives at this very moment? If the need and the opportunity match our gifts and engage our will, then perhaps it is we who are being personally called or guided by this convergence to help change things for the better. This isn't a passive role or what Underhill calls "limp resigna-tion"—waiting for heaven to come to us—nor is it an egotistically assertive role. It's an alignment, attunement, and willingness to graciously help co-create the greater good revealed to our spiritual imagination.

Ajahn Sona is far from being either egocentric or passive in his Buddhist view of human agency. He explained:

> The first thing is that it's not inevitable that individuals or groups evolve upwards. You can go up toward wisdom or devolve. There's nothing built in or automatic that you can sit or ride on. Both the individual and the community must work. If you're in

touch with generosity, compassion, and presence of mind, things should flow. It's the wrong aspirations—our befuddled hopes and desires—that lead us to darkness. The right hopes will lead us in the right direction.

So we can't just talk about hope. Is it skillful or unskillful hope? There's delusory hope—hopes about the past and hopes about the present—because the past and the present can't be any other way; they are the way they are. So we give up hope about the past and present. Regarding the future, our conviction is that good results come from good causes. That's right hope.

To have good hope means having basic faith in causality. If I'm doing skillful things now, then I will have a skillful result, and that is the right hope. But when we hope against hope that we will get good results from no efforts at all, that's wrong hope. We keep hope for the future that's about being present and realistically here.

Perceiving possibility, in other words, is by no means a denial of current reality, and it takes concrete action—not mere wish—to realize possibility. As Ajahn Sona says, "Good results come from good causes" and from "faith in causality." If we're doing skillful things now, we'll have good results later.

The Optimizing Force

Being skillful, in Hameed Ali's view, means learning to work hand in hand with the optimizing force: "In the Diamond Approach, we talk about the optimizing force in the sense that guidance basically opens up and supports the optimizing of our experience, our development—which means, really, the greater actualization of our potential."

Hameed includes the various qualities and dimensions of true nature that he has enumerated and explored elsewhere—such as compassion, will, strength, peace, forgiveness, and acceptance—among the essential aspects of our potential to become a "complete human being." These track pretty well with the Christian fruits and gifts of the Spirit or the Buddhist virtues. How they manifest specifically through us depends on what's called for by the particular situation at hand.

"Guidance," Ali tells us, "basically assists the process [of optimization]—assists us individually to participate in the process, to harmonize with it. But it doesn't have a particular form it's moving toward. It keeps developing one form or another depending on the moment, where its intelligence wants to go."

Hameed's insistence that intelligence and spontaneity are working together in the evolutionary process—by seeing what's needed in the moment—rises above the current debate between "intelligent design" creationists and evolutionists. There really is no conflict if we see that intelligent *designing*—as an active verb—is going on all the time in a creatively spontaneous way in the evolutionary process.

Neither in the individual human as microcosm nor in the greater cosmos is there a definitive advance plan. Rather, says Ali, "It is inherently open. The potential is infinite. The moment you make a blueprint, you make potential finite. And my impression of it is that there is no end to evolution. It's all changing; it's all emerging. I like the idea of emerging intelligence. The guidance is really like the discerning eye of this dynamic, evolutionary intelligence."

It Has No Way to End

Not having a plan makes navigating by spiritual guidance a subtle matter of flowing with the creative process itself. It happens in midair as it were, and without a safety net, unfolding moment by moment from the Source or Ground of our Being.

Reverend Cynthia Bourgeault, who if there were a spiritual equivalent to the Cirque du Soleil would be its dazzling trapeze star, has no difficulty with the high-wire act of divine co-creativity. It's there in the very language she speaks: "As you are able to keep yourself still, then God in His wonderful creativity is able to move through your finitude to do what He wants to do anyway—the wonderful, passionate creativity that flows through with absolute integrity when I get out of the way. But I think we may make the whole thing too highfalutin. Maybe all God wants to do in human form is touch a snowflake." Wonderful enough in its simplicity! And meanwhile, Reverend Cynthia shifts from the speculative notion of evolution as happening in linear time to "what I actually know—which is that the destiny of any human being is totally fulfilled in the opening of the heart to the Beloved Divine in each instant."

This instant, not the one just past. Awakening to what's here, to who is here now in this changing, moving universe, isn't a one-shot deal. "*Creation* as the 'rule of being' is the pre-eternal and continuous movement," philosopher and theologian of Islamic studies Henry Corbin wrote, "by which being is manifested at *every instant* in a new cloak."[2] Hence, the peril of a frozen identity or a fixed position—you're left holding the old cloak from which Being has vanished.

Rabbi Tirzah Firestone spoke with us of "a draw toward an unending wholeness. God is infinite. Growth is endless. It happens all the time—the current of the river that draws you."

"It's not a destination," said psychologist Linda Backman, "but a process." And she should know, having escorted her clients through a multitude of what seem to be past lives and the reflective times between them. The threshold, the liminal period between no longer and not yet, the time of pure openness and pure possibility, can be every moment to the degree that we learn to dwell in it. Guidance invites us to live with an open heart—and with our heels lightly off the ground—so that we're ready to move easily in any direction without even a moment's notice.

This is the threshold stance—the vision-quest stance. It's neither passive nor assertive; rather, it's attentive and responsive. "We are always growing, and we'll continue to grow forever," Father Thomas Keating affirmed, "in the knowledge of God. So it has no way to end. And the fact is that this is God's idea and not ours. It's His creation. So we're invited into a level of life that is both complete and always being completed. It's endless. Eternity is not a long time; it's no time at all. It's a whole different situation."

Fractions of a Teaspoon, Step-by-Step, Moment-by-Moment

Whatever situation we're in requires trust, humility, openness, and courage to engage with it in an evolutionary way, since we rarely—in fact, never—know exactly where we're going.

"It can be very entertaining to speculate on where it's all going, but that's really beyond me—and finally, none of my business," Quaker educator Patricia Loring explained in a way that brought us down to earth. She continued, "My business is discerning my way forward in my relationships here and now, step-by-step. It's overwhelming to think of my actions and life *vis-à-vis* the complexity of life and needs on our planet. It's virtually impossible to conceive that I as an individual can have any meaningful effect on anything that needs doing."

And yet, she finds hope in scientific theories that dispel the sense of futility that can so easily paralyze us in the face of our relative helplessness to change things: "In the notions of the new complexity and cosmology, I find growing trust that there are propensities in the nature of things that defy the randomness on which statistical odds are based. Those propensities may or may not come to fruition, depending on the conditions in which they arise. . . . [In this] I find secular support for my spiritual faith that acting in hope against the odds can be crucial in a world like ours."

So, is it really that simple? Can we choose to move against the current of our own conditioning and against the odds in a direction we may sense as evolutionary—even though we can't see more than partway down the road? This is Patricia Loring's hope and faith in a freedom that is really a form of *obedience,* in its Latin-root meaning of *ob audire*—to listen to or hear. She continued:

> In Deuteronomy [30:19–20] there's a speech that's attributed to God. He said something like, "I've set before you *today* life and death. Choose Life!" To choose to suit ourselves is Death. To choose Life is to choose to give ourselves over to God's order and guidance. The choice I'm making is to give myself—not to what I or anyone else may conceive to be the order of things, or even to an order I would like to see established, but to an order that is

given to me to be carried out in fractions of a teaspoon, moment by moment.

What dies, what gets stuck, when we identify with anything less than the soul's infinite potential is the free, spontaneous flow of that potential into manifestation. Freedom from our instincts and conditioning, as Patricia makes clear, isn't a licensed tyranny of whim, but rather an alignment of our will with the evolutionary force of guidance. It's freedom to obey a higher directive. Patricia continued:

> Many people ask, "What do you want?" I don't think discernment is about what *I* want. It's a matter of sensing where the invitation of Life is in the next moment. It may not be what I want, but having tasted Life, I will trust it, place my faith in it. I wouldn't prefer to be in any of the other places that I might have gone with my life; but I can say that only from here. It's not a question of what I want, not what's most pleasing, not what I imagine would make me happiest. It's what feels most true, right, and alive—and gives me peace.

What feels most true and alive can only be ascertained by being present in this very moment. Nothing else, past or future, truly exists. This is part of the difficulty of thinking about evolution as a forward movement through chronological time into the future. The Quakers are constantly reminding themselves not to outrun their guidance—to be patient.

Sister Rose Mary Dougherty also talked about this: "I think there's a delicate balance between just this moment—ourselves being good just as we are in this moment—and yet living into the possibility of the fullness when all of our little biases and unfreedoms are borne away. I find it hard to talk about a goal [that we're evolving to] because that puts me into a striving mode, a step-by-step *If we do this, we'll get somewhere else.* It implies that where we are right in this moment isn't good enough. So I'm back and forth on this one."

Sister Rose Mary recalls Thomas Merton saying, "Everything is right here."

"So we don't do something to get it," she continued, "or to get somewhere else. So if there is a goal, it's about living the full realization of this moment."

Joan: At this point, I admitted that every career path I've followed "has developed out of paying attention to where the road opens in the moment."

Gordon: I added that saying everything is here is not saying that here is a static place. Everything is here and alive and moving, and we're part of that movement. The *now* is in motion.

"Yes, yes," Sister Rose Mary agreed.

"Alive," I repeated.

Vision—the Creativity of the Heart

Joan and Gordon: Granting that the *now* is in motion, that it contains what Patricia Loring calls a "movement toward greater possibility," how do we discern and become part of that movement? We've addressed this already in our discussion of discernment, but here—in concluding this chapter on evolution—we want to focus on the role of *vision*.

This brings us to the faculty of imagination—the faculty that directly *perceives,* and can therefore help realize, possibility. Knowledge, what we think we know, is always about the past. But as Albert Einstein said, "Imagination is more important than knowledge." It represents our freedom to see and co-create an optimized future rather than having it simply "happen to us" like fate. Imagination in this sense is the actual organ of guidance, the organ of human evolution.

Michelangelo could see the shape of his statue *David* already present in the stone before he liberated it with hammer and chisel. His dramatic sculptures of *Prisoners,* heroically emerging from the marble in which they're still partly embedded, are apt symbols of imagination as nature's self-liberating process of creative emergence.

The "Flower Lady of Harlem," Bernadette Cozart, is another example of how spiritual imagination can bring potential into manifestation. She wasn't in denial about the toxic, refuse-strewn vacant lots she saw when she first moved to Harlem. But she also saw their *potential* to become community gardens where herbs could be grown by elders and youngsters working together to realize something new. She helped create more than a hundred plots that grew souls along with herbs.

When Mother Teresa picked up an infant who was practically dead from never having been lovingly held, the eyes of her heart saw "the body of Christ" in that child. It seemed miraculous that an abused and abandoned baby could then suddenly come to life with a radiant smile that was the infant's potential all along. But that potential had first to be *seen* before it could be realized—the function of our spiritual imagination.

In our culture at the present time, we still confuse imagination with fantasy or unreality. But mystics—such as the poet William Blake and the great Sufi saint Ibn al-'Arabi—understood it as the creative ability to see and bring forth a deeper reality than our five senses can perceive. That deeper reality is the *sacred* in all its rich aspects and dimensions—that which is most vibrant and alive, mysterious, and ready to be born.

Contemporary philosopher Richard Tarnas documented the failure of philosophy's mental modes of knowing to contact anything *real* after more than 4,000 years of Western intellectual history. He turned his attention to imagination as the self-knowing, self-revealing force of nature itself. He writes: "In its most profound and authentic expression, the intellectual imagination does not merely project its ideas into nature from its isolated brain corner. Rather, from within its own depths the imagination directly contacts the creative process within nature, realizes that process within itself, and brings nature's reality to conscious expression."[3]

The spiritual imagination, through which we perceive the sacred within the secular, was expressed in the famous lines of the poet William Blake: "To see a World in a grain of sand / And Heaven in a wild flower."

Islamic scholar Henry Corbin, translating the work of Ibn al-'Arabi, writes of *theophany*—the appearance of God or the sacred in a form that we can recognize—and the *theophanic imagination* as the instrument through which the Divine makes itself known: "Active Imagination is merely the organ of the absolute theophanic Imagination . . . whose real Subject is the Godhead revealing Himself to Himself. . . . The organ of this theophanic Imagination in man . . . is the heart and the creativity of the heart."[4]

The creativity of the heart is more than poetic language; it offers us a guiding vision for the future. There's a widely shared understanding of human development as a progressively more inclusive circle of identity and relationship. The trajectory of development moves from egocentric (me only), to ethnocentric (my group), to world-centric (all people and creatures), and beyond that to an intimate communion of the personal self with all that lives—with Life itself. The limiting factor to our development at any given time—the hindrance to a fully open heart—is the degree to which we're stuck in partial identities: *my* religion, *my* ethnic tribe—what Father Thomas Keating calls over-identification with one's group.

Transcending these over-identifications so that we can realize harmonious interdependence is a big job for the creativity of our hearts. Here is Keating's imaginative vision of how the creativity of the heart can co-create a healed, coherent world:

> The invitation is extended to us not only to enshrine within ourselves the presence of God, but to collaborate in making it available or awakening in everybody the virtue of the oneness of human nature. We're called to be not just the heirs, but collaborators or co-creators or co-healers, you might say, enabling the whole of the human family to participate. And so what will manifest who we really are is the light of our own beauty and truth and goodness as the image of God. We don't need God to judge us because the light itself will judge us and decide whether we're ready for the Land of Love where selfishness has no place.

"In the medicine," our shaman friend Oriah Mountain Dreamer told us, "we talk about *chulaquai*—a word that means the 'spark-of-life, life-force energy that ignites us and illuminates the path toward a greater sense of wholeness.' We're born two-leggeds, and if we wake up, we become a human being, a journey that's never really ended. The difference hinges on our ability for heart-to-heart communication. Becoming human is the capacity for compassion, the inclusion of everyone and everything that is. That's what moves us forward in infinite ways."

Reverend Suzanne Fageol summed up this evolutionary vision even more succinctly: "The shift is from small, self-seeking behavior to operating more in terms of the greater good." She then clarified: "It's not me *or* them. It's a co-creative partnership. How can I be served while serving others?"

We talked about synergy and how the anthropologist Ruth Benedict, observing the Blackfoot tribe in Montana, used it to describe that point where altruism and selfishness become indistinguishable. Reverend Suzanne continued: "So many traditions have taught: *Lose yourself, sacrifice yourself, for the good of the whole.* The shift I see now helps both me and everyone else to thrive. There's a mutuality there so that we all thrive. Then I become part of an energetic field of thriving that can change things."

The force of habit, of instinctual hardwiring, social conditioning, and ego identity—these are hard patterns to interrupt. Yet freedom, what makes us human beings rather than automatons, requires that we break the chains of habit. And the habit of selfishness may be the hardest to dispense with. "What we're doing here [at the Center for Purposeful Living]," Susan Baggett told us, "is to explore ways that ordinary human beings can live as souls in a sacred way." She was referring to the capacity to love and serve. The Center trains volunteers—students from a host of countries—in the life of service as a spiritual path, one that parallels karma yoga, although they don't call it that.

"We look at the old habits and patterns that block our way to change," Susan's colleague Thomas White added. "We work on a grounded level, and *reversing the flow* is a key concept of how we evolve. If we're less selfish today than yesterday, we've created something new."

This seems audaciously simple, yet it works. They teach their students how to voluntarily reverse the flow of their attention and concern from self to the greater good that includes others in need.

179

And compassion, as an intelligent form of guidance that operates without judgment or diagnosis but by *feeling with,* can see exactly what's needed in any given situation.

The key point in all these visions of our possible evolution—the full development of our humanness and our humanity—is that it's not just a matter of "I" who evolves, but of "we" who evolve together.

"Togethering," is the way Reb Zalman Schachter-Shalomi expressed it. "It's our job," he said. "How good it is when brothers and sisters are present in harmony in a post-triumphalist way when religions are learning to cooperate with each other. The thinking has been that when the Messiah comes, you'll find out how wrong you've been. That's not the goal today. The ultimate goal is for humankind and all of sentient life—the lion and the lamb, and so forth—to live in harmony together."

The "post-triumphalist" harmony that Reb Zalman alludes to requires transcending the sectarian religious blinders that currently plague our world. Truth, as the ancient Jews recognized, was once a mirror held in the hands of God; the glass shattered, and now each of us carries only a piece. To repair the mirror that holds the whole truth of who we are and what we may become together, we need the humility and openness to welcome and incorporate everyone's piece. This was the prophetic vision of Ibn al-'Arabi, the medieval Sufi teacher, as rendered by his modern translator and commentator Henry Corbin:

> The "day of Resurrection" . . . has an initiatic meaning: it is the moment when the individual soul comes to understand his unity of essence with the divine totality, the day on which the forms of the particular faiths cease to be veils and limitations and become manifestations in which God is contemplated because they express the capacities of men's hearts. This creativity of the heart (*himma*) is the ability to see the Divine through its metamorphoses of theophanies—its moment-by-moment revealings. To understand dogma as *mazhar,* a symbol, is to "unravel" its dogmatism, and that is the meaning of Resurrection.[5]

Harmony, Not Unity; Convergence, Not Consensus

Will the "unselfish gene" ultimately flourish? If so, we'll be able to see and act beyond our narrow identities and participate in a future where the larger, richer life of this planet can unfold. Occasionally we're graced with a sight of the promised land—even when we can't enter and stay there permanently. This was our good fortune when we attended the 2004 Parliament of the World's Religions in Barcelona, Spain. The Parliament's stated mission is a vision for what our world can become: "Harmony, not Unity; Convergence, not Consensus."

Participants were invited to attend a concert of sacred music from all the world's religions, to be held in the plaza beneath renowned architect Antoni Gaudí's great cathedral, the Sagrada Família, on the Thursday evening of the event. There was space for about 3,000 people, and every seat was occupied. The warm opening welcome was given by the archbishop of Catalonia, in a place where, just a half millennium earlier, his predecessors among these same Spaniards and Catalonians had begun their Inquisition against the Jews and Muslims. This evening seemed like a complete and conscious reversal of that dark time.

The lights were trained on the steps and balconies of the church as first one speaker, then another came forward to present their blessings to all on behalf of their religions. Each time, a child from the Children's Parliament would appear on a higher balcony holding a large globe of light, until finally there was a long, crowning array of lights held high above the seated audience. The stunningly beautiful music and dance that followed seemed to transcend all the religious distinctions that have historically divided us.

There was the beautiful operatically trained voice of a Spanish nun from Montserrat, whose music deeply pierced the listener's sweet heart and opened it like a pomegranate with all of its jewels exposed. There was the American Indian voice of Joanne Shenandoah, representing the noble soul of the Seneca tribe. Sufi dervishes spun in dramatic movement to the music of flutes, and Japanese drummers were perfectly synchronized as they played their great instruments with the athletic precision of martial artists. Every note was beautifully different, and together they harmonized as a rich symphony of the human spirit.

Nearly three enchanted hours passed, and finally, nearing midnight, the last group of performers came onstage: Sheva, named for the number seven in both Hebrew and Arabic. The band was made up of seven musicians—Jews and Arabs—from Israel. The crowd greeted them with resounding applause. Their music was an ecstatic ode to peace that rose into the Barcelona night sky from the base of that great cathedral. It was as though all the walls of belief that had divided us through the ages came down at last; we were finally together in our essential, triumphant, and joyous humanity. A musical ensemble of Jews and Muslims, 500 years after their people's expulsion from Spain, were now—in this very spot—lifting the hearts of all who were present. It was a taste of our deepest shared desire—our evolutionary possibility—fulfilled.

A woman well into her 70s, who told us that she had never danced before, was up on her feet gyrating to the beat and beaming pure bliss. This jubilation was not only an evolutionary possibility, we realized; it was happening here and now. We—and it seemed, all who were in attendance—*recognized* it as fulfillment, *recognized* ourselves in each other.

If he'd been there, Bob Marley would surely have sung his popular song "One Love." That's the lodestar toward which the Soul's Compass within the human heart is directing us. It's our *entelechy,* that big "Harvard word" that means "the realization of potential, the supposed essential nature or guiding principle of a living thing."

Chapter Thirteen

SIT DOWN AND SHUT UP: CONTEMPLATIVE WISDOM FOR WORLD LEADERS

We asked the Sages, "If you were to advise today's world leaders about how to find guidance toward a life-enhancing future, what would you suggest?"

"Well, I'm not anybody," Father Thomas Keating responded half-jokingly, "but if they asked me, I would suggest to sit down and shut up. Meaning," he quickly explained, "let God speak in you or just listen for a few minutes."

Can it be that something as deceptively simple as deep listening, and the humility it takes to do so, is the essential link between leadership and guidance? Reverend Cynthia Bourgeault thought so when she advised world leaders "to spend 20 minutes a day in solitude, in silence, with the heart open and the telephone off." Paraphrasing the 17th-century French philosopher Blaise Pascal, Reverend Cynthia went on to share his view that "all of the problems in the world can be reduced to this—man's inability to sit by himself in a room for a single half hour."

The Sages as a group acknowledged that the authority we lend our external leaders to help us realize our best possible future is reliably placed only if those individuals—in turn—are listening deeply to the source of all true authority, the wise inner silence from which spiritual guidance flows. The mental conflict between competing positions and interests, the agitation of either/or thinking, and the need to choose must be quieted for a leader to connect with the beneficent spirit—the impulse toward wholeness—that is the heart's intelligence.

Genuinely open leaders who can invite and sustain such intimate contact aren't insulated by power or driven by self-seeking agendas. Rather, they serve the unfolding of our common good by being exceptionally present in their innermost selves to what's real and possible in our shared historical moment. In this chapter, we'll consider what blocks such perception of possibility, what enhances it, and how leaders as listeners can help guide us along our hearts' path toward a more free and just world that is reflective of our true nature.

Co-creating a Positive Future

The point of asking a question about leadership was to acknowledge that there's a collective as well as an individual dimension to spiritual guidance. How do *we* move forward *together* in a way that aids us and this planet in becoming the best that we and it can be, even in the face of today's adversity? A leader's legitimate role as chief listener and inquirer—as facilitator of collective guidance—is to help us all *attend to what matters most:* to the emerging challenges and opportunities that call at this particular moment for our collectively wise and creative response.

The challenge side of the balance sheet, as we know from today's generally pessimistic view of the future, is daunting. Global warming, overpopulation, and mass species die-offs at a rate not seen since a giant asteroid extinguished half the life-forms on Earth 65 million years ago are unsettling augurs of what lies ahead. Exponential technological growth is still outpacing our abilities to predict or control its life-altering consequences for better or for worse. The perils of our current situation, as the above few examples illustrate, are much more obvious than the possibilities for breakthrough that exist just as surely at this time. This is why we so urgently need a new, shared vision and the encouraging leadership to help us discover it.

But first we have to be present to the current situation rather than merely to our hopes and fears, which tend to be residues of past experiences projected forward. These function like filters that distort the ability to perceive fresh solutions to existing problems. As a result, we're often moving at warp speed toward an unknown tomorrow, with our eyes firmly glued to the rearview mirror. Such perilous "rear-sightedness" creates a kind of repetition compulsion—we get what was, rather than what might be. And in the words of the prophet in the King James Version of Old Testament, "Where there is no vision, the people perish" (Proverbs 29:18).

When we can't see our way forward, our will is effectively frozen and we're not free. Shared vision, which enlightened leaders help us discover and articulate, is the clarification of collective will, providing guidance for right action. Where such clarity is absent—where robust, creative, full functioning is therefore not taking place—we as a society need to inquire about what's in the way. What are our hidden assumptions about the future, and how empowering or disempowering are they?

A sobering and helpful way of assessing our assumptions about the future was discovered by the Dutch cultural historian and philosopher Fred Polak and explained in one of the most important books of the 20th century, *The Image of the Future*. Polak's study of the rise and fall of world cultures revealed that the most reliable indicator of any civilization's continuing vitality or imminent decline could be found in its dominant images of the future. These hypnotically riveting projections of collective hopes or fears tend to operate, Polak showed, *as self-fulfilling prophecies*.

In response to Polak's findings, the eminent futurist and social scientist Willis Harman undertook a massively funded research project at Stanford University in 1973 called "Changing Images of Man." It was his premise that most of the problems we face on this planet are merely symptoms, mirroring back to us our flawed representations of who we are in relation to ourselves, to each other, and to the living world of nature. These distorted images—essentially I-It rather than I-Thou views of reality—produce equally distorted perceptions of future possibilities.

Harman and his colleagues believed that the systematic correcting of these distortions could—if widely engaged in—be a powerful
springboard for positive social change. Meanwhile, however, the
predominant view of the future embodied in our images is that
"it" is what's "happening to us." In other words, we're victims of
an impending negative future that's coming toward us like fate.
An I-Thou view, in contrast, invites us to co-create a positive future
using our imaginative capacities in partnership with a benign universal will.

The trauma of World War I, which married technology to terror, was a turning point in our dominant imagery of the future.
It dashed the nearly universal optimism that had preceded it, and
utopias virtually disappeared from that point onward, replaced by
pervasive fears of technological progress gone wild or hijacked—like
the planes on 9/11—by the primitive dark side of human nature.
Today we no longer confidently equate technological "progress"
with the certain advancement of human civilization.

This shift in our images of the future is displayed powerfully
in cinema. Fearful showdowns between the embattled spark of
human freedom and the powerful winds of a dark, impending fate
span from Fritz Lang's 1927 film *Metropolis* to contemporary movies
such as *The Matrix, Minority Report, Koyaanisqatsi,* and *The Sum of
All Fears.* Iconic news photos—the atomic mushroom cloud, for
instance, or the burning Twin Towers—also lodge in our collective
emotional limbic system and create lingering fear and trauma that
shrink our perceptions of possibility.

Even if these frightening images aren't self-fulfilling prophecies, we surely need new visions of the infinite and divine potential
within us . . . and of the beautiful world we can help create to reflect
it. Those visions—and "the way opening" that can bring them to
fruition—may arise from the kind of prayerful, shared silence that
the Quakers and other Sages describe.

"The more people cultivate silence, the more peace we will
have," said the Peruvian psychotherapist and Incan shaman Cecilia
Montero. "But we need to cultivate the cooperation of taking care
of the planet," she continued. "Everybody has to work together
to take care of the earth, our habitat." Cooperative listening and

shared inquiry invite the collective guidance that ought to be the goal of authentic leadership. The intelligence that emerges from dwelling in our essential questions together isn't conformity, but a richly diverse understanding of possibilities that can inspire creative action on many fronts. But, as with individual guidance, there are blocks to overcome in engaging that intelligence and implementing the solutions it suggests.

Blocks to Inspired Leadership

Sufi Sheikh Kabir Helminski identified victim mentality as a major block to guidance. He explained:

> I see so many sides of the world situation today where the problems are made worse by unspiritual attitudes. One is being the victim. When I speak to mainstream Muslim groups, I tell them to stop seeing themselves as a victimized minority. It's not a spiritual posture.
>
> Another spiritual disease is self-righteousness. The remedies are unselfish generosity, mercy, and forgiveness, which are the ways to establish justice. I don't know why justice is so hard to come to in this world—why we can't stand in each other's shoes. We see only our own demands and complaints, rather than the pain and suffering that our own actions are creating.

Yogi Mukunda Stiles also spoke of the inability to stand in one another's shoes. "The biggest problem in humanity," he said, "is not seeing how much pain we're causing and how much pain we're in. If a person can watch pain being inflicted and really get it, it turns you around. There was a captivating story in yesterday's news about a cow that escaped from the slaughterhouse and got onto the highway. Everyone tried to catch her. She was running away from the slaughterhouse, and everyone there voted to save her life. That's a practical example of what we don't get."

Cows frightened in the road, refugees fleeing across borders, poverty in our midst, habitats destroyed. Perhaps a major difficulty in today's televised world is that we see the violence on the evening news—but not the pain. We don't get it. To "stand in each other's shoes" is to transcend our narrow sense of identity . . . our attachments to beliefs, possessions, formative experiences, and ethnicities—all that distinguishes "us" from "them."

"The only guarantee of world leadership that's really going to be life enhancing," the founder of the Diamond Approach to Self-Realization, Hameed Ali, told us, "is that it has to be selfless, which means truly caring, not caring out of vested self-interest." Not only does this seem an almost superhuman requirement, but the competitive career ladder to powerful positions in world affairs seems designed to exclude anyone who might have that qualification. "These days," Hameed said, "we don't get leaders like that. It seems that people who are selfless don't become leaders. To get to that place requires so much of the ambition of the self-centered person."

Self-centeredness makes it hard to see other people's viewpoints. "The Buddha's principle of right view entails not clinging to right view," Buddhist monk Ajahn Sona summed up the paradox of clinging to an opinion without the humility to inquire into the other person's point of view, and calling it guidance.

Right view is not right when you cling to it. So if you are prompted, through delusion, greed, and ill will, to defend your right view, you will *lose* right view. Love is never defended by hate. Peace is never defended by war. So we encourage people to defend their faith through the sacrifice of nonviolence, the giving of patience—of infinite patience, which doesn't have a withdrawal date.

Religions and countries are preserved by veneration of wisdom and the wise. They endure longer than those who merely venerate their own existence above all else. So we have to have the absolute conviction that there's something more important than existence itself. You cannot guarantee long-term existence by being desperately attached to it. That's where the Buddha is such a clear teacher, saying, "Do not defend my doctrines. If someone criticizes me and you get angry, you've just lost my teaching. If you defend my religion by violence, you're not a disciple of mine."

"Get your spiritual practice together" was Reverend Suzanne Fageol's advice to world leaders. "Are you operating out of your separate self or in partnership with Spirit? It's about inclusion. We have to respect diversity, because we're all interdependent. One of the criteria I'd look at is whether world leaders are moving toward exclusion or inclusion. Inclusion is where evolution is moving to. If you're touting special interests and excluding some people, that's not a spiritual stance. We have to dialogue in a way that we're willing to be changed by that dialogue."

"Stop criticizing and blaming. Change your focus from what needs to be torn down to what needs to be built up." This is what our friend international mediator Bill Ury suggests as a way to transform the dialogue, advice that's echoed by poet Daniel Ladinsky.

"Drop the knife," is the wisdom Ladinsky suggests for world leaders, "for if you can, a great world teacher you will become." Daniel was talking about the positive heart of leadership. He continued:

> Real leadership—that is what the intelligent, or awake, heart brings to the table. That is what the true teacher can also give. And I think it is important to say here that I feel the goal is to become one's own true teacher. For a faith-based person that can only happen if you find the Nameless within yourself and can then converse with it as easily—and as clearly and intimately—as you and a friend can chat and share all kinds of secrets.
>
> The heart having intelligence may seem something of an odd notion, but I feel that is where the deeper—the greater—intelligence/guidance/wisdom begins: in the heart. And to me, loving and intelligence is the same.

Reconciling Power and Love

Heart intelligence is what the Sages agree is needed to replace blame and judgment with the compassionate understanding necessary to implement enlightened social action. We're living in an interdependent world without walls that is, nevertheless, fractionating violently along tribal and sectarian fault lines. Taking off the blinders and replacing harsh judgment with cooperation requires what international mediator Mark Gerzon calls "leaders beyond borders"—leaders who treat boundaries as points of contact rather than lines of separation and mutual distrust.[1]

He cites Nelson Mandela as an example. Mandela befriended his white prison guard by resolving to treat him with the utmost respect. Later, after his historic release, Mandela invited the guard to his presidential inauguration. This public act of forgiveness and reconciliation set the tone for healing the racial divide that had shamefully plagued apartheid South Africa. Mandela's willingness to forgive and befriend the *other* released him from the narrow confines of a limited identity—a victim stance. This leader-embodied attitude became a beacon for South Africans of all races, the opening to a future where justice and compassion were new possibilities.

Adam Kahane, a designer and facilitator of processes through which businesses and governments can overcome blocks and solve their most difficult problems, has worked in more than 50 countries, with executives and politicians, generals and guerillas, civil servants and trade unionists, community activists and United Nations officials, clergy and artists. Kahane is the author of *Solving Tough Problems: An Open Way of Talking, Listening, and Creating New Realities.* Nelson Mandela said of the work: "This breakthrough book addresses the central challenge of our time: finding a way to work together to solve the problems we have created."[2]

Gordon: I heard Kahane give a lecture in which he told a story about how what he calls "tough problems" might be solved. He was presiding over a truth-and-reconciliation process in Guatemala after years of brutal civil war and genocide. The participants in the gathering came from all sides of the struggle. Former victims and oppressors were *sitting together*—listening to one another for perhaps the very first time.

One participant related, in a quiet and non-accusatory way, a horrifying discovery. Present at the exhumation of one of many mass graves, he'd asked a forensic investigator if the small bones they were looking at had been forcibly fractured. "No," the scientist replied, "but pregnant women were among those killed, and the many small bones such as these belonged to their fetuses."

The long silence that ensued after this horrific revelation was recounted matter-of-factly and without anger lasted for what seemed like five minutes or more, according to Kahane. In a follow-up session several years later, the participants still remembered that deep, ego-dissolving silence as a turning point and referred to it as "a large communion," which, in their Catholic culture, they understood as the experience of becoming one body. Such was the power of that silence, and the opening it created for a new, compassionate way of *being with* one another.

This story, for Kahane, illustrates by dramatic contrast a major problem about power: its insulating effect. In his previous corporate life at Royal Dutch/Shell in London in the 1990s, he said, he'd been oblivious to how much power he and his giant employer wielded in the world. "Power," he explained, "was the water I swam in."

Like the fish that is proverbially the last to discover water, Kahane was ultimately shocked into recognizing—when he saw the painful consequences firsthand—that power for its own sake effaces the soul of others, as well as the depth of one's own true humanness. Where power reigns supreme, there is no mutual respect or acknowledgment, and an I-It rather than an I-Thou relationship ensues. In Kahane's mind, this is why his corporation, in its global irresponsibility and obliviousness to consequences, became guilty of "institutional violence." This is also why he left it for a life of global service to humanity.

"I opened up," was the way he put it, and that's what he said he meant by love.

Joan and Gordon: Spiritual guidance, as we've been exploring it in our conversations with the Sages, is an "opening up" because it blows the self-serving and self-blinding seal off of ego-appropriated power. It renders that power open and subservient to something higher. The relationship between leadership and guidance closely parallels the relationship between power and love. This is the question that Kahane pursued in his lecture: *How can we reconcile power and love?*

Kahane quoted Martin Luther King, Jr., from an August 16, 1967, presidential address to the Southern Christian Leadership Conference: "One of the greatest problems of history is that the concepts of love and power have usually been contrasted as opposites—polar opposites—so that love is identified with a resignation of power, and power with a denial of love." King was speaking both as a minister and as a Nobel Peace Prize laureate, addressing other clergy who were morally averse to the overt exercise of power. His stand against the Vietnam War was in contrast to the conventional attitude that politics and religion shouldn't mix. "Now, we've got to get this thing right," he continued. "What is needed is a realization that power without love is reckless and abusive, and love without power is sentimental and anemic."

The bridge between power and love in the story of reconciliation in Guatemala that Kahane recounted was *telling the truth . . .* not in an absolute sense, but—to paraphrase visionary philosopher Dr. Marshall Rosenberg's definition of nonviolent communication—*humbly speaking the truth of the situation as it was actually observed and felt by one person, without judgment or diagnosis.* When others could listen to that truth without defensiveness, it became a "large communion" of deep compassion. Listening with the ears of the heart and speaking it in a non-accusatory way that could be heard were key to the breakthrough.

When power grows deaf and becomes dissociated from reality, it becomes corrupt and insensitive. And when love grows hesitant and silent in the face of injustice, it becomes betrayal. "We must speak," said Martin Luther King on another occasion, "with all the humility that is appropriate to our limited vision, but we must speak."

Speaking Truth Together

Sister Rose Mary Dougherty provided several examples of venues where leaders could speak their truth in a safe way and be listened to respectfully. The capacity to *listen one another into deeper wisdom* is one of the skills of spiritual companioning that Sister Rose Mary speaks of with the humble authority that makes her such a fine teacher.

"A few years back, I was invited to a Merton retreat," she told us. She continued:

> Thomas Merton, before he died, had this dream—and he wrote about it—of getting world leaders like Gandhi and Martin Luther King together in dialogue. He even wrote some directions for doing this, and then he died before it could happen. Somebody came across this journal and they invited a group of world leaders—political and spiritual leaders—and I was one of the people there.
>
> When we started the conversation, people were asking questions like, "What is the United States going to do about this responsibility for globalization?" But by the time we finished, something had shifted entirely, because we would spend half an hour in silence together, and then people would go out for a half hour of silence by themselves, and then we'd come back for half an hour of conversation in small groups. Something shifted in the way people were listening to one another.

What Sister Rose Mary was describing was a different kind of space, deliberately created to facilitate deep listening and wider inclusion. This is a social invention of deep significance that could, if established at the highest levels of power, deepen the dialogue among world leaders and bring them into a more harmonious accord where authentic spiritual guidance might arise. Sister Rose Mary mentioned another of these forums she'd experienced, "Space in Politics," directed by Reverend Douglas Tanner in Washington, D.C.

"It's a place, a safe place," she explained, "where particular congresspeople, and some of the senators, get together for prayer and for small-group sharing about their freedoms, their un-freedoms, about the positions they're taking, what's going on in their lives. And there's something happening in that atmosphere: It allows people to listen and begin to trust across party lines." The famed social scientist and Quaker Kenneth Boulding called this kind of meeting a "hearing aid." It's an inspiring alternative to adversarial battling for supremacy and has the potential to open all parties to a higher form of collective intelligence.

We were delighted to discover, as Boulder Friends Meeting member Deanne Butterfield told us, that the Quaker House located near the United Nations headquarters in New York serves as an international "hearing aid" of the type Boulding was referring to: "Delegates and anyone associated with them can come off the record and talk, and Quakers will sit with them and moderate. People can say what they think in confidence, so we talk with these leaders about how they personally lead their lives."

Quaker Mary Hey added, "Those meetings are for them to think and reflect. As our service to the world, it's promoting love, honesty, and respect. That's what we try to bring to world leaders. They have the capacity to do the right thing if they have the support. Many leaders have been influenced by a single Quaker to do something unpopular. Knowing they're held and supported has made a difference." And when anyone lives their Light, as our Quaker Sages continually assure us, the Light increases.

Spiritual guidance can be described as the organ of spiritual imagination that enables leaders to perceive, in concert with those they serve, the noblest potential in the current reality—the most encouraging opening to newness. The Latin phrase *Potentia est potentia* translates as "Potential is power," but this is true only when potential is perceived, aligned with, and acted on.

Sister Rose Mary told us how—in facing the rubble left by World War II—the educational mission of her religious order, the Sisters of Notre Dame, had become one of enabling people to reach their highest potential. She said: "I would want to send every world leader to a crash course in something like that, beginning with their own deepest, highest potential, and then have them create ways that our nations can realize that."

"That's a magnificent vision," we agreed. "With enlightened world leadership, we could implement a specific aim to begin with our children, enabling them to bring forth their unique gifts and talents. What a different world it would be if that could be the central organizing task of humanity going forward from this point in history."

"That's what I really do believe," Sister Rose Mary agreed, "and in order for that to happen, our leaders need to come to a sense of their own deepest potential and not be led by the expectations of others."

Leadership development, in other words, and personal spiritual development have to be understood as two sides of the same coin. Helping leaders expand beyond role identities and touch their deepest human essence is key to such progress. After all, "How can a role love a role?" organizational psychologist Jack Gibb once asked an audience of business leaders.

From Head of State to Heart of State

Rabbi Rami Shapiro suggested that our leaders "should all go for a walk." He explained how that simple act can help people transcend their roles and meet in a more real, intimate way: "Ronald Reagan told this story about meeting with Gorbachev at a high summit meeting and nothing was happening. They go for a walk, and by the time they come back, all is solved. It's probably an apocryphal story, but there's truth in it. Instead of sitting in a formal setting, go for a walk in the park and talk as human beings. Instead of being a head of state, be a heart of state."

This isn't a new idea. The birth of American democracy, which we're inclined to think of today in purely secular terms, was mystically rooted in heart wisdom. The understanding was that all human beings, by virtue of the soul's divine nature—or what the Quakers call "that of God" in us—have access both within themselves and in community to spiritual guidance. This optimistic assumption, as a basis for the country's independent right to self-determination, as stated in the Declaration of Independence, rested partly on the experience of mystical communities such as those of the Quakers.

Jacob Needleman, professor of philosophy at San Francisco State University, writes in his remarkable book *The American Soul:*

"The doctrine of the self put forward by mystical communities like the Quakers dictated that every individual seek to consult the inner divinity for guidance in the conduct of life. But what *is* that inner God?" Needleman asks himself. When he looks back at his earliest experience of real autonomy, he recalls a "mysterious sense of an *independent awareness* within myself that was at the same time an awareness *on the side of God.*"[3]

This recognition is the entrance point to spiritual maturity—acknowledging the existence of a vast, unconditioned, witnessing awareness within. It opens out to; is informed by; and, as Needleman states, is "recognized by the universe."[4]

In other words, there's an infinite intelligence we can look toward that can look back and confirm that we're on the right track. In seeking to do the right thing, the young Needleman's "need to act came from the sense that really good or right action could emanate, and perhaps could only emanate, from that inner mind which was myself and was on the side of God!"[5]

The fundamental human capacity to attune to spiritual guidance was a central pillar of both Hebraic and classical Greek thought, the two streams from which Western culture and modern democracy emerged. "Judaism and Hellenic spiritual philosophy called all human beings to search in themselves for a capacity of the mind in which objective perception and moral will converge into one power."[6]

The Hebrews, in order to love and serve this higher unity of the good and true that in their theistic framework was the will of God, knew that they had to strive with all their minds, hearts, and might for *understanding.* Plato called this godlike power *reason,* by which he meant the ability to intuit what is both ethically good and ultimately true. And Needleman notes that while *reason* was the dominant value upon which the United States was founded, the founders were not referring to today's impoverished understanding of it as "the tyrant of merely logical, mechanistic thought."[7] They had a much more heartful form of knowledge in mind, the ancient name for which is *conscience.* Needleman describes conscience, which he's careful to distinguish from superego (the voice of our critical parent within), as "the exquisite and essential subtlety of the feeling/valuing component of the mind"—what we're calling the Soul's Compass.[8]

The miracle is that where two or more human beings are gathered to listen for guidance together, the filter of personal limitations can yield and sudden sunlight shine through to show the way forward. This happened among the founders of the American democracy when framing the Constitution. They listened to one another. "To 'listen' another's soul into a condition of disclosure and discovery," wrote the Quaker Douglas V. Steere, "may be almost the greatest service any human being ever does for another."[9]

The founders of the U.S. were able to listen together for shared guidance at a time when the noble experiment of democracy could just as easily have failed for lack of an appropriate and agreed-upon form to build it on: *the United States Constitution.* We're in a similar situation today on a much larger scale, divided by our perceived differences yet drawn ever more closely together by the inescapable fact of our global interdependence. This is a moment in world history that is, in the words of the late psychologist Erich Fromm, pregnant with possibility. It's a time for all of us, especially with help from our world leaders, to collectively "listen one another toward" global wholeness and drop the knife of blame and victimization.

As we open the ears of our hearts to neighbor and stranger alike and to the hidden treasure of possibility within us all desiring to be known, the compass of spiritual guidance may help us bring a future of wisdom and compassion into being—a civilization with a heart.

PART II

Introducing the Sages

*"Wisdom is not a product of schooling
but of the lifelong attempt to acquire it."*

— Albert Einstein

THE SAGES

We present the Sages to you now with great delight and a little trepidation as well. How can such brief introductions capture even a hint of their essence? In the hopes of doing so, we focused less on standard biographies and more on the unique ways that Life flows through them. Our wish is that something of who they really are—beyond pedigrees and degrees—will come through as you become "officially" acquainted with these extraordinary human beings, whose wisdom you've been absorbing in Part I of the book.

After each introduction, we've included a final excerpt from the conversation we had with that person. Weaving this last tapestry from the 27 interviews was a joy. We hope that it will serve both as a review of *Your Soul's Compass* for you and as another opportunity to appreciate the common Mystic Heart from which almost all of the Sages speak.

Swami Adiswarananda

Swami Adiswarananda has been a senior monk of the Rama-krishna order since 1963 and Spiritual Leader of the Ramakrishna-

Vivekananda Center in New York City. He joins Reb Zalman Schachter-Shalomi and Father Thomas Keating as one of our three elders. The Swami was the first of the Sages to be interviewed, and his scholarly clarity and evident good humor got us off to a wonderful start.

The Swami referred to the spiritual life, and to our journey of Self-realization, as *The Great Adventure*. The moment of waking up from the trance of ordinary life and realizing that something far more mysterious and real is at work is the start of that adventure. And according to the Swami, there's a certain grace involved in the moment of awakening:

> There is, in coming into one's spiritual path, an element of divine intervention. That intervention is a glimpse of the truth that comes like Light through a sudden crack in the wall. It is a taste of something higher that enables you to renounce what is lower—an awakening or revelation. This is a precondition for living The Great Adventure.

Once we have tasted the exquisite freedom of true nature, we have a basic sense of orientation. We know which direction to go in—that of peace. After all, who wouldn't prefer to be relaxed, creative, and peaceful rather than fearful and uptight? Nonetheless, the conditioned pull of the ego is strong, and the tendency remains to go back to sleep again. The next Sage is a master of using the practice of inquiry to stay awake.

Hameed Ali

Hameed Ali, who writes under the pen name of A. H. Almaas, is the founder of the Diamond Approach to Self-Realization, which is taught internationally through the Ridhwan School. *Ridhwan* is an Arabic term meaning "the manifestation of contentment in the complete human being."

Hameed was completing a doctorate in physics at Berkeley in the 1960s when he had a life-changing experience that led him to devote himself to an exploration of the spiritual journey. "It is important to understand that I did not develop my work by organizing it at the beginning," he has explained, "looking at the various theories and integrating them. It was a living and organic process of development that was guided by Spirit."[1] In our conversations with him, Hameed defined spiritual guidance as an indication that we're on the right track in our spiritual journey:

> *Spiritual guidance is not the same thing as when people talk about guides who tell you what to do—"This is wrong"; "Don't do that"; "This person, not that person"; "Do this investment." It isn't really that way. Spiritual guidance is basically spiritual. It's connected classically or traditionally with the angel of revelation, so it's connected with revealing truth. Guidance doesn't tell me what to do. It mostly indicates that I'm on the right track. It works by revealing <u>the truth of the moment</u> in a way that takes the consciousness deeper or closer to the Spiritual Ground.*

What Hameed calls "love of the truth" is the humble realization that we don't know what will happen next, coupled with a courageous curiosity that's willing to see whatever reveals itself. Our next Sage also spoke of spiritual guidance—albeit in a different way—as feeling for the forces that are operative in the moment.

Rabbi Rami Shapiro

Rabbi Rami has been called a Stand-Up Mystic, the Jewish Alan Watts (a famous and very funny philosopher of comparative religion who died in 1973), and a Holy Rascal. He's a prolific and stunningly brilliant writer, a teacher of religious studies at Middle Tennessee State University, and a spiritual guide, providing what he calls, with his predictable wit, "roadside assistance for your spiritual journey." Strongly grounded in Judaism, he has depth and breadth in many of the world's great spiritual traditions.

Rabbi Rami defined guidance in a simple, clear way:

What is spiritual guidance? I can experience it, but to define it is more challenging. Maybe it's discovering or experiencing the grain of the moment—like the grain of wood—what the forces are that are operative in this moment so that I can engage them directly and cleanly without having to go across the grain.

While Rabbi Rami can't easily define spiritual guidance as a concept, he knows very clearly when it's happening. It's an experience—a verb rather than a noun. The lack of words for experiences of a Greater Reality is the plight of the mystic, who has to rely on music, art, and poetry to describe the landscape of Being: that essential state of contentment and wisdom that comes from resting in one's own true nature.

Daniel Ladinsky

Daniel Ladinsky is a poet and a renowned translator of spiritual poetry, of which several luminous volumes are available. Our favorite is *Love Poems from God: Twelve Sacred Voices from the East and West*. Daniel is a particularly skillful artist who mixes words, rather than colors, on his palette to create images that are spiritually alive. Daniel referred to the late Hindu holy man Meher Baba, his teacher, as a golden compass. Daniel wrote: "His death a few years back seems to have no effect on how we can still be near, and my ability to talk with him—as it were. One of my wilder Hafiz renderings comes to mind [referring to a translation he did of the mystic poet]: 'Love Kicks the Ass of Time and Space.'"

Daniel provided two definitions of guidance. The first was "advice or information aimed at understanding or resolving a problem or difficulty." The second focused on guidance as leadership or direction that comes from the heart:

The heart having intelligence may seem something of an odd notion, but I feel that is where the deeper—the greater—intelligence/guidance/wisdom begins: in the heart. And to me loving and intelligence is the same.

Spiritual guidance as a loving intelligence—a Soul's Compass that orients us to both our own inner goodness and to the True North of God or Ultimate Reality—was a theme that carried through most of the interviews. For Taj Inayat—a Sufi whose spiritual worldview is based on caring—guidance and love are also one and the same.

Taj Inayat

Taj Inayat is the vice president of the Sufi Order International and the spiritual companion of the late Pir Vilayat (the word *Pir* refers to the spiritual leader of a Sufi order). Sufism is an ancient mystic tradition that predates Islam but has also become the inner, mystical stream within Islam. Its philosophy and practices center on divine love and cultivating the intelligence of the heart.

Sheikh Ahmad Zarruq, a 14th-century Sufi who wrote *The Principles of Sufism,* defined *Sufism* as "a science whose objective is the reparation of the heart and turning it away from all else but God."[2] Sufis rely on guides or mentors to help initiates, or *mureeds,* find their way and select practices that are suitable for them. Taj is a Sufi guide who weds the wisdom of the revered spiritual teacher Hazrat Inayat Khan with the insights of modern psychology.

Taj's responses to our questions seemed to come less from her brilliant mind than from a deep, felt experience, which poured through the phone connection and took us with her into the exalted states of divine love that she was describing. Her tone of voice grew soft when she spoke of the connection between guidance and love, and her words flowed like nectar from some secret source:

> *Love has everything to do with guidance. This guiding light, this light intelligence, illuminates our journey toward the Great Becoming—it's loving light, the Hidden Treasure (God) desiring to be known. Creation is an exhalation of a sigh of compassion that creates the universe, not a big bang. Love is the ground, love is the journey, love is the end. God is love, lover, and beloved.*

Sufism is a relational path. In order for love to happen, there has to be a beloved. Whether the beloved is partner, pet, or God, the dynamic is one of love. Out of that comes the realization of the Universe as love.

Taj is like a living embodiment of the Sufi logo, which is a winged heart. But the Sufis are joined as divine lovers by mystics of many other religious traditions. The next Sage speaks of following the "vector of love," which leads us home to true nature and union with the Divine.

Sister Rose Mary Dougherty

Rose Mary Myoan Dougherty is a School Sister of Notre Dame. She is a senior fellow for spiritual guidance at Shalem Institute for Spiritual Formation in Bethesda, Maryland, where she has worked for many years. She is a student of the contemplative way and offers guidance in contemplative practice.

As a dharma heir of Roshi Janet Jinne Richardson, CSJP (Congregation of the Sisters of St. Joseph of Peace), she is a sensei (Zen teacher) in the White Plum Asanga. Her Zen name means "subtle peace," and she imparts that peace in retreats and meditation "sits" and to patients at Joseph's House, a hospice for formerly homeless men with AIDS, as well as offering retreats and group spiritual direction for hospice caregivers. Sister Rose Mary defined spiritual guidance for us as:

> . . . *an inner direction, a leading, that comes to me from that place where I'm living in my true Self. I would call it the Holy Spirit, the Guidance of Love. It's something that takes me more deeply into myself and to the heart of the world in loving service and compassion. . . . I don't see or hear it as separate from myself. I think of those words from Deuteronomy: "Don't say who will go and get the word and bring it to me, no the word of God is already there planted deep within you. All you need to do is listen." So it's something that's deeply a part of me.*

Although Sister Rose Mary is a Catholic as well as a Zen teacher, her insights about guidance were remarkably similar to one of our Jewish Sages. It was this meeting on common interspiritual ground that we enjoyed the most about the interviews.

Rabbi Zalman Schachter-Shalomi

Reb Zalman Schachter-Shalomi is a wisdom teacher in his 80s who literally wrote the book on *From Age-ing to Sage-ing.* He's a founder of the Jewish Renewal movement, which breathed new life into today's Judaism.

Reb Zalman is one of the few remaining rabbis who still carry the wisdom of pre-Holocaust Judaism. His genius is in holding an ancient and disciplined lineage, while simultaneously bringing it to life in a new way suitable for modernity—a way that's practical, fun, and true to the Mystic Heart. Born in Poland in 1924, he was raised in Vienna and escaped to the United States with his family in 1941 after their release from an internment camp in Vichy, France. Ordained as a Hasidic rabbi in 1947, he's a brilliant scholar who knows multiple spoken languages in addition to the unspoken language of the heart.

He described spiritual guidance as the teaching that comes from the inside, as an intuitive "knowing" for which we have no words, but have to experience on a more mystical level that arises out of silence:

> *There's so much noise today in the world, it's hard to go to the place where the mind is so clear that it can listen to more subtle places. So we have to go and calm the mind so we can really listen in order to be able to hear from the right hemisphere. That's where you have IN-tuition—and I like to spell it out—the teaching that happens on the inside.*

Our next Sage speaks directly to the calm mind that Reb Zalman describes. Her mysticism is representative of an indigenous culture in Peru—the ancient Inca. That culture, as well as other indigenous traditions, flourished in times when the world was less noisy and alignment to the more subtle realms was more easily accessed. She speaks to the necessity of coming into a condition of internal quietude where harmony replaces stress.

Cecilia Montero

(Maria) Cecilia Montero is a psychotherapist, academician, and spiritual guide. She was trained as an Altomisayoc (Andean shaman) of the Inca tradition by her maternal great-grandmother from the age of two. Much of her training was in silence in order to awaken her inner knowledge of sound—which, she was taught, carries the blessings of the grandmothers and the grandfathers of her culture, who are the keepers of the Sacred Sound of Mother Earth.

In the Inca tradition, *Sami* are coherent waves of Intelligent Creative Force that guide Life Energy. Cecilia was taught that connecting with Sami—the actual force of spiritual guidance—leads us on a path of growth and harmony, rather than furthering the insatiable desire nature that overtakes us when we're stressed. She began in her perfect, barely accented English:

> *We can get very technical, but for this purpose we want to keep it simple, not academic. This force (Sami) is available to everyone. It can be felt in one's body and one's being, and with the practice of meditation, it can be felt in one's thoughts and one's mind. It takes different forms. It can even be felt like an earthquake, and it has felt like that to me at times. At other times it's like a soft wind, an insistent thought, or a little intuition.*
>
> *In Inca tradition, energy is divided into refined energy and energy that is not harmonized—hucha in Spanish—when one doesn't live in harmony with nature and other people. One feels sick, unhappy, and stressed-out. Yet harmony is available to everyone and permeates the Universe. Sami is sublime, infinite, pure energy. That's what can be felt in different ways.*

It is the force of guidance. If it's the lower-vibratory-rate force, it's not guidance. That's more human, based on desire and disharmony.

That energy that Cecilia calls Sami is usually felt as clarity, ease, or a state of being that's referred to as *nondual* in some Eastern traditions. Instead of feeling separate, stressed, or striving, as in the egoic state, in the nondual state there's a sense of being knit into a larger wholeness—a coherent intelligent field, like Sami. Our next friend speaks directly to the nondual state in which we're one with spiritual guidance.

Yogi Mukunda Stiles

Yogi Mukunda is sprightly and elfin, overflowing with good-humored smiles and laughter. We conducted two interviews with him—one was at his home, and the other was at a Nepalese restaurant in Boulder, Colorado. At the end of that second two-hour conversation, a woman who had been listening discreetly from across the room approached Mukunda earnestly and asked him to be her teacher.

He is, indeed, a captivating Sage who emanates gentle authority and a loving presence. Mukunda is a scholar and practitioner of Kashmir Shaivism, a Hindu religious philosophy in which the practitioner seeks union with God as the Divine Beloved. The underlying thinking is "nondual," which is a translation of the Sanskrit word *advaita*.

Mukunda is not only a Hindu scholar, but also an outstanding teacher of hatha yoga and the originator of a very refined system of structural yoga therapy. For Mukunda, spiritual guidance takes the form of connection to a Living Presence:

It's about being connected to a Higher Power that takes the form of feeling like a Divine Presence. When Spirit is there, the world dissolves. [To follow spiritual guidance] there must be a sense of what love is, and then you can look for it. So the language of love is very important.

Love spoke clearly to awaken guidance for the next Sage, who had "cleaned out and cleaned up" from a drug habit in her 20s. She told us that she made a powerful decision to choose Life and awakening, rather than going back to sleep. The result has been a clear and powerful intention to follow spiritual guidance in every aspect of life.

Nina Zimbelman

Nina Zimbelman is a metaphysician and medical intuitive who was recommended enthusiastically by our friend Sara Davidson as a woman who takes spiritual direction very seriously. She'll literally pick up and move to the other side of the earth when that's the guidance she gets. That introduction piqued our curiosity and seemed an appropriate credential for an interviewee.

Nina explained how love, the Spirit of Guidance, first came to her in a classic type of sudden-awakening experience:

> *One day the presence of pure love came into my space and began to communicate with me—to speak to me in my inner awareness. It was so amazing to experience love. This field of unconditional love opened up to me, and in that space everything was different. I could love the unlovable. I didn't judge. I could accept things. Slowly, this became an embodiment of wisdom. This is the field of unconditional love that is the Universe.*
>
> *When this first happened, I projected it as something outside of myself—I called it Baba [a Hindu term for a saint or holy man]. As you stand in those spaces and allow them to teach you, and as you surrender to those teachings—which are totally different from manmade teachings—you become something different.*

Nina's definition of guidance is nontheistic. She speaks of wisdom, rather than of God. It's the pure experience of love, for her, that opens the door to a wisdom that helps her accept life, rather than resisting it. Our next Sage, a Buddhist monk, has a similar understanding of spiritual guidance as a connection to wisdom.

The Venerable Ajahn Sona

Ajahn Sona is a Theravadan Buddhist monk and abbot of the Birken Forest Monastery in Canada, near Kamloops, British Columbia. Formerly a classical guitarist, he's a humble, delightful teacher who is ever compassionate, insightful, and funny. His pithy one-liners could be a book in themselves.

He talked about the importance of having a *Kalyana Mitta,* or soul friend on the spiritual journey. As he described it, the word derives from the same root as the Pali *metta,* or loving-kindness, and means "the beautiful one who loves you." The reason why this friend is beautiful is that he or she embodies the beauty of wisdom. Such companions are the type of people it's good to associate with, because they can help you cultivate mindfulness and serenity, which are preconditions for attuning to guidance. Ajahn Sona explained:

> *Guided, from a Buddhist point of view, means guided by wisdom, rather than guided by God—which in the end might come down to the same thing. If we talked long enough about this, we might agree, but [regardless of what you call it] we've got to find that voice of wisdom. So what the Buddhists do is to ask, <u>Is my action rooted in greed or non-greed? Ill will or non-ill will? Confusion or clarity?</u> Then you're going to be able to distinguish between actions that are based on the ego and actions that are based on wisdom.*

To Ajahn Sona, the spiritual journey is one of becoming more conscious and letting the awakened, compassionate heart be your guide. One of his pithy one-line teachings is: "When we sleep, we grind away at duty, but if we awake, it's beauty." The spiritual journey as a moment-to-moment awakening—or *watchfulness,* in

Christian terminology—is spoken to beautifully by the next Sage, who defines guidance as being unconditionally present to your life no matter what's happening.

Reverend Dr. Cynthia Bourgeault

The Reverend Dr. Cynthia Bourgeault is the principal teacher and advisor to the Contemplative Society, a retreat and conference leader, a writer, and an Episcopal priest. One of her books, *The Wisdom Way of Knowing: Reclaiming an Ancient Tradition to Awaken the Heart,* is a perennial favorite of ours.

She and her cat stayed overnight with us during her annual March trek from her winter teaching at the Aspen Chapel in Aspen, Colorado, to her hermitage in Maine. There she not only chops wood and carries water (a Zen teaching that reminds us that paying attention to mundane activities is a way to enlightenment), but continues to build her own off-the-grid buildings with tools charged by energy generated from solar power.

Reverend Cynthia is a deep well of wisdom—a Sage steeped not only in the Christian tradition, but also in a much broader interspiritual perspective. She explained:

> *Real guidance and heart awareness comes from relaxing your grip on the outcome and staying present to Source. Guidance is not about making the right choices; it's about uninterrupted presence with the Divine as we are in this moment. Then right action falls out of us like water running down a hill.*
>
> *Thomas Merton made the distinction between choice and spontaneity freedom. Choice is: <u>Do I buy a Cadillac or a Buick?</u> Spontaneity is to be unconditionally present to your life no matter what's happening. Then nothing can throw you out of your center. Then you can do no wrong. Whatever happens to you becomes the means to your enlightenment.*

Listening to Reverend Cynthia, we had a deep yearning for the heart awareness that she spoke of. That alignment with Source, the "uninterrupted presence with the Divine as we are in this moment," is the only real refuge and safe haven. Our next Sage continues the theme of spiritual guidance as uninterrupted presence with the Divine—that state called Beingness that follows from connection to true nature.

Oriah Mountain Dreamer

Oriah Mountain Dreamer was given her name through experiences she had in the shamanic tradition in which she studied and practiced for many years. Oriah is also a poet and best-selling author. Her insightful poem "The Invitation" touched the heart of people's longing to live an authentic life and sped across the Internet like lightning. It became the inspiration for the first book in her best-selling trilogy: *The Invitation, The Dance,* and *The Call.*

She's a serious student of many of the world's great wisdom traditions and a woman deeply committed to living her guidance with steadfast courage and integrity. Oriah and her husband, Jeff, live a quiet, simple life in a relatively remote area of Canada. Practices that help her align with Source—what she calls an opening of the heart to wholeness—provide spiritual guidance, which she described as:

> . . . *receiving a sense of direction from an essential aspect of what I am and a Divine Whole that's greater than that—greater than the sum of the parts. Over and over it's an opening of the heart to this wholeness that gives us guidance. This has led me to a growing love of the truth for its own sake, not for the wonderful things that the truth will bring, like the alleviation of suffering or building community—all good things—but just touching Beingness for its own sake. While it does lead to more intimacy, it's an end in itself, rather than a means to an end.*

The next Sage is another model of Beingness and how to touch into this state by "consenting" to the presence and action of God in your life.

Father Thomas Keating

Father Thomas Keating is a Catholic priest and Trappist monk who resides at St. Benedict's Monastery in magnificent Snowmass, Colorado. He's one of the founders of the Centering Prayer movement (a Christian contemplative practice of inviting relationship with God) and a major voice in the interreligious dialogue and interfaith spirituality.

When we interviewed Father Thomas, he was infinitely gracious, and although tired after a month of traveling and teaching, he gave us two very spirited hours. Eighty-three at the time of our conversation, he had energy that was like champagne: It bubbled through him with an excitement that was delightful. When we commented on the wisdom that came in spite of fatigue, Father Thomas replied, "That's because it's not mine. It functions, I guess, irrespective of how I feel. I'm just a little bushed, but I regenerate because it's not my message—I'm just repeating it. It energizes me." He explained the attitude that favors spiritual guidance:

> *It's basically being silent and listening—that is to say, it's a listening attitude, a welcoming receptivity that comes out of surrender to God or the love of God, which wants to do God's will. One wants to please God and to serve other people, and so one is receptive to the inspiration coming from grace, which is not only something to do, but also the empowerment that enables you to do it. It's highly dynamic and very relational— a growing sensitivity to living with God or walking in the Divine Presence.*

Spiritual guidance, by definition, isn't about getting where *we* want to go. It's about letting the winds of wisdom fill our sails and take us where they will. That doesn't mean that we're just along for the ride, though. Wisdom calls upon our gifts in a co-creative partnership that culminates in sacred action that's only ours to give. Our next Sage has a great deal to say about this divine partnership.

Reverend Suzanne Fageol

Reverend Suzanne Fageol is a retired Episcopal priest, among the first women to be ordained in the Anglican Church. She has lived and ministered in Africa, England, and the United States. Reverend Suzanne is both a spiritual director and a supervisor of spiritual directors. She's on the faculty of the Lorian Association in Seattle, which offers a master's degree in contemporary spirituality and spiritual direction, and she also teaches the art of discernment and spiritual guidance to our students in the Claritas Interspiritual Mentor Training Program. One of her core teachings concerns how clinging to an agenda prevents recognizing and moving with the guidance that's always present:

> *Spiritual guidance is the fruit of the soul connecting with that which is ineffable—Mystery—and the wisdom that comes forth from that partnership. It requires trust that the answer will come and a release of the outcome. Sometimes it comes in hints, and I have to put it together, and sometimes it comes—boom! But if nothing comes, the first thing I have to ask is: <u>Am I attached to the outcome? Have I closed down the partnership?</u> That's the biggest reason for no reply, so I have to stay open to what the answer will look like.*

Our next Sage is an expert at helping her students let go of their agendas. Staying in our center as a witness to what we're feeling, thinking, and experiencing—without mistaking our thoughts and feelings for Ultimate Reality—invites partnership with wisdom.

Sally Kempton

Sally Kempton was a famous journalist in the 1970s.[3] Brilliant and witty, she was writing for *The New York Times, Esquire, The Village Voice,* and other prestigious publications in her 20s . . . then everything changed in the blink of an eye. As described on her Website, "One evening in 1971, while sitting in her

Manhattan living room, Sally Kempton was overcome by a feeling of all-encompassing, unconditional love that seemed to come out of nowhere. She had never known that love like this was possible. The experience lasted for 24 hours, and turned her life around."

In 1974, she entered the ashram of Swami Muktananda and became a Hindu monk in the tradition of Siddha Yoga, where she spent many years as Swami Durgananda. Now back in the world again, Sally is recognized as a powerful meditation guide and a down-to-earth spiritual teacher who integrates yogic philosophy with daily life. She's an authentic inner explorer who for more than 20 years has inspired students to make breakthroughs in their own practice. She explained spiritual guidance as an intuitive way of knowing that operates when the mind backs off because it's not sure of what to do:

> *I experience guidance most powerfully at times when I'm not sure what I should do or how to move forward, and I give in to allowing the energetic pull of a certain direction to draw me. If I can do that with a deep intention to sense the path as it unfolds, I usually feel as though I'm being guided at every level. This is a subtle energetic sensing, as if you're a blind person moving along a road in the dark, trusting the road to unfold. There aren't necessarily words or visions; it's just that the path opens at certain points, and you follow the openings. . . . It's a way of knowing that comes from the nonpersonal, intuitive level of awareness, and it's usually worth following.*

The nonpersonal, intuitive level of awareness is given many names. Among them might be Rabb, one of the 99 names of God in the Islamic tradition. Our next Sage, a Sufi sheikh and musician, told us that Rabb is the aspect of God that the opening line of the Koran, "In the name of God, the most merciful and compassionate," refers to—the Sustainer and Educator of all Universes—the energy of guidance itself.

Sheikh Kabir Helminski

Kabir Helminski is a Sufi sheikh of the Mevlevi order, which traces its lineage back to the 13th-century Persian poet-saint Mawlana Jalal ad-Din ar-Rumi. Kabir has an M.A. in psychology and an (honorary) Ph.D. in literature from Selçuk University in Konya, Turkey. A translator of many books on Rumi, as well as several collections of Sufi writings, Sheikh Kabir is also a skilled and inspired musician who has brought the art of the Turkish whirling dervishes to people of many cultures.

With his wife, Camille Helminski, he is cofounder and director of the Threshold Society, a nonprofit educational foundation with the purpose of facilitating the experience of Divine Unity, Love, and Truth in the world. He explains that in Sufism, guidance is a natural function of God's mercy as Sustainer and Educator of all beings:

> *The Divine Being, which is also called <u>Rabb</u>—the Divine Lord or Sustainer—has a primary function of guidance. <u>Rabb</u> comes from the same root as the Hebrew <u>rabbi,</u> or "teacher." There is a function in the Universe that is educating. Every Universe is evolving from darkness to light and from ignorance to realization. So this is a force to cooperate with. In the Sufi tradition, we understand that one of the most important functions of the Divine is to guide each soul, each consciousness, to greater and greater realization.*

A key question that comes up on the spiritual path is: *What are we being guided to?* Is Self-realization an individual undertaking, or do we have a larger life purpose that involves others? Our next Sage, a Buddhist scholar and interspiritual educator, addresses just these questions.

Dr. Edward Bastian

Ed Bastian is president of the Spiritual Paths Institute, which offers a master's degree in interspiritual studies. His doctorate is in Buddhist studies and Western philosophy. Dr. Bastian lived for several years in Tibetan Buddhist monasteries, where he studied Indian philosophy and religion. Later on, he produced a series of award-winning television documentaries on the religions of Asia for the BBC and PBS.

Ed's scholarly wisdom is precise, and he held our feet to the fire when we were tempted to make generalizations that might have blurred important distinctions between Hinduism and the three branches of Buddhism. In speaking of Mahayana Buddhism, in particular, and where that path may lead, he told us:

> *The idea of Buddha nature is important. We have that seed within us to become a Buddha. What does this really mean? If you're already a Buddha, why don't you know it? It's like an acorn that has a shell: We have to uncover the obstructions to the potentiality so that it can actualize itself and grow. So a lot of Buddhist training is about removing the obscurations to the seed of your enlightenment so that you can become a Buddha. What extraordinary hubris—but how hopeful it is to think that way. We could all become Moses or Jesus or Mohammed or Solomon. That's the goal.*

When we reach that goal, he explained, we're in the best circumstances to help other people become free of delusion and suffering. One of the clearest articulations of how we might develop the compassion to do so came through Rabbi Tirzah Firestone.

Rabbi Tirzah Firestone

Rabbi Tirzah is an author, psychotherapist, and spiritual leader of Congregation Nevei Kodesh in Boulder, Colorado. Widely known for her groundbreaking work on the reintegration of the feminine wisdom tradition within Judaism, she teaches meditation and spirituality all over the world. Her background is a fascinating mix of Kabbalah and Jung.

She gave a wonderful definition of what it is to find spiritual guidance by going beyond the surface of our various ego identities and locating the core Self that unifies them all:

> *Spiritual guidance is a face-to-face encounter. G-d is facing us and we are facing G-d, which sets up a spiritual field that allows our deepest selves to emerge. . . . There's no singular word for <u>face</u> (<u>panim</u>) in Hebrew. It's plural—you can't say "face." The understanding is that we have many faces, and our job is to go inside and find the unifying principle, the core Self. When I'm facing another person and I can really drop my agendas and roles and just sit with them, a powerful field emerges, and there's a direction that happens as the inessential voices are pared away. The picture that comes to mind is from the many to the One.*

The next Sage has yet another way of describing how guidance is related to love. Unlike the majority of the Sages, she isn't a contemplative. The wisdom she shares is instead based on many years of working with clients who come seeking guidance for the soul's journey.

Dr. Linda Backman

Linda Backman has her doctorate in psychology and was in private practice for 30 years. Following the death of her second son as an infant, she became interested in the possible continuity of the soul. Linda is trained in numerous traditional and nontraditional techniques, including hypnotherapy, Life Between Lives spiritual-regression therapy, past-life-regression therapy, and shamanic soul retrieval.

We were interested in her perspective on spiritual guidance because of the large number of people (more than 600) whom she has regressed specifically to what she believes is the stage of existence between lives. This is a stage, according to Dr. Backman, when we understand where we've been on our spiritual journey and where we're going. We meet with teachers and other souls who comprise part of a learning group and have a chance to understand and integrate the experience of our recent incarnation. To receive spiritual guidance from these teachers and souls, she advised:

> *. . . you have to look for uncanny details and synchronicities. Being a healthy skeptic is important, as well as the willing suspension of disbelief. We hold ourselves in between not knowing and the belief that souls can communicate. They communicate a pure perspective, and the pure perspective is love. Those words are synonymous. Each of us works toward pure perspective as we walk the path of soul growth. We're seeking love. What is Spirit at its purest?* <u>*Love*</u> *is the explanatory term, but it's love that we can't fully comprehend while we're in bodies. We can only see the tip of the iceberg.*

Trusting love, she explained, is a key attitude that allows spiritual guidance to function. For those people who believe in God, their image of that deity as loving or punitive will, of course, affect the functioning of guidance. If we think of God as vengeful, says the next Sage, then guidance can't come through. But if we trust in God's graciousness, then we can more easily discern the movement of Spirit in our lives.

Dr. Wilkie Au

Dr. Wilkie Au is a former Jesuit priest. He is professor of theological studies at Loyola Marymount University in Los Angeles, a spiritual director, and the author of several books. His approach to discernment—the question of whether what we believe to be guidance is authentic or not—is meticulous and thoughtful. It spans the inner realms of our own intuitive felt sense, the importance of involving another person or persons in our search, the Christian fruits of the Spirit, and a good knowledge of our habitual ways of thinking and acting. Dr. Au also speaks with great wisdom about what blocks us from hearing guidance:

If we think that Reality is hostile and threatening, then our response will be hostile and paranoid. But if we think Reality is indifferent, has no investment in us, we still have to roll up our sleeves and get it done. But if we see Reality as gracious, there's more of an ability to flow, surrender, and move with what happens in our life, trusting that in the end all will be well.

For Christians, we know that in the end there will be new life. If we believe that, we can loosen our grip on the steering wheel and trust more in being guided. Our images of God are important. If we trust that God has our happiness in mind and can be trusted, then we can move with divine guidance; but if we have distorted images of God as punitive, mean, vengeful—the Promethean God—then we're not going to be willing to trust whether it comes through direct revelation or through the guidance of others. We'll want to control instead.

The next Sage, like Dr. Au, has a special interest in discernment. As a Quaker, she speaks often and elegantly of patience as a way of connecting with Spirit and determining whether what we hear is authentically inspired or not.

Patricia Loring

Patricia Loring is a contemporary Quaker writer and educator. Her books on listening and discernment are widely used both by the Religious Society of Friends (the "proper" name of the Quakers) and by others seeking to follow the lead of spiritual guidance.

She comes from the tradition of the unprogrammed Quakers, who have no clergy or church as such. Instead, they are organized as Meetings (with a capital *M*) who hold meetings (with a small *m*) for worship and what are called "meetings for worship with attention to business." In this part of our interview, Patricia was speaking about how a Meeting examines ideas and lets them ripen over time:

Nothing is done in a hasty manner. There's a chance for all the emotional and instinctual drive to dissipate and the clarity of what's there—and where the motion of the heart is—to become apparent. Time seasons things. <u>Seasoning</u> is another Quaker discernment word. You let things become seasoned as much as you can before making a decision. One of the greatest helps is to just sit with it, or—another Quaker expression—hold it in the Light. This is different from the kind of meditative sitting in which you're simply open. You're bringing a specific question before God, or into that Light, and waiting to see how it's illuminated.

The fruit of following spiritual guidance for the Quakers is often enlightened social action—acts of compassion that enhance the dignity and human rights of others. We were so impressed with the intention of the Quakers to live spiritually guided lives that we asked a friend, who is also a Friend (the way Quakers refer to one another), if she'd introduce us to some of the people in her Meeting who might be willing to be interviewed. She found three volunteers, each of whom is an accomplished professional, but to preserve the humility that is so much a part of the Quaker way, we'll dispense with discussing their professional credentials and let their words speak for them.

The Boulder Quakers

Mary Hey, Deanne Butterfield, and Denny Webster are all members of the Boulder Friends Meeting. On the day of the interview, the five of us (the three Quakers and your two authors) gathered in the den of our friend Sara's home near downtown Boulder. We began with 20 minutes of silence, but despite the quiet beginning, a lot of excitement was generated as the three women warmed to our questions. We had only two hours together, since one of the women was on her way to take part in a peace vigil on Boulder's Pearl Street Mall and another was going to a training session for volunteer counselors at the county jail.

Mary Hey described the unprogrammed Quakers as a prelude to our conversation so that we'd have a context:

> Quakers are called seekers and have no creed. Without a creed, we're not forced to fit our lives into a series of tenets. There are three of us here because it's difficult for any of us to speak as Quakers, since the tradition is invisible from the outside. You have to get deeper into it to understand what it's about. We're Protestants, but we're in a unique spot, a different kind of sect. What Zen is to Buddhism, we are to Christianity, although not all of us are Christian. There are many strains of Quakers.
>
> We at the Boulder Meeting are at the most liberal end. Some Quakers are extremely conservative—Bible-based hellfire and damnation. This is the result of their seeking and where people moved in their spiritual lives as a result. There are now three major groups of Quakers, the first two of which have ministers: the conservatives; a middle group that's similar to a mainstream type of Protestant denomination; and the unprogrammed Quakers, which is what we are.

The three women then shared their thoughts on spiritual guidance. Mary Hey continued:

> We seek inner guidance in a contemplative meeting for worship, seeking together. The insights that one has are tested against the group, so the guidance isn't like, "Make up your own religion." By speaking out of the silence and sharing insights with the group, the group then acts as a sounding board to test the truth of the insight.

"Quakers say there's 'that of God' in every person," added Deanne Butterfield. She explained:

> Because there's that of God in each of us, we each experience and can access different parts of the Divine. When the five of us gathered here sit together seeking access, then the presence of

Spirit is amplified. That's why we worship together rather than just do solitary meditation as our worship.

Denny Webster explained the process of sitting together in worship at a silent meeting and waiting for the inner sense that it's time to speak aloud from Spirit:

> *You might be moved to consider whether you'll speak, and someone else will say what you were thinking. Sometimes when I'm struggling with whether I must speak, someone else will say it. We don't know the mechanics of how this happens—we call it a gathered meeting—but it seems as though the space is enlivened, and it's a really extraordinary experience.*

We were so impressed with the simplicity, honesty, and integrity of the Quakers that we attended several of their meetings for worship. The silence was profound as we sat together in an elliptical room with a bank of high windows that gave the space the illusion of being an eye, which—we were told—was the architectural intent. The group sees together, comes to clarity, patiently waits for confirmation that the spiritual guidance is authentic, and then puts the guidance into action.

The final two Sages are part of the founding group of the Center for Purposeful Living. Like the Quakers, they lead lives of service and social action, which they believe are in accord with their souls' purpose.

Susan Baggett and Thomas White

Susan Baggett and Thomas White are members of the Center for Purposeful Living (CPL), which grew out of the founding circle's need to be of service to others. Susan is an accountant by day and Thomas is a lawyer, but their real vocation is service.

For 14 years, they cared for the terminally ill, first in a private home and then in a hospice building that they purchased. In the process of this—and several other—service projects, they developed extraordinary skill in the dynamics of how groups work best together and how individuals become responsible human beings who recognize and live their purpose in life. CPL has been named as a Presidential Point of Light. They're a shining example of how people of like mind can create community, make decisions based on spiritual guidance, and run successful all-volunteer businesses that make a positive difference in people's lives.

Susan Baggett's initial thought on spiritual guidance was the following:

> It's recognition from one's own soul that can be perceived in many different ways—through ourselves, through others, or in the context of different situations. The guidance can come in so many ways—through illness or through beauty. Some of our experience is caring for the terminally ill, where we come face-to-face with what really matters. That, for instance, took us into much deeper territory than we might have normally gone.

Thomas White summed up the underlying philosophy of CPL as acting on the guidance you get and learning to choose the unselfish path:

> Looking at my own life, spiritual guidance has often come in the form of opportunities, like our soul saying, <u>Here's a chance for you to do something, now. I want to see if you carry through.</u> If we don't, the soul's going to go fishing. Why waste time on an ego that isn't listening? . . .
>
> If we're receiving guidance, what's it asking us to do? There's a choice between our selfish desire nature versus our heart nature, and in making those choices, we evolve. What we want to do is to choose the path of the heart, and then we're following our guidance. When we choose the unselfish road, versus the selfish road, then we're serving our purpose.

❉

Our sincere thanks to these, the Sages, who—in following their own guidance—took the risk of sharing their wisdom with us in the hopes that we'd be able to transmit it to you. We've tried our very best to do that, and we hope that in spite of our limitations, you've received at least a taste of their authentic transmissions of the Mystic Heart. Our introductions to the Sages were, of necessity, short. But in these wondrous days of Internet access, you can learn more about them all and pursue both the books and public teachings that many of them have to offer.

※　※　※

Afterword

Cultivate Contentment—
Being Responsible to Guidance

"If there's any duty, it's to find the beautiful mind."
— The Venerable Ajahn Sona

W hen time allowed, at the end of our interviews we asked the
Sages whether there were any last thoughts they wanted to
share. Sometimes the greatest treasures emerged in these final few
moments.

Nina Zimbelman observed with her typical clarity: *"What's the
gift of guidance, and what's the responsibility to guidance?* because they
go hand in hand. If we choose to live a spiritually guided life, then
that's a gift, but there's a huge responsibility in honoring that gift.
. . . Sometimes we want the gifts, but not the responsibility."

Buddhist monk Ajahn Sona's concluding words spoke directly
to honoring that responsibility: "Keep asking what leads to lessen-
ing of greed, ill will, and delusion. Cultivate contentment over
wanting, which leads to violence. To want is to lack. From contentment comes generosity and inner peace. If I cultivate want, no

matter how much I get, I'll always feel as if I'm lacking. You have to understand the folly of craving and want. People misunderstand letting go of this as having no ambition, but the contented person has access to energy that's drained when you're worrying about having enough. The person who is content will spread peace."

Part of cultivating contentment—the beautiful mind of which he speaks—is choosing to take a rest once in a while in order to leave the noise behind. For example, the holiest day in the Jewish year is the Sabbath, even though it's celebrated once a week. Time is set aside to worship, celebrate with family and friends, and put down the heavy yoke of the world. Sabbath gives rhythm to life and access to silence that refreshes the soul and invites alignment with the Spirit of Guidance.

"The Buddha didn't just say that people should be enlightened wherever they are," Ajahn Sona told us in ending our conversation.

> You know, you have to have some compassion for yourself. You have to set up environments that are conductive to the increase of goodwill and clarity. And you have to associate with people who will bring you in the right direction. The critical factor is that you have to have a place and real people, because reading a book is fine, going to work in downtown Chicago is all right, but we really have to have the kindness to get ourselves out from time to time and remember what it's like to calm down.
>
> So the critical thing that's missing is places to go. We can never have too many places, and they should be available to people. These are springing up everywhere—little living-room sanghas, retreat centers, interfaith and interspiritual centers—someplace to go and be inspired and to feel safe and to have your mind moved to calmness by the environment. We can't forget the actual concrete structures that have to be in place.

Interspiritual teacher and Buddhist scholar Ed Bastian's last words about being responsible to guidance concerned cultivating the sincere wish to liberate others from suffering. In order to actualize the wish, he explained, our behavior has to reflect it: "You're not discerning about: *Does my kid need a new bike?* or *Does this person want me to spend a lot of time doing something to make them happy?* The question is: *If I do this, will it help them toward enlightenment?* If not, then maybe I'm doing it for another reason. It helps to create a decision hierarchy for why you agree or don't agree with a course of action. We need to have the same pact toward ourselves. The bottom line is: *Does this action help to enlighten me?"*

Father Thomas Keating used a wisdom saying of Jesus to summarize how we can be responsible to guidance. He explained: "In Matthew 10:39 [King James Version], it is written: 'He that findeth his life shall lose it: and he that loseth his life for my sake shall find it.' If you want to save your life—I presume this means the false self—life as you understand it, you'll bring yourself to ruin. So the pursuit of all those over-identifications with our possessions and our instinctual needs will bring us to ruin. And they do. They're the source of all human misery, social sin and injustice, indifference, and all the rest of it. But anyone who brings himself or herself to nothing will find out who they are."

He continued:

> *No thing* means that we're not identified with any particular name, including our idea of ourselves. Nothing means that you become everything, and this is Who God is. He, too, has an aspect of nothingness. The Father, in the Christian theology, is sheer emptiness containing infinite possibilities. And so, to become no thing is to become what God is—no particular thing—so that He can then be present in us in everything. And so, to become nothing is really more important than to become a saint. To become enlightened, the Ultimate that we're called to is greater than any specific goal. And it's so simple: It's just the ordinary being human, nothing greater, if we can do that without attachment.

"And so," the 83-year-old Sage finished, "that saying [of Jesus] has meant a great deal to me. I'm spending these last few days, weeks, months, or maybe a year or two of my life wanting to be no thing. Nothing. So I recommend it. It doesn't make life exactly any easier, but it makes more sense than anything I've done so far."

Taking what we've learned to heart, we too aspire to be no thing. Nothing special. While authors generally try to write best-sellers, we've agreed that we have no attachment to this book. It has its own destiny, and we release it. Writing this work has been a privilege that extended over two years and taught us so much about the interior places where we're free and those where we're still bound by ignorance, fear, and desire. The writing has sharpened our understanding of how to live a spiritually guided life and honed a keen intention to do so.

Our deepest wish is for your freedom and the freedom of all beings. In orienting toward this potential, we will all contribute to manifesting Brother Wayne's vision of a civilization with a heart.

— **Joan Borysenko** and **Gordon Dveirin,**
Boulder, Colorado

The Interview Questions

1. What is spiritual guidance?

2. What is your personal experience of spiritual guidance, if you'd be willing to share that?

3. How does the heart, the mystery of love, factor into what we understand as guidance?

4. How does one distinguish between action that comes from the ego and action that is guided?

5. Is doubt a help, a hindrance, or both?

6. Is there a particular role for community in helping us come to right action?

7. What are the greatest blocks to listening to and acting upon guidance?

8. What are the practices for seeking guidance?

9. How do you understand the relationship between contemplation and action?

10. Is there something within your tradition that corresponds on the individual and collective levels to an entelechy, or principle of becoming, a force that drives evolution into a form like an acorn becoming an oak?

11. What is a human being—and creation at large— evolving toward? What's the ultimate goal to keep in mind?

12. If you were to advise today's world leaders about how to find guidance toward a life-enhancing future, what would you suggest?

Spiritual Mentoring and Resources for Guidance

After reading so much about spiritual guidance and the importance of spiritual mentoring, you might be interested both in some background about how the art of spiritual mentoring developed and in resources for finding appropriate mentors. People generally work with a spiritual companion for just one hour a month, but the impact can be profound and transformational.

Dr. Janet Quinn, cofounder of the Claritas Interspiritual Mentor Training Program—our colleague and friend—is the Claritas Spiritual Director in residence. The meticulous training and supervision in spiritual mentoring that our students receive is due, in large part, to her care and diligence. We're grateful for her permission to include the following description of spiritual mentoring, which she wrote to introduce people to its history, intention, and practice.

Spiritual Mentoring: An Ancient Practice in Modern Form
by Janet Quinn, R.N., Ph.D.

The Early Spiritual Directors

If you lived somewhere near the deserts of Egypt and Syria in the 4th century, and if your heart was restless in its holy longing for deeper connection with God, Spirit, and the Holy Mystery, you might have felt called to make a long, hot pilgrimage over difficult terrain to see one of the desert Ammas and Abbas for spiritual guidance. These "mothers" and "fathers" were serious folks when it came to the spiritual journey. They left the safety but also the chaos of their cities for the stillness of the desert, where they hoped to live a deeper life, a life grounded in, centered in, and guided by Source, the Ultimate Reality, God, the Holy Spirit. They hoped that in the desert they could follow the lead of the Psalmist who wrote: "Be still, and know that I am God." And while they tried to leave the world behind, people hungry for the same spiritual experience found them and sought them out for their mentoring in living the spiritual journey.

When you arrived, they would have welcomed you as if they were welcoming the Divine itself, and they would have sat with you in your longing, listening deeply with you for where it might be leading. In the end, they would have "given you a word," the story goes, a seed thought or a teaching story inspired by the Spirit to meditate on as you made your trip back into the dailiness of your life. Thus was the ancient Christian tradition of spiritual direction birthed, by men and women hungry for meaning and purpose and, most of all, for authentic connection to what they experienced as the Source of all. Similar sacred relationships between those more seasoned in the journey and those seeking guidance have existed in all the world's religious traditions, although they have not necessarily had a formal name for it.

Contemporary Forms

Today there are many terms used to describe this art of offering support for the spiritual journey, and there are also various forms. There is a wonderful expansion of this work into an interspiritual context, emphasizing the deep unity of wisdom that exists at the core of all the world's spiritual traditions. Spiritual direction, spiritual mentoring, spiritual guidance, spiritual companioning, and soul-friending are all terms used to describe this process of the two listening for the One. Whatever the language, the art of spiritual direction seems to be enjoying a type of renaissance. There are an increasing number of programs designed to train spiritual directors, and there seem to be growing numbers of people looking for spiritual guidance. Why might this be?

Why Spiritual Direction?

Some of us long for a safe harbor to explore the deepest questions of our lives, questions about God, Spirit, Ultimate Reality, meaning, and purpose and calling. It is not therapy we are after, but something with a larger context. It isn't that we need to be fixed, but rather heard, held in a sacred space of unconditional love, and trusted to find our own deepest connections with Spirit. It is not so much that we think anyone has the Ultimate answers—and that is what makes seeking spiritual guidance through the usual mainstream churches so difficult for some of us—it is more that we just need a place where we can be heard, where we can hear ourselves, and where someone will help us notice the movement of the Spirit within our ordinary lives and listen for the wisdom and guidance available from within our own deep heart. We, like those early pilgrims, seek a soul-friend from whom we might receive a word; a gentle sweep of a hand suggesting a place to look; or a practice or a prayer to guide us on this, our most important journey.

Perhaps spiritual mentoring is a call because, for many of us, the state of our life or the state of our world begs response, but discerning what is a True response, one that comes from our True nature and not our egoic needs, wounds, and habits, is tricky business. We need the support of someone who can help us discern what is True for us, listening with us for what some would call "God's will."

There are as many personal reasons for seeking spiritual mentoring as there are people seeking it. Ultimately, spiritual mentoring is holding the space for another to come into deeper relationship with God, the Absolute, the Ground of Being, and to manifest that deepening in their lives. Spiritual direction, spiritual mentoring, and spiritual companioning are names for a form of relationship between not two but three—the person seeking mentoring, the mentor, and God, who is the real Mentor/Director in the relationship.

Resources for Locating Spiritual Guides

- Janet Quinn is a Spiritual Director (mentor or guide) with a deep interspiritual perspective and roots in Roman Catholicism. She has been a practitioner of Centering Prayer, a contemplative prayer form, for 20 years and is also is a mureed (an initiate) in the Sufi Order International. She has availability in her practice of spiritual direction for in-person and/or phone sessions. She also has openings for supervising other Spiritual Directors. You may contact Dr. Quinn at: **janetquinn@aol.com**.

- Reverend Suzanne Fageol was interviewed as one of the Sages for *Your Soul's Compass*. Her roots are in the Anglican Church, in which she's an ordained Episcopal priest, but her branches are interspiritual. You can contact her either for spiritual mentoring, supervision, or information about the Lorian Association's Master's Degree in Spiritual Direction (for those who have already completed a certificate program). Please contact her at: **spirit@whidbey.com**.

- For training in the art of interspiritual mentoring, please check our Website for the Claritas Institute for Interspiritual Inquiry: **www.claritasinstitute.com**. The Website includes a list of our graduates who have practices in interspiritual mentoring, including brief descriptions of their orientations.

- Spiritual Directors International (SDI) is the trade organization for Spiritual Directors. Their Website (**www.sdiworld.org**) has information about spiritual direction, and a list of Spiritual Directors around the world. They also publish an excellent quarterly international journal with peer-reviewed articles called *Presence*.

Endnotes

Preface

1. See Wayne Teasdale's seminal book on interspirituality, *The Mystic Heart* (Oakland: New World Library, 2001).

Introduction

1. The story of the prince who awakens to his true Self in the Hymn of the Pearl is also known alternatively as the "Hymn of the Soul" or the "Hymn of the Robe of Glory." We have cited here from G. R. S. Mead, *Echoes from the Gnosis*, vol. X, "The Hymn of the Robe of Glory," couplet 67 (The Gnostic Society Library, 1908).

2. Ann Weiser Cornell, *The Power of Focusing: A Practical Guide to Emotional Self-Healing* (Oakland: New Harbinger Publications, 1996), p. 3.

3. Francis S. Collins, *The Language of God: A Scientist Presents Evidence for Belief* (New York: Free Press, 2006), p. 217.

4. Ibid., p. 217.

5. Ibid., p. 217.

6. Ibid., p. 218.

PART I

Chapter One

1. Wayne Teasdale, *The Mystic Heart* (Oakland: New World Library, 2001), p. 26.

2. Thomas Keating, "Guidelines for Interreligious Understanding," *Speaking of Silence: Christian and Buddhists on the Contemplative Way,* edited by Susan Walker (Mahwah, NJ: Paulist Press, 1987), pp. 127–128.

3. Father Thomas Keating gave this eloquent summary of the three steps on the spiritual journey at the end of the film *One: The Documentary.*

Chapter Three

1. Rose Mary Dougherty, S.S.N.D., *Group Spiritual Direction: Community for Discernment* (Mahwah, NJ: Paulist Press, 1995), p. 125.

Chapter Four

1. All biblical references, other than those that may be quoted by the Sages, are taken from the New Revised Standard Version (NRSV) of the Old and New Testaments.

2. Albert Einstein, Banesh Hoffman, and Helen Dukas, *Albert Einstein: The Human Side* (Princeton, NJ: Princeton University Press, 1981).

Chapter Five

1. *Time* magazine, "God vs. Science," Nov. 5, 2006: p. 55.

Chapter Six

1. Patricia Loring, "Spiritual Discernment: The context and goal of clearness committees," *Pendle Hill Pamphlet* 305: 14–15 (Wallingford, PA: Pendle Hill Publications, 1992).

2. Anthony de Mello, *The Way to Love: The Last Meditations of Anthony de Mello* (New York: Doubleday, 1992), pp. 108–109.

3. Francis S. Collins, *The Language of God: A Scientist Presents Evidence for Belief* (New York: Free Press, 2006), p. 119.

4. Rami Shapiro, *The Sacred Art of Lovingkindness: Preparing to Practice* (Woodstock, NY: Skylight Paths Publishing, 2006), p. xii.

Chapter Eleven

1. *The Journal of John Woolman, Part 1: 1720–1742,* The Harvard Classics (New York: **www. Bartleby.com**, 2001).

2. Swami Adiswarananda, *The Four Yogas: A Guide to the Spiritual Paths of Action, Devotion, Meditation, and Knowledge* (Woodstock, NY: Skylight Paths Publishing, 2006), p. 12.

3. Thomas Merton, *Letter to a Young Activist.* The entire text of this short letter is available at **http://www.perc.ca/PEN/1998-03/s-note book.html**.

4. A. H. Almaas, *The Pearl Beyond Price* (Berkeley, CA: Diamond Books, 1998).

5. The metaphor of the light versus the lampshade comes from the work of Gerald Jampolsky, M.D., who writes about *A Course in Miracles.*

6. Jacob Needleman, *The American Soul: Rediscovering the Wisdom of the Founders* (New York: Jeremy P. Tarcher/Putnam, 2003), p. 95.

7. Ibid., p. 104.

8. Ibid., p. 107.

9. Ibid., p. 107.

10. Ibid., p. 106.

Chapter Twelve

1. Evelyn Underhill, *The Spiritual Life* (Seattle: Morehouse Publishing, 1997), p. 74.

2. Henry Corbin, *Alone with the Alone: Creative Imagination in the Sufism of Ibn 'Arabī* (Princeton, NJ: Princeton University Press, 1969), p. 200.

3. Richard Tarnas, *The Passion of the Western Mind* (New York: Ballantine Books, 1991), p. 434.

4. Henry Corbin, *Alone with the Alone: Creative Imagination in the Sufism of Ibn 'Arabī* (Princeton, NJ: Princeton University Press, 1969), p. 183.

5. Ibid., p. 114.

Chapter Thirteen

1. Mark Gerzon, *Leading Through Conflict: How Successful Leaders Transform Differences into Opportunities* (Cambridge, MA: Harvard Business School Press, 2006).

2. From his biography for Generon Consulting; see **www.generon consulting.com**.

3. Jacob Needleman, *The American Soul: Rediscovering the Wisdom of the Founders* (New York: Jeremy P. Tarcher/Putnam, 2003), p. 44.

4. Ibid., p. 44.

5. Ibid., p. 45.

6. Ibid., p. 48.

7. Ibid., p. 50.

8. Ibid., p. 49.

9. Douglas V. Steer, *Gleanings: A Random Harvest* (Nashville: Upper Room Books, 1986), p. 111.

PART II

The Sages

1. The quote cited came from the interview "At the cutting edge of using psychological concepts in soul work is spiritual teacher Hameed Ali," by Pythia Peay. It is published in the *Southern California Diamond Approach Newsletter*. Please check their Website for it: **http://www.dia mondheartsocal.com/CB_Interview.shtml**.

2. Some of the information about Sufism—in particular, the quote of Sheikh Ahmad Zarruq—was quoted from an article in Wikipedia on the Internet.

3. Some of the biographical information about Sally Kempton was adapted from our mutual friend Sara Davidson's book *Leap!: What Will We Do with the Rest of Our Lives?* (New York: Random House, 2007).

Acknowledgments

Every book owes its existence to the lineage of people who have gone before and have handed their wisdom down. We're tremendously grateful to the 27 individuals, most of them lineage holders from venerable traditions, who took the time and care to share those traditions with us. You met them all in the preceding pages. Most of the Sages didn't have the opportunity to review their interviews, and we want to acknowledge once again that any inaccuracies that might have crept into their material were ours, not theirs. We spent many months combing through the interviews and cross-referencing material. It was a prodigious task, and we sincerely hope that we've honored the gift they've given us with accuracy and appropriate context.

This book owes its existence, as an interspiritual inquiry, to the late Brother Wayne Teasdale. He died in October of 2004, just a few months after we'd been with him at an Interfaith Conference in Vancouver, B.C., organized by Dr. Hong Leng Chiam, to whom we are deeply grateful for her devotion to the interspiritual dialogue. Sometimes we have no idea what seeds we've sown. This book, and our Claritas Interspiritual Mentor Training Program, are flowers that bloomed from Wayne's far-flung seeds. He had no idea that either project would come from our friendship, and we hope that they honor his memory.

A number of other people added to the text either directly or indirectly. We especially want to thank Janet Quinn for all that she's taught us about spiritual mentoring; for her deep and caring friendship; and for her partnership in designing, birthing, and being the committed Spiritual Director in residence at Claritas. Our thanks, too, to our beloved Claritas community—those in training and those who are graduates. You inspire us with the realization of what's possible in community. Each of you is a gift that we're very grateful for, and we're in awe of the gifts you bring.

Thanks to our other good friends and colleagues at Claritas: Kathleen Gilgannon, our registrar who helped plan the program from its inception and whose skill and deep commitment makes it all happen; Karen Drucker, musician in residence, for her gift of weaving music out of love; Reverend Suzanne Fageol, who teaches discernment and spiritual mentoring; Joan Drescher, our artist in residence; and Kathy Gracenin, who offers her "cup of grace" through movement. One of our Claritas graduates, Reverend Dr. Ruth Ragovin, gave us a spectacular gift. She spent two precious days reading the first draft with a very practiced editorial eye and gave us invaluable feedback.

Our friends and family—who saw us much less frequently than we would have liked—supported us in every possible way. Thanks to Chris and David Hibbard, Sara Davidson—who also gave us critical input on the manuscript—Rachael Kessler, Josie Evans, and our children and their spouses: Justin and Regina, Andrei and Nadia, Natalia and Shawn, and Ben and Shála. And a special thanks to Joan's loyal, efficient interspiritual assistant, Luzie Mason.

Without Hay House, and the vision of its president, Reid Tracy—and Louise Hay, its heart and founder—we would not have had the opportunity or the means to undertake this project. Thank you from the bottom of our hearts. And thanks to our editors, Jessica Kelley, Alex Freemon, and Jill Kramer, and to all the people—from Charles McStravick, who designed the beautiful cover, to the rest of the art department who collaborated in designing the book, to Jacqui Clark and the publicity department—whose work and commitment to spiritual growth have made it possible for this book to reach you.

⊛ ⊛ ⊛

About the Authors

Joan Borysenko, Ph.D., is an internationally known speaker in spirituality, integrative medicine, and the mind/body connection. She has a doctorate in medical sciences from Harvard Medical School, is a licensed clinical psychologist, is the author of many books, and is the cofounder of the Claritas Institute for Interspiritual Inquiry and director of its Interspiritual Mentor Training Program.

Website: **www.joanborysenko.com**

❀

Gordon Dveirin, Ed.D., is the president of Dveirin & Associates, a consulting firm in organization and human development. His interests span educating the social, emotional, and spiritual lives of children; training leaders; and facilitating new visions of possible global futures. Cofounder of the Claritas Institute for Interspiritual Inquiry and its Interspiritual Mentor Training Program, he is coauthor (with his wife, Joan Borysenko) of *Saying Yes to Change*.

❀ ❀ ❀

Notes

Notes

Notes

Notes

Notes

Notes

Notes

Notes

Notes

Notes

Notes

Notes

Hay House Titles of Related Interest

⚙

All of the above are available at your local bookstore,
or may be ordered by contacting Hay House (see next page).

⚙

We hope you enjoyed this Hay House book.
If you'd like to receive a free catalog featuring additional
Hay House books and products, or if you'd like information
about the Hay Foundation, please contact:

Hay House, Inc.
P.O. Box 5100
Carlsbad, CA 92018-5100

(760) 431-7695 or **(800) 654-5126**
(760) 431-6948 (fax) or **(800) 650-5115 (fax)**
www.hayhouse.com® • **www.hayfoundation.org**

Published and distributed in Australia by: Hay House Australia Pty. Ltd.,
18/36 Ralph St., Alexandria NSW 2015 • *Phone:* 612-9669-4299
Fax: 612-9669-4144 • www.hayhouse.com.au

Published and distributed in the United Kingdom by: Hay House UK, Ltd.,
292B Kensal Rd., London W10 5BE • *Phone:* 44-20-8962-1230
Fax: 44-20-8962-1239 • www.hayhouse.co.uk

Published and distributed in the Republic of South Africa by:
Hay House SA (Pty), Ltd., P.O. Box 990, Witkoppen 2068
Phone/Fax: 27-11-467-8904 • orders@psdprom.co.za • www.hayhouse.co.za

Published in India by: Hay House Publishers India, Muskaan
Complex, Plot No. 3, B-2, Vasant Kunj, New Delhi 110 070
Phone: 91-11-4176-1620 • *Fax:* 91-11-4176-1630 • www.hayhouse.co.in

Distributed in Canada by: Raincoast, 9050 Shaughnessy St., Vancouver, B.C.
V6P 6E5 • *Phone:* (604) 323-7100 • *Fax:* (604) 323-2600 • www.raincoast.com

Tune in to **HayHouseRadio.com®** for the best in inspirational
talk radio featuring top Hay House authors! And, sign up via the Hay House
USA Website to receive the Hay House online newsletter and stay informed
about what's going on with your favorite authors. You'll receive bimonthly
announcements about Discounts and Offers, Special Events, Product
Highlights, Free Excerpts, Giveaways, and more!
www.hayhouse.com®